DOUBLE ENTRY BY SINGLE
A NEW METHOD OF BOOK-KEEPING

THE DEVELOPMENT
OF CONTEMPORARY
ACCOUNTING THOUGHT

DOUBLE ENTRY BY SINGLE

A

𝔑𝔢𝔴 𝔐𝔢𝔱𝔥𝔬𝔡

OF

BOOK-KEEPING

F[rederic] W[illiam] Cronhelm

With an Introduction by
Basil S. Yamey

ARNO PRESS
A New York Times Company
New York • 1978

Editorial Supervision: LUCILLE MAIORCA

———◆———

Reprint Edition 1978 by Arno Press Inc.

Reprinted from a copy in the University
    of Florida Library

THE DEVELOPMENT OF CONTEMPORARY ACCOUNTING THOUGHT
ISBN for complete set: 0-405-10891-5
See last pages of this volume for titles.

Manufactured in the United States of America

———◆———

Library of Congress Cataloging in Publication Data

Cronhelm, Frederic William.
    Double entry by single.

    (The Development of contemporary accounting thought)
    Reprint of the 1818 ed. published by Longman, Hurst,
Rees, Orme, and Brown, London.
    1. Bookkeeping. I. Title. II. Series.
HF5633.C89 1978   657'.2   77-87267
ISBN 0-405-10896-6

Introduction

Cronhelm's *"Double Entry by Single"*

Cronhelm's book, published in 1818, is unusual in several respects: it certainly is not typical of contemporary text-books on bookkeeping and accounts. The quality of its author and his work did not go unrecognised. B.F. Foster in his *The Origins and Progress of Book-Keeping* of 1852, the first book concerned solely with the history of the subject, refers to "Cronhelm's very clever and elaborate work".[1] A few years later Hayne Carter described the author himself as "an ingenious and clever writer".[2] Yet the book seems to have had but little detectable influence on its successors. Perhaps its approach and treatment of the subject-matter were too novel to be found of use in more strictly instructional or pedagogic text-books. Perhaps, also, its impact was limited by the misfortune that befell the edition. "Shortly after its publication" the premises of the publishers were destroyed by fire "and nearly the whole edition was consumed".[3]

Little is known about Cronhelm. He must have had direct contacts with business, and indeed he explained in the preface of his book that his "New Method" was "the result of many years' experience in Accounts, and has been gradually perfected by a series of improvements in the Books of an extensive and diversified establishment".

Published expositions of the double-entry system generally proceeded on the basis of the organisation of the accounting records in terms of three account-books, namely memorial (waste book), journal and ledger. Exposition of this particular arrangement was found to be useful pedagogically, even though in practice most business firms must have had other arrangements of account-books that differed more or less materially from the "classical" pattern. These alterations were introduced to save effort, or to facilitate division of clerical labour, or to meet the requirements of the business activities of the particular enterprise, or to satisfy the whims of a particular accountant or merchant.

In the first published treatise on bookkeeping, its author, Luca Pacioli, observed that many smaller businesses used only the journal and the ledger and not all three "libri principali".[4] Ympyn, an influential Flemish author of the sixteenth century, likewise reported that "many are sufficed with two bokes, and leave the Memorial".[5] John Weddington, whose *A breffe instruction* ... was published in 1567, dispensed with the journal (although he said that merchants might use the journal also, "yf it please them to take somiche pains".). Further, he recommended that the memorial should be sub-divided into several separate books or parts, for particular types of transaction, "because marchantis of great dowingis ought to have many servantes to helpe them to write".[6] De la Porte, whose *La science des négocians et teneurs de livres* ... first appeared at the beginning of the eighteenth century, referred to two types of memorial, the "mémorial entier" and the "mémorial divise en plusieurs parties". He also listed and described fourteen different kinds of auxiliary or subsidiary account-books. He explained that while the three principal account-books were indispensible ("mémorial", "journal" and "grand livre"), there were also others which each could use according to the requirements of his business. These books were the "livres d'Aide ou Auxiliares", of which there was no fixed number.[7] John Mair, the most successful writer on accounts in English in the eighteenth century, followed the traditional expositional approach in terms of the three principal books. But he had an appendix on "the subsidiary books used by merchants". He wrote: "Yet Men of great Business find it convenient, either for abridging these [the principal books], or for other Ends, to use some others, generally called

Subsidiary or subservient Books". And he discussed eight of these and also a "copy-book of letters".[8]

Thus early writers on bookkeeping and accounts were aware that business-men did not always use all three principal account-books and often used additional account-books as well. It seems, however, that towards the end of the eighteenth century, at least in Britain, writers tried more self-consciously and deliberately to incorporate some of the bookkeeping practices and procedures of real business in the systems expounded and illustrated in their text-books.

In 1789 Benjamin Booth's *A complete system of book-keeping by an improved mode of double-entry* ... was published in London. Its author, "late of New-York, and now of London, merchant", explained that, "being cut off, by the late War, from the friendships formed in my youth; and prevented, by the Peace that succeeded it, from pursuing the line of business to which I had long been habituated", he decided to use his time and talents usefully for society by writing a practical treatise on bookkeeping in which his system of bookkeeping could be presented. It was "the result of thirty years experience", and would obviate "every objection that can be made to double-entry" since "it possesses both the facility and expedition of the single-entry, with all the advantages of the double. All extraneous matter being lopped off from the Journal, every article is brought to its respective account in the Ledger, by the shortest and most expeditious means. The Ledger, by this mode, is prevented from swelling to an enormous size (which must happen when the articles are posted separately) ...".[9] These advantages were secured by sub-division of the memorial into a number of specialised books of original entry and by monthly journalisation of the entries in each book of original entry. The memorial (waste book) itself was simply a book of original entry reserved for miscellaneous transactions, the entries in which for each month were re-grouped (one imagines, laboriously) to form compound entries in the journal.

Cronhelm knew Booth's work, and referred to it as "the first English work illustrative of the modern Italian Method" (p.xiii). As Booth did for his system, Cronhelm claimed also for his "New Method", although in different words, that it combined the brevity of single entry (without its imperfections) with the advantages of double entry (without its repetitions). As compared with Booth's treatment, Cronhelm's eliminates the monthly journalising of the entries in the various books of original entry. Each of the latter books serves as the direct posting medium to the various individual accounts to be debited or credited in the ledger. Further, each book of original entry serves as a ledger account for the item of property dealt with in it. "While the Ledger records the Stock [= Capital], the Personal, and a few other Accounts, the Day Books record the remaining parts of the property: the Cash Book shews the Cash in hand; the Bill Books shew the amount of Bills payable running, and of Bills receivable, in hand; the Book of Merchandise, shews the stock of Goods" (p.22). Booth's objectives are achieved more fully and economically.

Unlike some of the innovators of his times, Cronhelm had no doubts about the superiority of the principle of double entry. He was highly and tellingly critical of Edward Thomas Jones who had invented and patented his English System and hoped with it to overthrow the double-entry system (chapter VII). But Cronhelm was critical also of many of the contemporary expositions of double entry. And his chapter on the "Principle of Equilibrium" (chapter III) is well ahead of his time in the quality of its conceptualisation and analytical elaboration (although it is fair to say, without suggesting he was derivative, that Cronhelm was anticipated to some extent by a few earlier writers who had addressed themselves to the question of the inter-dependence of various categories of accounts in the double-entry system).

Cronhelm's "Sketch of the Progress of Book-Keeping" (pp.x-xiv) is of some interest as an early attempt to outline the historical development of the subject. It consists of some historical facts and several conjectures. It may be observed that, after the turn of the century, several authors of treatises on bookkeeping and accounts included short histories in their work.[10]

Cronhelm intended to publish a further book, "subordinate to the present Work". It was to contain "in full details the *materials* of the Five Sets of Books, arranged in order of occurrence, with *references* to specific rules for the entries". This intended book was to be for pupils, with the main book itself to "remain as a key in the teacher's hands" (p.ix). There is no record of the publication of the promised book, which in its approach would have had recourse to a teaching method used much earlier (and no doubt still used also in Cronhelm's time).

Notes

1. B.F. Foster, *The Origins and Progress of Book-Keeping ...*, London, 1852; reprint, Arno Press, New York, 1976, p.iii.

2. F. Hayne Carter, *Practical bookkeeping ...*, Edinburgh, 1861; 2nd. ed., Edinburgh, 1874, p.5.

3. Foster, *op. cit.*, p.iii.

4. Luca Pacioli, *Summa de arithmetica ...*, Venice, 1494, dist.IX., tract.XI, chapter 5.

5. J. Ympyn, *Nieuwe instructie ...*, Antwerp, 1543; *A notable and very excellente woorke ...*, London, 1547, chapter 4.

6. J. Weddington, *A breffe instruction* ..., Antwerp, 1567.

7. M. de la Porte, *La science des négocians et teneurs de livres* ..., new edition, Paris, 1753, p.125.

8. J. Mair, *Book-Keeping methodiz'd* ..., Edinburgh, 1736; reprint, Arno Press, New York, 1977, Appendix, chapter I. The number of books was increased to 18 in the same author's *Book-Keeping moderniz'd* ..., 1773.

9. B. Booth, *A complete system of book-keeping* ..., London, 1789, pp.5-6.

10. For example, P. Kelly, *The elements of book-keeping* ..., London, 1801 ("A short history of book-keeping"); A. Wagner, *Eduard T. Jones neuerfundene ... Englische Buchhalterey* ..., Leipzig, 1801 ("Geschichte der Enstehung und Erfindung der verschiedenen Systeme des Buchhaltens"); J. Isler, *Nouvelle méthode suisse* ..., Brussels, 1810.

DOUBLE ENTRY

BY

SINGLE.

[Entered at Stationers' Hall.]

DOUBLE ENTRY BY SINGLE,

A

New Method

OF

BOOK-KEEPING,

APPLICABLE TO

ALL KINDS OF BUSINESS;

AND

EXEMPLIFIED IN FIVE SETS OF BOOKS.

By F. W. CRONHELM.

London:

PRINTED FOR THE AUTHOR,

BY BENSLEY AND SONS, BOLT-COURT, FLEET-STREET;

AND PUBLISHED BY

LONGMAN, HURST, REES, ORME, AND BROWN,
PATERNOSTER-ROW.

1818.

TO

HENRY LEES EDWARDS, Esq.

This Work

IS GRATEFULLY AND RESPECTFULLY

INSCRIBED

BY

THE AUTHOR.

PREFACE.

In the commercial world, few things are more readily admitted, or more generally experienced, than the importance of Book-keeping. The ruin that rarely fails to punish its neglect, renders it indispensable to the individual; whilst, from its connexion with the stability and extension of trade, it becomes interesting even in a national point of view. Proportionate to its utility must be the value of the system that accomplishes its purposes with the greatest degree of conciseness and accuracy, and on the most enlarged scale of applicability. To these qualities the New Method of Book-keeping has firmly, but not arrogantly, laid claim : its pretensions may have been considered weighty, but they have not been hastily assumed; and, with respectful confidence, its vouchers are now submitted to the public.

The opposition of prejudice and established usage being the natural birthright of improvement, there may be no impropriety in premising that the *New Method* is not the production of mere theory unconnected with practice : it is the result of many years' experience in Accounts, and has been gradually perfected by a series of improvements in the Books of an extensive and diversified establishment. The advantages which it offers will be best explained by a comparison of its leading features with those of the Two Systems hitherto adopted in Accounts.

Single and Double Entry are terms which but partially describe these methods, referring not to the entire number of entries, but to those in the Ledger only. In Single Entry, each transaction requires *two* entries; one in the Day Book, and one in the Ledger. In Double Entry, or the Italian Method, each transaction requires *four* entries; one in the Waste or Subsidiary Book, one in the Journal, and two in the Ledger. The modern plan of Journalizing occasionally reduces one of the entries in the

Ledger to the fraction of a collective counter-entry; but it will be shewn hereafter, that, amongst other inconveniences, this occasions new repetitions in another quarter. Double Entry, however, possesses a completeness and proof of the Accounts, of which the other method is destitute. Hence, Single Entry is short and simple, but imperfect and unsatisfactory; whilst Double Entry is complete and systematic, but laborious and complicated.

The New Method excludes what is defective, and combines what is advantageous, in each of the others. It obtains by *two* entries the same results as the Italian System by *four*: it possesses the brevity of Single Entry without its imperfections, and the proof of Double Entry without its repetitions.

It will naturally be asked how this union of conciseness and proof can be accomplished. The inquiry leads us to consider the *true fundamental principle* of Accounts, and to extricate it from forms with which it has long been confounded.

The purpose of Book-keeping, as a record of property, is to shew the owner at all times the value of his whole capital, and of every part of it. The component parts of property in trade, are in a state of continual transformation and change; but, whatever variations they undergo, and whether the whole capital increase, diminish, or remain stationary, it is evident that it must constantly be equal to the sum of all its parts. This Equality is the great essential principle of Book-keeping. It will at once give the Reader a clear idea of the nature of that *proof* which is so highly, and so justly appreciated in Accounts. For, if the Stock Account be found equal to the collective result of all the other Accounts, the desired proof is obtained; but, if the least inequality exist between them, the Books must obviously be incorrect.

To admit this proof, however, the Books must be complete; that is, the whole capital, and every one of its parts, must have a distinct Account. Hence Single Entry is incapable of proof, because it attends almost exclusively to the Personal Accounts, omitting one or more of the Accounts of Merchandise, Bills, Cash, or Stock.

The clear and simple principle of *the equality of the whole to the sum of its parts*, has never before been laid down as the basis of Book-keeping. From its neglect have proceeded those vague and confused notions of Accounts, evinced in almost every treatise, by dividing them into *personal, real*, and *fictitious;* as if the whole capital and each of its parts were not equally real. In this classification, however, the Personal Accounts are treated as if neither real nor fictitious; whilst the Stock Account is actually said to be in the latter predicament; or, in equivalent words, the whole capital is pronounced an unreal and imaginary thing!

The equality of Debtors and Creditors is the immediate, but less obvious consequence of the principle laid down, and may be considered as the general law for its observance. Every transaction in business being virtually a transfer between two accounts, it must be entered to the debit of the one, and to the credit of the other. In Double Entry, these two balancing entries are made in the Ledger; and they comprise all that is systematic in the Italian Method. The entries in the Waste Book and Journal are merely preparatory arrangements, unconnected with the principle and proof of Accounts.

In the New Method, the two balancing entries are the only ones that occur. It has no introductory entries, no intermediate Book between the Day Books and the Ledger. All its Day Books being arranged on the plan of debit and credit, they are not merely, as in Single Entry, records of personal transactions; but each of them is, moreover, a regular Account of some component part of the property, shewing the Balance of Merchandise, of Cash, of Bills Receivable, or of Bills Payable. Thus, the first entry of a transaction in the Day Book, forms immediately one side of the balance, and, by the posted or secondary entry, the equilibrium is completed. The New Method is, therefore, Single Entry in *form*, and Double Entry in *principle*, obtaining every result of the Italian Method, with a saving of the whole Journal, and of all the counter-entries in the Ledger. Proportionate also to its greater brevity, must be its greater accuracy; for it is obvious that every repetition increases the liability to error, and the difficulty of detection.

Another important feature of the New Method is its universal applicability,—a point not resting on mere assertion, but proved beyond contradiction, by Complete Sets of Books for *Retailers, Wholesale Dealers, Manufacturers, Merchants*, and *Bankers*. All these Sets are governed by the same principle; but in the number of the Books, and in the arrange-ment of the Accounts, variations obtain according to the nature of the business.

From the pale of the Italian System, Retailers and Manufacturers have ever been excluded; but the New Method enables them to obtain that PROOF of their Books which has hitherto been deemed imprac-ticable; whilst Merchants and Bankers, who have acquired it by a series of elaborate repetitions, may now possess it by the most concise and simple form in which it is possible to keep Accounts. By inspecting the arrangement of the following Day Books, and the proof exhibited in the Inventory at the close of each Set, the man of business may see at a glance the plan of the New Method, and its easy application to any description of trade whatever.

Advantage has been taken of the numerous Sets of Books, to exhibit a greater diversity of commercial affairs than has appeared in any pre-ceding work. The financial system is varied in every set; losing concerns are stated, as well as profitable ones; and the entire settlement of an in-solvency is introduced, with Partnership Accounts on different principles.

In the course of this Work, some improvements are suggested, which, however important in themselves, do not form essential parts of the New Method. It may, consequently, be adopted either with or without them, at the discretion of the proprietor or clerk; and, for this reason, it is proper to give a distinct enumeration of them, namely:

1. Instead of the Balance Account, a distinct Book, called the In-ventory, for the extract of Balances, and proof of the Books.

2. Instead of the Profit and Loss Account, separate Accounts for Profit and for Loss.

3. A distinct Ledger for Partnership Accounts, so as to keep systematic Accounts of the Joint Capital, and of each Partner's Share; instead of leaving either the Capital or the Shares without a regular Account.

4. A new plan of routine, applicable in all cases when two or more persons keep the Books. In common posting there is no regular check

on the original entries; but this plan proves the primary, as well as the secondary entry, and affords an efficient preventive against fraudulent entries and erasures.

To facilitate the objects of the Teacher and the Student, the Author is preparing for the press a School-Book, subordinate to the present Work, of which it will not be an abridgment or epitome, but bear to it the same relation as a manual of arithmetic to the key. It will contain in full detail the *materials* of the Five Sets of Books, arranged in the order of occurrence, with *references* to specific rules for the entries. By this means, the pupil will be obliged to form the Accounts from the materials alone, without access to the constructed Books in the present Work, which is intended to remain as a key in the teacher's hands. In all other school-books, the materials and the books are bound together; and the learner has the opportunity of transcribing the latter, instead of constructing them. But the Book proposed will teach Accounts on the *true elementary plan* that has so long been successfully used in Arithmetic; and will facilitate in schools a formation of the Books, as similar as possible to their practical construction in the counting house.

F. W. CRONHELM.

Halifax, January 31, 1818.

SKETCH

OF

THE PROGRESS OF BOOK-KEEPING.

———————

THE necessity of some record of property, and of the transactions affecting it, must have been felt in the earliest ages of society. The nature of the first rude expedients for this purpose, may be inferred from the allusions of ancient authors, from the customs of yet uncivilized tribes, and from the practice of ignorant and uninstructed persons within the circle of our own observation.

Long before the invention of figures, men would begin to designate their simple possessions and debts, by collections of pebbles, of shells, or of small pieces of wood, in which size or colour would represent the kind of property, and number its extent. The explorers of Africa, and of the Pacific Islands, occasionally narrate these rude devices, in which we may discern not merely the dawn of Accounts, but the first germ of that symbolizing principle which has generated the noblest inventions, and the most fatal errors of mankind.

Another contrivance consisted of notches cut on rods or canes. These fixed and preservable marks were in some respects superior to loose counters, and bear to figures the same relation as sculptured sketches to written language. The ancient Peruvians used the kindred expedient of knotted strings, which they employed not only as numerical symbols, but also as historical hieroglyphics. To the age of notches, must obviously be referred the invention of tallies. It was truly an ingenious device, to split the rod, so that, by uniting its halves to receive the common indenture, each party might possess a *proof*, as well as record, of the transaction. The tallies were real, though rude Accounts Current, the conformity of which was ascertained at every new transaction; and they exhibit the first conception of a *check* on numeral records.

The practice of scoring presents us with a third class of expedients for registering Accounts. It was probably at first merely a picture of the counters or notches that preceded it; but it was an important advance, and opened the way to all those abbreviations and improvements that were crowned by our present system of numbers, the admirable invention of the Hindoos.

Of the primitive modes of recording accounts, we possess various testimonies, among which that of language is not the least observable. The word *calculate* is derived from *calculus,* the Latin term for *pebble:* when accounts disagree, we still say that they do not *tally*; and, when we have paid a debt, that we have rubbed off our *scores.*

The original pebbles disposed in parallel grooves, or exchanged for perforated beads strung on wires, were marshalled to the most intricate evolutions of numbers in the swanpan of the Chinese, in the abacus of the Greeks and Romans, and in the counting-boards retained in Europe long after the fall of the western empire. The swanpan is still the universal *ready reckoner* of China; and an instrument of the same description is used in Russia. During the years 1816 and 1817, a deputation from the Russian Commissariat resided in the West Riding of Yorkshire, to superintend the contract for re-clothing the Imperial army. These commissioners brought with them a counting-board, resembling the swanpan; and assured the Author that it is very prevalent in Russia. Its counters consisted of white and black beads strung on brass wires, and afforded the usual calculations of business, with considerable rapidity and accuracy.

The use of tallies is rapidly decreasing in England, before the wide diffusion of arithmetical knowledge; but it still exists in the Exchequer, and in the sequestered dairies of our northern counties. It was first applied to the national revenue by the Norman statesmen; and, guarded by the institutions of the Tally Court, it will probably long be preserved in the British Treasury,—a monument, isolated as the Egyptian obelisks at Rome, and exhibiting, amidst surrounding refinements, a rude but interesting vestige of the science and finance of the eleventh century.

The custom of scores is also much on the decline, but it may yet be traced on the chimney-board of the ale-house, and the wainscot of the village shop. It must, however, be observed, that the idea of durability seems to have been excluded from all these primitive attempts at accounts. When the balance was paid, the record was no longer preserved; the counters were swept from the board; the tallies were broken; the scores were rubbed out.

The Athenians were the most commercial of the Grecian states; yet, at the period of their highest refinement, they do not appear to have kept permanent accounts. The following interesting remark on this subject, is extracted from the

Supplement to the Encyclopædia Britannica, article Arithmetic,—a treatise, combining in rare degrees of excellence, science with elegance, and originality with erudition. " Æschines, in his oration for the Crown, speaking of balanced accounts, says, that *the pebbles were cleared away, and none left.* His rival, Demosthenes, repeating his expression, adds, that *as many counters were taken up as were laid down.* It is evident, therefore, that the ancients, in keeping their accounts, did not separately draw together the credits and the debts, but set down pebbles for the former, and took up pebbles for the latter. As soon as the board became cleared, the opposite claims were exactly balanced."

A similar inference of the want of durable accounts, may be drawn from the parable of the faithless steward in St. Luke's Gospel. He relinquished to his lord's debtor the true bill for one hundred measures of oil, and directed him to write quickly a new bill for fifty. But had there been any permanent record of the debt, or, in other words, had any books been kept, the fraud would have been unavailing, as it must have been detected by the account.

The custom of crossing out, which still exists among retailers, may be considered as a vestige of the fugitive record of accounts. In many cases, the first books would be merely a transfer of the chalk scores to paper; and the practice of rubbing out would be imitated as closely as possible, by drawing lines over them with the pen.

About the commencement of the Christian era, the Romans, however, had attained a permanent Method of Accounts, corresponding, in all probability, to that of Single Entry. A familiar passage in Pliny, describes the collection of debts and credits on opposite pages; and, in other writers, there are allusions to the practice of posting, and to a distinction of Books, analogous to that of Waste Book and Ledger. Thus, *nomina translata in tabulas,* denotes articles posted to the Ledger; *nomen jacens,* an unposted transaction; *adversaria,* the Memorial or Waste·Book; and *tabulæ accepti et expensi,* a collection of accounts, contrasting debt and credit, like those of the Ledger.

To the researches of the ingenious Simon Stevin, we are chiefly indebted for this view of the Book-keeping of the Romans; but his opinion that they derived it from the Greeks, is very disputable, and far from being supported by the practice at Athens in the age of Demosthenes. Though the Romans were not originally of a commercial character, it must be considered, that, at the period in question, they held united in peace as well as conquest, all the shores of the Mediterranean. This state of things would be highly favourable to the extension of ·commerce; and its effects are testified by history, in the numerous colleges or companies of merchants, established in the maritime cities of the empire. It is, therefore, not improbable that Rome herself deserves the honour of inventing the method of Single Entry: but, if an external origin must yet be sought, it may be no very presumptuous suggestion to indicate Carthage. That interesting, but unfortunate, republic, exceeded in commerce all the nations of antiquity; and, from her Asiatic origin and connexions, she possessed, in all probability, a system of numerals far more perfect than that of Rome. These circumstances may justify the inference, that her commercial records would enjoy a proportionate degree of superiority; and that, either directly, or mediately by her colonies in Sicily and Spain, she may have communicated the art to her rival and destroyer. The inglorious destruction of the Carthaginian records has placed this conjecture beyond determination, and, along with it, some of the most interesting questions that regard antiquity.

When commerce and literature began, in the fifteenth century, to revive from their long slumber during the dark ages, the progress of Book-keeping and of every science connected with numbers, was materially facilitated by the introduction of the Indian notation. That beautiful system, in which every figure increases its expression ten times by removing one place to the left, was brought into Spain by the Arabian conquerors of that country, thence communicated to Italy, and gradually diffused over Europe. Venice was in those days the great emporium of oriental and western commerce; and the adoption of the denary numbers by her merchants, was soon followed by the admirable, though complicated system of Accounts, named the Italian Method from the country of its invention, and Double Entry from the arrangement of its Ledger. Had it received a scientific denomination, it would have been called, from its balancing principle, the System of Equilibrium; or, with greater justice, it ought to have recorded the name of its inventor, now forgotten and unknown.

The first treatise on the subject appeared in Italian at Venice, in 1495, from the famous Lucas Paciolus, better known by his local name, De Burgo. This work, and the commercial connexions of Italy, gradually diffused the science. In 1531, John Gottlieb published at Nuremburg the first German treatise; and in 1543, Hugh Oldcastle bestowed the same benefit on England. Simon Stevin published in 1602, at Leyden, in the French language, his celebrated work on the application of Book-keeping to Finance. In 1736, Scotland had the honour of producing, in the Book-keeping Methodized of John Mair, the most complete and elaborate exposition of the old Italian Method, ever published. Benjamin Booth gave to the world in 1789, the first English work illustrative of the modern Italian Method. The latter system differs from the former, in dividing the Waste Book into various Subsidiary Books, and in journalizing each of them separately once a month. This

Method was rendered elementary, and adapted to schools, in 1801, by the popular treatise of Dr. Kelly.

It is unnecessary to enumerate the host of writers who, in every age and country, have followed the track of their predecessors. There are many of recent date, who are highly meritorious within the sphere of their pretensions, but the object of all has been to illustrate and exemplify the Italian Method. They may have smoothed or embellished the road, but they have not shortened it: satisfied with its eventually leading to the proof of accounts, they have implicitly followed its windings; and have either not perceived its circuitousness, or considered it as irremediable.

Mr. Jones's work furnishes a solitary, but unfortunate exception. In 1796, he published the " English System of Book-keeping," intended to overthrow the Italian; but, rejecting the essential principle of the science, he resembled the mariner who, at the outset of a voyage of discovery, should cast away the compass; and it is not surprising that the attempt was abortive.

Is it too much to hope, that England may yet enjoy the honour of perfecting the science of Accounts; and that, as she eclipses all that was wealth and glory in the commercial empires of the Mediterranean, so she may repay the debt of instruction, and restore to Italy the *Doppia Scrittura*, purified from its repetitions, and guarded from its liabilities to abuse?

CONTENTS.

PART I.
THEORY OF BOOK-KEEPING.

PART II.
EXEMPLIFICATIONS.

PART I.

THEORY OF BOOK-KEEPING.

CHAPTER I.

INTRODUCTION.

BOOK-KEEPING is the art of recording property, so as to shew at all times the value of the whole capital and of each component part.

As a method susceptible of harmony and system, it owes its origin to the invention of money. Without this universal symbol of property, Book-keeping would be merely a series of memoranda, incapable of that beautiful harmony between the whole and the parts, which now entitles it to rank amongst the exact sciences. Without the relation of money, a man might keep accounts of various kinds of property, and even of personal debts; but he could not collect the different parts into one whole, nor state his real worth by any other method than an enumeration of all his possessions and debts. Neither could he accurately calculate his Profit or Loss from one year to another, unless his property at each period should happen to be composed of parts similar in nature, with either no augmentations, or no diminutions.

An example may serve to familiarize these observations, and, at the same time, to give enlarged notions of the admirable utility of money, which not merely circulates and diffuses the productions of nature and art, but, introducing system and harmony into Book-keeping, commands (as with the creative wand of enchantment) a new science to spring into existence.

B

Discarding the use of money, the following Statement shews the property of the individual C, at the beginning and at the end of a year :

C's Stock, 1st January.	*C's Stock, 31st December.*
Item No. 1. — House and Furniture.	Item No. 1. — House and Furniture.
2. — 100 Packs of Wool.	2. — 120 Packs of Wool.
3. — 200 Pieces of Woollens.	3. — 150 Pieces of Woollens.
4. — 80 Cwt. of Cotton.	4. — 10 Cwt. of Silk.
5. — 100 Pieces Linens due from A.	5. — 20 Tons of Lead due from B.
Less No. 6. — 30 Tons of Iron due to D.	Less No. 6. — 8 Hhds. of Sugar due to E.

At neither period can C form any conception of the extent of his **property,** without enumerating the six component parts. Still more vague and uncertain will be his estimate of the Profit or Loss on the year's transactions. Beginning to compare the individual items, he will find that in No. 1. no alteration has occurred; that in No. 2. he is richer by 20 Packs of Wool, and in No. 3. poorer by 50 Pieces of Cloth; but in Nos. 4, 5, 6, the two Stocks consisting of different things not admitting comparison, there is an end to all certain conclusions; and the entire result must remain in obscurity or unsatisfactory conjecture.

But restoring the use of money, C becomes provided with a common symbol, by which he can reduce his various possessions and debts to one specific nature, collect the whole into one amount, compare these aggregates at different periods, and thus determine the real extent of his capital, together with his Profit or Loss. Let us repeat the example under this new form.

C's Stock, 1st January.	*C's Stock, 31st December.*
No. 1. — House and Warehouse, Value £1000	No. 1. — House and Warehouse, Value £1000
2. — 100 Packs Wool . . at £20 . . 2000	2. — 120 Packs Wool . at £20 . . 2400
3. — 200 Pieces Woollens . at 10 . . 2000	3. — 150 Pieces Woollens at 10 . . 1500
4. — 80 Cwt. Cotton . . . at 30 . . 2400	4. — 10 Cwt. Silk . . at 300 . . 3000
5. — 100 Pieces Linens due from A. . . . . . at 4 . . 400	5. — 20 Tons Lead due from B. . . . at 25 . . 500
£7800	£8400
6. — 30 Tons Iron due to D. at 10£ 300	6. — 8 Hhds. Sugar due to E. at 50 . . 400
	C's Worth £8000
C's Worth £7500	7500
	C's Profit this Year £500

CHAPTER II.

COMPLETE AND PARTIAL BOOK-KEEPING.

COMPLETE Book-keeping is that which gives a record of the whole property as one mass, and of all the constituent parts. If the account of the whole mass, or of any of its parts, be omitted, Book-keeping is partial and imperfect.

The component parts of property, are Money, Goods convertible to Money, and Personal Debts. The whole mass, or capital, is technically called Stock. Without entering into subdivisions, it will at present suffice to enumerate the objects of Book-keeping under four general heads; namely,

1. STOCK ACCOUNT.
2. MONEY ACCOUNTS.
3. MERCHANDISE ACCOUNTS.
4. PERSONAL ACCOUNTS.

The record of each class of Accounts is equally essential to the completeness and system of the Books, but not equally urgent as regards the interest and convenience of the proprietor.

Of all his Accounts, the Personal are those which most imperiously claim his attention: the evils occasioned by the neglect of other Accounts are remote and contingent; but immediate and inevitable injury must result from inattention to his Personal Accounts.

In all concerns, but more especially in those that invest the whole capital in trade, it is highly necessary to attend to the finances, and provide due resources against pending engagements: hence the Money Accounts are second in the order of urgency. The natural desire which every man of business feels to know his real capital, renders the Stock Account the third object of attention.

There remain only the Merchandise Accounts, which are little regarded, excepting by merchants and wholesale dealers, and even by these are frequently neglected. Retailers and manufacturers almost universally omit the record of this class of Accounts, from the erroneous opinion already mentioned, that the nature of their business renders it impracticable.

But whenever one of the parts of property is omitted in the Books, they must of necessity be partial and incomplete; there can be no dependence or harmony between the whole and the parts; the Stock cannot be procured from the Accounts

alone, and when it is obtained by valuations and inventories, it will stand unconnected and unproved in the Books.

In complete Book-keeping, the Stock or capital is known by its particular
Account, without enumerating and adding together all the component parts.
When, however, this general extract of the parts is made, their sum will correspond
with the Stock Account, if the Books are correct; and, thus, the parts and the
whole mutually check and verify each other.

Here, then, we may discern the great difference between Complete and Partial
Book-keeping, as regards their general extracts or inventories. In Partial Book-
keeping, the inventory is made to discover the Stock: in Complete Book-keeping,
the Stock is previously known; and the object of the inventory is the general proof,
as well of the Stock, as of all the other Accounts.

In Partial Book-keeping, the capital is ascertained by the single process of
collecting its component parts: in Complete Book-keeping, the capital is obtained
by two distinct processes; firstly, by the Stock Account; secondly, by the collection
of the parts; the correspondence of the two results proving the accuracy of the
Books. In Partial Book-keeping, the Profit or Loss cannot be discovered till the
Stock is collected, and it is then obtained by comparison with the preceding Stock.
In Complete Book-keeping, the Profit or Loss is declared by its Account, prior to
the Stock which is ascertained by the entry of the Profit or Loss.

Complete Book-keeping has hitherto been practically attained only by the Italian
method of Doublé Entry; the various forms of Single Entry in use being all more
or less partial and imperfect. But the New System of Double Entry by Single
accomplishes a record of Accounts, which combines with the brevity of Single Entry,
the completeness and proof of the Italian method. Preparatory to the description
of this New System, it is desirable to ascertain the real principles of Accounts, and
to disentangle them from forms with which they have long been confounded.

CHAPTER III.

PRINCIPLE OF EQUILIBRIUM.

IT is a primary axiom of the exact sciences, that the whole is equal to the sum of its
parts; and on this foundation rests the whole superstructure of Book-keeping. It
considers property as a whole composed of various parts: the Stock Account records
the whole capital; the Money, Merchandise, and Personal Accounts record the

component parts. Hence, in complete Books, there must necessarily and inevitably be a constant equality between the Stock Account on the one hand, and all the remaining Accounts on the other.

The introduction of Credit and Bills into commerce, produced two kinds of property directly contrary in their natures:

1st, Positive Property, consisting of Goods, Cash, Bills Receivable, and Debts Receivable.

2d, Negative Property, consisting of Bills Payable, and Debts Payable.

And as these two kinds of property mutually destroy each other, it is evident that the Stock, or entire capital, must always be equal to the difference between them, and be of the same nature as that which preponderates.

Hence arise three varieties of Stock or Property; the Positive, the Neutral, and the Negative; in the first two of which the proprietor is solvent, in the latter, insolvent. An example of each case is here adduced.

CASE I. POSITIVE PROPERTY.

Positive Parts: Goods	£2000	
Cash	1000	
Bills Receivable	500	
Debts Receivable	1500	£5000
Negative Parts: Bills Payable	8C0	
Debts Payable	1200	2000
Stock, Positive		£3000

The Proprietor is here solvent, with a surplus of £3000, his net capital.

CASE II. NEUTRAL PROPERTY.

Positive Parts: Goods	£2000	
Cash	1000	
Bills Receivable..	500	
Debts Receivable...	1500	£5000
Negative Parts: Bills Payable	1800	
Debts Payable	3200	5000
Stock, Neutral....................		£ 0

The Proprietor is here solvent, but worth nothing.

CASE III. NEGATIVE PROPERTY.

Negative Parts : Bills Payable £2000
                  Debts Payable 4000 £6000

Positive Parts : Goods.. .... £2000
                   Cash 1000
                   Bills Receivable 500
                   Debts Receivable 1500 5000

                   Stock, Negative £1000

The Proprietor is here insolvent for One Thousand Pounds, the amount of his deficiency.

From the view of property as a whole composed of positive and negative parts, constantly equal to the collective result of those parts, we must now ascend to a higher and more general consideration of it, as a mass of relations between Debtors and Creditors. The application of these terms is originally personal ; but it is extended by analogy to every part of property, and to the whole capital itself.

A man's positive property consists of Debts Receivable, Bills Receivable, Cash and Goods : and all these parts are consequently in the same relation to him as proprietor. But the first, or Personal Accounts, bear the relation of Debtors : therefore the others equally bear this relation ; and Bills Receivable, Cash, and Goods are Debtors to him for their respective amounts. So also with the negative parts : persons to whom he owes money being his Creditors, Bills Payable are also Creditors for their amount.

Thus all the component parts of property are distributed into Debtors and Creditors ; the positive parts constituting the former, and the negative parts the latter. The Stock, or whole capital, must also come under one of these classes ; for the proprietor, being Creditor for all the positive parts of his property, and Debtor for all the negative parts, must, upon the whole result, be either Creditor for the excess of positive parts, or Debtor for the excess of negative parts ; in other words, Creditor for the excess of Debtors, or Debtor for the excess of Creditors ; the direct inference from which is the Equilibrium of Debtors and Creditors throughout the Books.

But without thus deducing it from the connexion of the Accounts, this correspondence is immediately evident from the very signification of Debtor and Creditor, which being relative terms, the one always implies the other, and cannot exist without it. If, therefore, for every Debtor there must be an equal Creditor, and for every Creditor an equal Debtor, the respective sums of these equalities must also be equal.

To illustrate this principle, let us repeat the examples of the three cases of property, under a different arrangement.

CASE I. POSITIVE PROPERTY.

POSITIVE PARTS, OR DEBTORS.		NEGATIVE PARTS, OR CREDITORS.	
Goods	£2000	Bills Payable	£ 800
Cash	1000	Debts Payable	1200
Bills Receivable	500	Stock (Proprietor's Capital)	3000
Debts Receivable	1500		
	£5000	——Equilibrium——	£5000

CASE II. NEUTRAL PROPERTY.

POSITIVE PARTS, OR DEBTORS.		NEGATIVE PARTS, OR CREDITORS.	
Goods	£2000	Bills Payable	£1800
Cash	1000	Debts Payable	3200
Bills Receivable	500	Stock (Proprietor's Capital)	0
Debts Receivable	1500		
	£ 5000	—— Equilibrium——	£ 5000

CASE III. NEGATIVE PROPERTY.

POSITIVE PARTS, OR DEBTORS.		NEGATIVE PARTS, OR CREDITORS.	
Goods	£2000	Bills Payable	£2000
Cash	1000	Debts Payable	4000
Bills Receivable	500		
Debts Receivable	1500		
Stock (Proprietor's Deficiency)	1000		
	£ 6000	——Equilibrium——	£6000

Should it be inquired why the Stock appears to be negative when the property is positive, and positive when the property is negative; this seeming contradiction will be removed by the following consideration. In these general relations of Debtors and Creditors, the estate or concern itself is abstracted from its proprietor, and becomes a whole, of which the Stock or proprietor's Account is now also one of the component parts. If, therefore, his property be positive, the Concern is

Debtor to him for that property, the same as to any other person ; and he classes among its other Creditors. If, on the other hand, his property be negative, or himself insolvent, the Concern is Creditor, and he classes among the other Debtors.

We are now arrived at the most comprehensive view of the subject, having generalized the three specific cases of property into one. For, when we thus abstract a Concern from its Proprietor, and place the account of Stock or entire capital among the component parts, the Concern itself is constantly neutral, consisting of a mass of relations between Debtors and Creditors, in perpetual and necessary equilibrium. The Concern thus abstracted, is always a cypher ; and all its component parts are equally and mutually dependent upon each other, and upon the whole. It is no longer merely the Stock which is the result of all the other Accounts collected together : every Account has the same property, and may be found or proved in the same manner. For example, if in Case 1. the Account of Goods be required, it is ascertained by collecting all the other Accounts into one result ; thus,

```
Creditors :  Bills Payable ........................  £  800
             Debts Payable  .....................     1200
             Stock.. ............................     3000
                                                    ————————
                                                    £5000
Debtors :  Cash ................. ........£1900
           Bills Receivable..........    500
           Debts Receivable .........   1500          3000
                                                    ————————
          Result :  Goods ..................... ...........£2000
                                                    ════════
```

By a similar process any other Account may be obtained; and hence it is evident that each of the Accounts is equal to the aggregate of the remainder, and that all are in mutual dependence and harmony.

The same reasoning may be more concisely expressed in an algebraic form. Let a, b, c, &c. represent the positive parts, or Debtors ; l, m, n, &c. the negative parts, or Creditors ; and s the Stock, or proprietor's real worth. Then, as the whole is equal to the sum of its parts,

$$a + b + c, \text{ \&c.} - l - m - n, \text{ \&c.} = \pm s.$$

By transposition, we obtain

$$a + b + c, \text{ \&c.} - l - m - n, \text{ \&c.} \mp s = 0,$$

or that general equation, in which the whole Estate is neutral or a cypher, and includes the Stock as one of its component parts. Here too, it may be observed that the transposition of s changing its sign, explains the reason why the Stock, when positive in itself, becomes negative or creditor as a component part of the estate, and positive or debtor when negative.

Again, by transposing any one of the terms in the general equation, it may be proved to be equal to all the rest. Thus,

$$b + c, \&c. - l - m - n, \&c. \mp s = -a;$$
$$a + b + c, \&c. - m - n, \&c. \mp s = l;$$
$$a + b + c, \&c. - l - m - n, \&c. = \pm s.$$

Hence the truth of that general proposition already laid down, that any debtor or creditor in the books is equal to the collective result of the other debtors and creditors, an affection which has been commonly supposed peculiar to the stock account.

In tracing the principle of equality, we have hitherto considered property in a state of rest; but we shall find it equally essential to property in motion. This is evident from two considerations:

Firstly, At any two periods of time, as the beginning and the end of a year, the equilibrium of debtors and creditors exists in the concern considered in a state of rest. From the axioms, that if equals be added to equals the sums will be equal, or if equals be taken from equals the remainders will be equal; it is evident that the same equilibrium must exist in all the intermediate occurrences.

Secondly, The same thing is apparent in the very nature of all transactions relating to property. The component parts of property in trade are in a state of continual fluctuation and change. In purchases, cash is converted into goods; and in sales, goods are re-converted into cash. Or, if credit is allowed, the changes are still more numerous. Purchases create personal creditors and goods; sales convert goods into personal debtors; receipts convert personal debtors into cash; whilst payments destroy cash and personal creditors. The introduction of bills would multiply the changes by an intermediate stage between personal debts and cash. But all these creations, metamorphoses, and destructions of the parts, resolve themselves into the single case, that in every transaction two accounts are affected, the one receiving what the other communicates. The imparting account is always creditor, and the recipient always debtor; so that in each occurrence debtor and creditor must perfectly equilibrate.

We must proceed to shew that the harmony of debtors and creditors is not disturbed by profits and losses, or, in other words, by the augmentations and diminutions of the capital. Each alteration in the whole mass can be produced only by a correspondent alteration in one of the parts; and hence two accounts are always affected by the change, namely, the stock account and the account of the part, between which the equality of debtors and creditors is maintained. Thus, when a legacy is received in money, Cash is debtor, and Stock creditor; when the sale of goods exceeds the cost, Merchandise is debtor for the surplus or profit, and Stock is creditor; when the sale falls short of the cost, Merchandise is creditor for the deficiency or loss, and Stock is debtor. In all these cases, there is a transfer between the whole and the part, the one receiving what the other transmits; but, as it would be inconvenient to record in the stock account every individual alteration of capital, the transfer is made periodically; and, when the profits and losses proceed from various sources, accounts are opened to collect the particulars, and transmit the general result in one entry to the stock. Till the time of this transfer, the profits and losses remain latent in the particular accounts, without at all disturbing the equality of debtors and creditors, which exists in all the transactions that have produced the profits and losses. Thus, goods bought of A. for £900, and sold to B. for £1000, leave a profit of £100, which remains latent in the merchandise account till the periodical transfer. Debtors and creditors are in the mean time perfectly equilibrated; for in the purchase, Merchandise is debtor £900, and A. is creditor £900; whilst in the sale, Merchandise is creditor £1000, and B. is debtor £1000.

The Equilibrium of debtors and creditors having been demonstrated, as well from the nature of these relations, as from the axiom that the whole is equal to the sum of its parts; and having been shewn to exist essentially in property, in every state, whether of motion or of rest; we may justly lay it down as the fundamental principle of Book-keeping—a principle not of art or invention, but of science and discovery; not of mere expediency, but of absolute necessity, and inseparable from the nature of accounts.

Mr. Jones has attempted to ridicule it as the "common saying, that for every debtor there must be a creditor;" but we shall see hereafter that he was guided imperceptibly by the principle which he imagined to reject, but which it is impossible to banish from complete accounts.

CHAPTER IV.

PRINCIPLE OF ADDITIONS.

From ascertaining a necessary principle of accounts, we must now proceed to investigate one that is merely expedient. The augmentations and diminutions of the various parts of property, may be recorded by two different processes; the first and most obvious of which is to add immediately every increase, and subtract immediately every decrease. Let us exemplify a personal account kept on this plan.

conceding to established custom the introduction of every debtor entry with the preposition To, and of every creditor entry with the preposition By.

	B.		Debtor.	Creditor.
1817.				
January 1.	Dr. To Goods		£400	
6.	Cr. By Cash		200	
		Dr.	200	
11.	Dr. To Goods		300	
		Dr.	500	
16.	Cr. By Cash		200	
		Dr.	300	
21.	Cr. By Goods		500	£200
26.	Dr. To Cash		....	100
		Cr.	....	£100

This method has the advantage of shewing at every entry the actual state of the account; but, consisting of alternate additions and subtractions, it has great liability to error: for the improper operation might easily occur, adding what should be deducted, or deducting what should be added.

The second method consists of additions alone, and, on account of this uniformity of process, has justly been preferred. Each account is here considered as composed of positive and negative parts; and its space in the book being vertically divided, the left side is entitled Debtor, and the right, Creditor. In the left column are entered all the positive parts, or debits, and in the right column, all the negative parts, or credits. The former example is repeated upon this principle.

	Dr.		B.		Cr.	
1817.				1817.		
Jan. 7.	To Goods......	£400		Jan. 6.	By Cash.....	£200
11.	Ditto.......	300		16.	Ditto	200
26.	Cash.......	100		21.	Goods....	500
26.	Balance	100				
		£900				£900
				Jan. 26.	By Balance ..	100

Here the debits being £800, and the credits £900, it is obvious that B. is creditor for the difference £100, being the same result as in the former method, unattended by its exposure to error. Much time is also saved, as the different transactions are simply entered, without any further operation, till the state of the account is required, when both sides are added and equipoised, by entering the difference between them as balance. The balance is immediately transferred to the opposite column, in order to equilibrate its entry, and shew the result of the account.

To avoid equivocal expressions, the term balance is restricted in this treatise to the sum thus entered, to make the two sides equal; and therefore, by *Balance*, the reader will always understand the *make-weight*, or result of the account. For the same reason, the term *Closed* is applied to accounts, only when they equilibrate without entering any balance. The promiscuous use of the word balance for things so different as the equilibration, the result, and the close of an account, has occasioned much indistinctness and confusion. For instance, " When there is no balance to bring down, there is a balance of the account, for it balances without entering any balance."

After thus considering the method of Additions, it must be acknowledged highly useful and expedient; and, though not a principle of necessity, like the Equilibrium, it deservedly ranks as the secondary law of accounts.

The whole system of Book-keeping being constructed on these two principles, our next inquiry must be directed to the shortest and most simple method of applying them to accounts.

CHAPTER V.

ITALIAN METHOD.

THIS system consisted originally of Three Books:

1. The Waste Book, which opens with an inventory of the property in the concern, and proceeds to give a simple narration of all its transactions, in the order of time.

2. The Journal, which is an abstract of the Waste Book, with a formal statement of the debtor and creditor resulting from every transaction.

3. The Ledger, or register of the component parts of the property, as well as of the whole capital, each account having a separate folio or space allotted to it.

The contrivance by which the equilibrium is maintained, is to post every Journal entry twice to the Ledger, namely, to the debit of one account, and to the credit of another. This double entry in the Ledger has become the appellative of the system, in contradistinction to the single entry in the Ledger, made in those imperfect books which do not record every component part of the capital.

The inconveniences of recording all transactions indiscriminately in one Waste Book, and of not being able to ascertain the state of Cash, Bills, &c. till the entire processes of journalizing the Waste Book and posting the Ledger are completed, have occasioned an alteration in the old Italian Method. Instead of one Waste Book, several Waste or Subsidiary Books are used, each appropriated to a distinct class of affairs, as the Purchase Book, Sales Book, Cash Book, Bills Payable, Bills Receivable, &c. All these books are journalized once a month, so that the Journal is no longer a day book, as its name imports, but a monthly abstract; and its appellation is consequently improper.

It may, however, be doubted if this alteration be a positive improvement; for, though it affords great facilities in the first stage of the accounts, it occasions considerable delay and encumbrance in the subsequent processes. The whole month must be closed before the Journal entries can commence; and, before they can be completed, a considerable part of the next month will elapse : then follows all the double posting, so that the arrears of the Ledger will be never less than five or six weeks, and probably often seven or eight. Thus the state of an account can seldom be ascertained from the Ledger alone, but must be traced through the Journal, and all the Subsidiary Books. This is a serious inconvenience.

The whole month's similar transactions relating to one account, are classed together in the Journal, and posted in one sum to the Ledger. Hence the latter deals too much in generals; and the particular information which it ought to give, is too frequently buried in " Sundries" upon " Sundries." To remedy this inconvenience, Book-keepers are actually driven to the necessity of repeating many of the personal accounts in a separate book, called the Account Current Book, which is merely a Ledger of particulars. This tedious repetition is a sufficient comment on the impolicy of generalizing the Ledger.

From these disadvantages the old Italian method is free : its Journal and Ledger may be entered up daily or weekly, according to convenience; and its Ledger is full and explicit in information.

We must now consider some defects which are common to all the forms of this system.

In the first place, it is a process of much time and labour to repeat the record of a transaction so many times : once it appears in the Waste, or Subsidiary Book, once in the Journal, and twice in the Ledger; making in the whole four entries. It is due to the modern Italian method to observe, that it curtails in some of the accounts, part of the double posting to the Ledger : thus, the receipts and payments for the whole month, are equilibrated by collective counter-entries. Other transactions, however, have not this facility; and whatever may thus be saved from the fourth, will be lost in the fifth repetition in the Account Current Book.

Secondly, this frequent repetition increases the liability to error; and it must be noticed, that, in general, there is no systematic check between the Journal and the Subsidiary Books.

In the third place, the process of journalizing is frequently iutricate and perplexing, on account of the various methods of arranging the debtors and creditors in equilibrium. To this subject, elaborate treatises have been devoted, in which the merits of the rival arrangements have been debated with all the majesty of proposition, theorem and problem; demonstration, corollary and scholium. In the search of judicious arrangement, ingenious writers have wandered far from simplicity, as may be seen in those complicated combinations, entitled " Sundries Drs. to Sundries." In fact, the more ingenious the accountant, the more will he be distracted with the various methods suggested by his fertile invention; and the more frequently will he find himself in the situation of the traveller, embarrassed by a multitude of roads to his destination, and hesitating which to choose.

As regards the Journal, the most favourable view of the Italian method is perhaps to be found in the manuscript of Mr. Black, an ingenious professor of Book-keeping, well known in the counties of York and Lancaster. In his Journal, distinct columns are allotted to the debtors and creditors, which, being added forwards to the end of the month, are shewn to be equilibrated, and also equal to the aggregate additions of the subsidiary books; thus establishing a systematic check between those Books and the Journal. The counter-entries of his Journal are also much simplified, by discarding the tedious preambles and cumbrous phraseology which are so prevalent in that book. His arrangement of the Bills cannot, however, be recommended on account of their numerous repetitions. They are entered first in the Bill Book; secondly, in the Cashier, or Cash Book; thirdly, in the Journal; and after this twice in the Ledger. Thus they undergo five entries; and though this number includes a collective counter entry, the repetitions continue most laborious, exceeding even those of the regular Italian method. If any thing could justify or compensate unnecessary repetitions, it would be the elegant arrangement of Mr. Black's Cashier: but, in Book-keeping, brevity and simplicity are objects anterior to masterly combinations. From the best constructed set of Books, it would be easy to make extracts, that, for some particular objects, might exhibit arrangements superior to any thing in the books themselves: but such arrangements are not therefore entitled to be inwoven into their regular system, by the ever prohibitable means of repetition.

After enumerating the defects of the Italian system, candour must acknowledge, that, notwithstanding its slow and intricate operations of Journalizing and Double Posting, notwithstanding its want of simplicity and of determinate rules, it is founded on the just and beautiful principles of Equilibrium and Additions; and that it accomplishes a systematic, self-verifying record of Accounts. The name of its inventor is unknown, but the applauses of four centuries have justly been bestowed upon his art; and, unless a shorter and more simple method be devised for obtaining the same results, it will continue to deserve the preference of the commercial world.

CHAPTER VI.

EXPLANATION OF THE NEW METHOD.

THE New Method consists in keeping all the Day Books by Debtor and Creditor, and in posting them directly to the Ledger, without any intermediate process.

In common Single Entry, the Day Books (excepting the Cash) are mere memoranda of personal transactions; but in the New Method, by altering the arrangement of the same entries, the Day Books become also regular accounts of property. Thus it requires no additional labour in the Books; and yet, by this simple means, it obtains every result of the Italian System; for it observes the great law of Equilibrium in the clearest manner, every entry having a distinct counter-entry, and the harmony of Debtors and Creditors being evident in the very nature of the posting, the constant rule of which is to transfer from the left side to the right, and from the right side to the left.

Its discovery was suggested by considering the results of a common Cash Book, kept by Single Entry. On examining the entries in this Book, and their counter-entries in the Ledger, it will be seen, by the following comparative example, that they accomplish the equality of Debtors and Creditors, as completely as all the repeated processes of Journalizing and Double Entry in the Italian System.

CASE I.—*Cash Transactions recorded by Single Entry.*

CASH BOOK.

(1)		Dr.	Cash.						Cr.			
Jan. 5	1	To John Smith £	150	0	0	Jan. 10	2	By Bolland and Co. £	100	0	0
15	3	To William Binns	400	0	0	20	4	By Peter Bland....	275	0	0
25	5	To Samuel Brown	250	0	0	30	6	By Thomas Howorth	300	0	0
						31		By Balance	125	0	0
			800	0	0			£	800	0	0
Jan. 31		To Balance.... £	125	0	0						

LEDGER.

(1)		Dr.	John Smith.					Cr.			
					Jan. 5	1	By Cash..........£	150	0	0

(2)		Drs.	Bolland and Co.					Crs.			
Jan. 10	1	To Cash ......£	100	0	0					

(3)		Dr.	William Binns.					Cr.			
					Jan. 15	1	By Cash.........£	400	0	0

(4)		Dr.	Peter Bland.					Cr.			
Jan. 20	1	To Cash ......£	275	0	0					

(5)		Dr.	Samuel Brown.					Cr.			
					Jan. 25	1	By Cash..........£	250	0	0

(6)		Dr.	Thomas Howorth.					Cr.			
Jan. 30	1	To Cash ......£	300	0	0					

Result: Debtors......£ 800 | 0 | 0   (Equilibrium) Creditors ..£ 800 | 0 | 0

CASE II.—*The same Cash Transactions recorded by the Modern Italian Method.*

SUBSIDIARY BOOK.

		Dr.	Cash.						Cr.		
Jan.	5	To John Smith ...£	150	0	0	Jan.	10	By Bolland and Co. £	100	0	0
	15	To William Binns	400	0	0		20	By Peter Bland	275	0	0
	25	To Samuel Brown	250	0	0		30	By Thomas Howorth	300	0	0
		£	800	0	0			£	675	0	0

Additional Entries in the Italian Method.

(1) **JOURNAL.**

		1	*Cash Dr. to Sundries.*			
			For the following Sums received this Month.			
Jan.	5	2	To John Smith ....£	150	0	0
	15	4	To William Binns.......................	400	0	0
	25	6	To Samuel Brown	250	0	0
			£	800	0	0

		1	*Sundries Drs. to Cash.*			
			For the following Sums paid this Month.			
Jan.	10	3	Bolland and Co. ....£	100	0	0
	20	5	Peter Bland	275	0	0
	30	7	Thomas Howorth	300	0	0
			£	675	0	0

LEDGER.

(1) Dr. Cash. Cr.

Jan.	31	1	To Sundries .. £	800	0	0	Jan.	31	1	By Sundries ....£	675	0	0
								31		By Balance.....	125	0	0
										£	800	0	0
Jan.	31		To Balance ...£	125	0	0							

(2) Dr. John Smith. Cr.

							Jan.	5	1	By Cash........£	150	0	0

(3) Drs. Bolland and Co. Crs.

Jan.	10	1	To Cash......£	100	0	0							

(4) Dr. William Binns. Cr.

							Jan.	15	1	By Cash.......£	400	0	0

(5) Dr. Peter Bland. Cr.

Jan.	20	1	To Cash......£	275	0	0							

(6) Dr. Samuel Brown. Cr.

							Jan.	25	1	By Cash........£	250	0	0

(7) Dr. Thomas Howorth. Cr.

Jan.	30	1	To Cash ......£	300	0	0							

Result: Debtors ....£ 800 0 0 (Equilibrium) Creditors.. £ 800 0 0

D

These two processes accomplish the same result, but the first is superior in three particulars :

Firstly, In simplicity and brevity, saving the whole process of Journalizing and the Cash Account in the Ledger.

Secondly, In the mode of equilibrating the Debtors and Creditors. In the Italian Method, all the Personal Debtors are equipoised by a single counter-entry to the credit of Cash, and all the Personal Creditors by a single counter-entry to the debit of Cash; but in the shorter method, each individual Debtor in the Cash Book has a corresponding Creditor in the Ledger, and each individual Creditor a corresponding Debtor. The Complex Method maintains the equilibrium merely in the whole collectively: the Simple Method has, besides this general harmony, a particular equilibration of each individual entry; and, consequently, it more definitely, if not more completely, observes the great fundamental law of Accounts.

Thirdly, In the prevention and detection of error.

Supposing Thomas Howorth's payment of £300, to be erroneously posted £200, the equality of Debtors and Creditors would be destroyed in the Simple Method, and the error detected by calling over, or comparing the Ledger with the Cash Book. If the Journal entry be correct in the Italian Method, the conformity will be equally destroyed, and the error similarly detected; but if the error originate in the Journal itself, it will no longer disturb the harmony of Debtors and Creditors, and its discovery will become more remote and contingent. By avoiding the repetition that occasions it, this liability to error does not exist in the shorter method.

In the comparison which has been instituted, every possible advantage has been shewn to the Italian System. Neither the Waste Book nor the Account Current Book is introduced, yet all writers admit the necessity of the latter, and some contend for the use of the former, as a history of the business and a connective index to the Subsidiary Books. The use of these two books would occasion no less than six entries of one transaction; and would extend the Italian process to three times (instead of twice) the length of the other method.

Having satisfactorily ascertained the equilibration of the Cash Book by Single Entry, our next object is to inquire if the Day Books which contain the other branches of business can be kept on the same principle, so as to afford a general equilibration of the Accounts by Single Entry. We have so long been accustomed to other forms of these books, that, on first proposing the question, we are apt to consider this assimilation to the Cash Book as impracticable; but now, after its accomplishment, nothing will seem more easy and natural. For, in any of the other Day Books, what is there to prevent its being debited for what is received, and credited for what is withdrawn? The book of Bills Receivable is debited with Bills Received;

it is credited with Bills Remitted, and Cash received for Bills falling due. The book of Bills Payable is credited with Acceptances, Promissory Notes, and Drafts on Bankers; it is debited with Payments of Bills falling due, and Bankers' Acceptances. The Book of Merchandise is debited with Purchases, Charges and Profits; it is credited with Sales, Re-charges, and Losses. The following short examples will more fully illustrate the assimilability of all these Books to the Cash Book.

Dr.   BILLS RECEIVABLE.

Received.	Fo.	From.	No.	By	Date.	Trm.	Order.	On.
March 2		To J. White	11	J. King	Jan. 7	2 m.	Birch and Co.	Chalmer and Co.
4		To Janson and Co.	12	Jarrold and Co.	Feb. 1	3 m.	S. Janson . . .	T. Flood.
15		To Farmer and Co.	13	J. Smith	20	2 m.	Davy and Co.	Lloyd and Co.
20		To W. Sims	14	Cook and Co. . .	Jan. 22	2 m.	N. Pitt	T. Bell.
25		To Watts and Co.	15	D. Hill	Mar. 20	3 m.	F. White . . .	Ogle and Co.
March 31		To Balance	13	. . . .	. . . .	. . .	. . . .	. . . .

Dr.   BILLS PAYABLE.

Date.	Fo.		No.	Amount.			Accepted.	Fo.	Drawers.
April 20		To Cash paid	21	£350	0	0	April 5		By Sykes and Co.
27		To Cash paid	22	150	0	0	10		By S. Lyon.
30		To Balance	20 & 23	600	0	0	15		By Gordon and Co.
							15		By R. Sampson.
				£1100	0	0			
							April 30		By Balance. . . . . . .

Dr.   MERCHANDISE.

	Fo.			PURCHASES, &c.					
Jan. 5		To Jackson and Co.	18	Tons Lead, ... at	£20	£360	0	0
15		To Melville and Co.	42	Ditto . . . . at	21	882	0	0
20		To Ab. Peters.	. . .	Carriage	. . .	35	0	0
30		To Duncan and Co.	. , . .	Discount 5 per Cent.	. . .	39	0	0
31		To Profit.		. . . .	. . .	175	0	0
			60	Tons	. . .	£1491	0	0
Jan. 31		To Balance. . . ·.	20	Tons of Lead		£440	0	0

PER CONTRA. *Cr.*

Due.	Amount.			Date.	Fo.		No.	Amount.		
March 10	£500	0	0	Mar. 7		By J. Smith remitted.....	12	£150	0	0
May 4	150	0	0	10		By Cash, received for .....,	11	500	0	0
April 23	375	0	0	25		By Cash, received for	14	200	0	0
March 25	200	0	0	28		By C. Conder, paid him ...	15	100	0	0
June 13	100	0	0	31		By Balance	13	375	0	0
	£1325	0	0					£1325	0	0
....	£375	0	0							

PER CONTRA. *Cr.*

No.	Order of.	Date.	Trm.	Due.	Amount.		
20	J. Dearden.........	April 1	2 m.	June 4..................	£200	0	0
21	P. Harris.	Jan. 17	3 m.	April 20..................	350	0	0
22	T. Rogers.	Feb. 24	2 m.	27............	150	0	0
23	Chaloner and Co.	Mar. 27	2 m.	May 30	400	0	0
					£1100	0	0
20 & 23	....	....	....	....	£600	0	0

PER CONTRA. *Cr.*

Date	Fo.	SALES, &c.				Amount.		
Jan. 10		By Roberts and Smith.......	10	Tons of Lead ...... at	£25	£250	0	0
20		By Duncan and Co.	30	Tons of Lead ...... at	26	780	0	0
25		By Melville and Co.	....	Abated 10s. per Ton....	....	21	0	0
31		By Balance...............	20	Tons of Lead, worth ...	22	440	0	0
			60	Tons.................	....	£1491	0	0

It is unnecessary to exhibit the Ledger entries for these three Books, or to state their respective processes by the Italian Method; for the comparison will obviously be similar to that of the Cash Accounts, and lead to the same inferences.

We have, therefore, discovered a Method of Single Entry, which supersedes the circuitous and laborious processes of Journalizing and Double posting, hitherto supposed to be the only means of equilibrating Accounts. In this New Method, the Day Books are assimilated to each other and to the Ledger, being all kept by Debtor and Creditor: whilst the Ledger records the Stock, the Personal, and a few other Accounts, the Day Books record the remaining parts of the property: the Cash Book shews the Cash in hand; the Bill Books shew the amount of Bills payable running, and of Bills receivable, in hand; the Book of Merchandise shews the stock of Goods.

The scientific accountant will discern much beauty and simplicity in this general assimilation of the Books. He will perceive the great process of Equilibration regularly and uniformly carried on, commencing in every primary, and completed in every secondary entry: he will observe it easily and naturally emanating from the arrangement and method; whereas, in the Italian System, it is superinduced by an artificial and laborious contrivance. Here the Equilibrium flows on continuously through the whole mass of accounts; there it is obtained only by breaking them up, and equipoising them in detached fragments; as may be seen at a glance in the endless preambles and intersections of the Journal. The general practicability of the New Method, is another criterion of its merits which ought not to be overlooked. Its principles and its forms apply with equal facility to the minutest Retail, and the most extensive Mercantile Transactions; to the diversified Accounts of Chartered Companies, and the still more complicated Finances of the State.

The laborious process of the Journal has directed the attention of a few writers to the possibility of avoiding it, and of forming the Ledger by Single Entry. It is due to Mr. Tate and Mr. Black to mention, that in the Merchandise Accounts they suggest a method of accomplishing these objects, by posting immediately to the Ledger the periodical additions of the Books of Purchases and Sales. But in the Bills, Mr. Black's repetition of them in the Cash Book is equivalent to their entry in the Journal, and Mr. Tate appears to hesitate between the unsatisfactory expedients of recording them at once as Cash, or of keeping the Bill Book as a mere Memorandum Book. The Book in which Mr. Tate ascertains the result of each lot of Merchandise, is a complete repetition of all the Purchases and Sales; and, therefore, little is gained in this instance by the suppression of the Journal. It must also be observed that the New Method is very different from the plan of entering in the Ledger the periodical additions of the Day Books. Each of these Books becomes a complete Account in itself, recording some particular branch of property. Its additions are not transferred to any other Account; and, though it is convenient to carry forwards the distinct amounts of its Debtors and Creditors to the regular periods of proving the Books, yet this mode of continuation is not necessary; for its Balance may at any time be taken, as that of a Ledger Account, without deranging the system of the Books.

Mr. Jones is the only writer who has hitherto attempted a substitute for the Italian Method, and exemplified his plan by a regular set of Books. Though "The English System" succeeded only in the subscription which it raised for its author, it deserves to be noticed, and shall be examined in the following chapter.

CHAPTER VII.

EXAMINATION OF MR. JONES'S SYSTEM.

STRONGLY impressed with the defects of the Italian Method, Mr. Jones applied with laudable perseverance to the construction of a new system. Unfortunately for this undertaking, his views of the subject were not comprehensive and scientific; his attention was directed to externals; and, confounding the Form with the Principle of the Italian Method, he had the misfortune to reject the great fundamental law of Equilibrium. Oppressed by this radical error, it is really astonishing that he accomplished any thing: at the same time it must be observed, that all he did accomplish, was by the secret assistance of the very principle which he ridiculed and rejected. So strongly was he prepossessed in favour of his system, that he appeared really to consider it as infallible: in the fervour of his prejudice, he denounced its opponents as defective, less in sagacity, than in moral rectitude; and he even hinted to the Legislature the expediency of making it the law of the land. It is not surprising that these ridiculous and acrimonious insinuations were resented, nor that the unwarranted pretensions of his book laid it bare to the shafts of his antagonists. The work, however, is highly curious; and, the angry controversy which it excited having subsided, a calm review of it will be no loss of either profit or amusement.

" The English System" consists of a Day Book and Ledger, ruled in a particular manner. The Day Book contains three columns; one on the extreme left of the page for Debtors; one on the extreme right for Creditors; and an inner column on the right for the first reception of both Debtors and Creditors, before they are entered in their appropriate columns. This preparatory column is further intended to prove the additions of the other two, to the aggregate of which its sum must always be equal. From the additions of the Debtor and Creditor columns, the result of the business is ascertained.

The first impropriety that appears in this plan of the Day Book, is the combination of dissimilar things; purchases being added with receipts, and sales with payments; so that, at first view, it is difficult to conceive how any harmonious result can be obtained from these incongruous assemblages. But, on closer examination, it will be seen by the following extracts from the Book, that the threatened confusion is avoided, by immediately neutralizing every personal Cash or Bill entry, with a counter-entry in the opposite column to the Cash or Bill Account.

Dr. Sundry Accounts.			Fol.		Drs. and Crs.			Cr. Sundry Accounts.		
			Jan. 2	Cr. Notes and Bills Payable, accepted John Antonio's Draft for Wine due 1st. Sept.	£1000	0	0	£1000	0	0
£1000	0	0	2	Dr. John Antonio, Oporto, for my Acceptance of his Draft	1000	0	0			
			17	Cr. Thomas Jones, Bath, received of him....	50	0	0	50	0	0
50	0	0		Dr. Cashier for money received of Jones	50	0	0			
400	0	0	Apl.23	Dr. John Vernon, Manchester, remitted him .	400	0	0			
				Cr. Cashier for said remittance	400	0	0	400	0	0
£1450	0	0	.....	.... Addition of these Extracts	£2900	0	0	£1450	0	0

This specimen will sufficiently shew that all the personal Cash and Bill entries are immediately equilibrated by counter-entries. But how is this accomplished? By mere repetition. Each of these transactions is entered twice in the Day Book; and, every Day Book entry being posted to the Ledger, it also comes twice into that Book. Thus the heterogeneous addition of all Accounts in one Day Book, occasions four entries of the money transactions; and the boasted simplicity and brevity of this System terminate in a repetition, equal to that of the Italian Method itself.

All personal receipts and payments being, however, neutralized by this awkward contrivance, it is evident that the Day Book remains as to its results a Book of Merchandise alone, capable of shewing by the addition of its Debtors and Creditors the profit or loss on the business, and the stock of goods on hand. But all this is governed by the unperceived influence of the rejected principle of Equilibrium. In the first place, the money transactions are obviously equilibrated in both the Journal and the Ledger. As to the remaining accounts, the creditors in the Day Book being virtually at the debit of Merchandise for purchases, &c. do really equilibrate their posted creditors in the Ledger; and the debtors in the Day Book being virtually at the credit of Merchandise for sales, &c. do really equilibrate their posted debtors in the Ledger. Thus it is by means of the rejected principle alone, that the result of the business is ascertained.

From the manner in which this Day Book is opened and closed, there is reason to doubt whether Mr. Jones himself perfectly understood its nature and office. He has no stock of goods at the opening of the business, and, at the conclusion, he appears to be at a loss what to do with the stock then existing. At last, an account is actually opened in the Ledger for " Stock of Goods unsold," where this troublesome concern is deposited. Now, supposing the business to be continued, the stock of goods will be sold in the regular course of trade, and the sales be entered as usual in the Day Book; but unless the " Stock of Goods unsold" be brought back from the Ledger to the Day Book, the apparent result of the business will be completely false. Had Mr. Jones understood the nature of his book as an account of Merchandise, he would have carried down the stock of goods in the book itself as its proper balance, and not have let it abscond to a sinecure account in the Ledger, either to be fetched back again to its appropriate station, or to disconcert the next year's result by its elopement.

The columnar arrangement of the Day Book appears to promise more than it accomplishes. The central column merely proves the additions of the other two columns; but it is no check against entering debtors in the creditor column, or creditors in the debtor column; a mistake to which the promiscuous assemblage of debtors and creditors on the same page renders the book extremely liable.

It must also be observed, that the examples of the Day Book are petty inland transactions of the most simple kind, and that its construction renders it inapplicable to general purposes. At all events, it is not easy to conceive how it could be adapted to a mercantile consignment or account sales, involving a series of debtors and creditors, besides the net result of the transaction; nor has its author thought proper to solve the difficulty.

In Mr. Jones's Ledger every account has five columns for debtors, and five for creditors. Four are devoted to the daily postings from the Journal, each containing the entries of three months; and the fifth receives the sum of each month's entries. All these columns are added and carried forward through the Ledger, to shew that the amounts of debtors and creditors in this book correspond with those of the Day Book. No account is equilibrated, the balances being merely entered as memoranda in the blank space, or rather in a sixth column, which is also added forwards

E

throughout the Ledger, to shew that the difference between the debtor balances, and the creditor balances, leaves the same profit or loss as the difference between the debtors and the creditors in the Journal. But to this irrelevant correspondence, Mr. Jones sacrifices the very accuracy of his books; for, to accomplish it, he omits to post the moieties of profit to the accounts of the two partners Abraham Bold, and Charles Wise, so that the balances of these two accounts are absolutely false; and hence it is that there appears any difference between the debtor balances and the creditor balances. Had the profit been posted, there would have been equality of debtors and creditors.

Each addition of the Ledger occupies three lines at the foot of every page: thus, in ten years, this book would be nearly filled with additions; or, at all events, it would be necessary to allot to this purpose a considerable portion of its pages. Upon the whole, it is a most inelegant and cumbrous arrangement. These endless additions, united with the four-fold entry of the money transactions, render the English System quite as laborious as the Italian Method itself.

Mr. Jones was so deceived by the conformity of the Ledger debtors to the Day Book debtors, and of the Ledger creditors to the Day Book creditors, as to consider it tantamount to an infallible proof of correctness; but, not to mention that he has no check on the original entries in the Day Book, this conformity does not even prove the accuracy of the posting. It is a check merely on that class of unapparent errors which compensate between debtor and creditor, but not on those which compensate in the same relation. If A's account in the Ledger be over-debited £100, and B's account be short-debited the same sum, the amount of debtors in the Ledger will still correspond exactly to those in the Day Book.

CHAPTER VIII.

CLASSIFICATION, ARRANGEMENT, AND ROUTINE.

THE unscientific divisions and inappropriate appellations which occur in preceding treatises on Book-keeping, being calculated to excite confused and erroneous notions in the student, it may not be useless or irrelevant to devote a little attention to these improprieties.

In the titles of Books, the terms Journal and Waste Book are exceptionable in their modern application. Journal, signifying a daily record, is improperly applied to a monthly abstract. The latter meaning, however, is so strongly associated with the term, that, to prevent misconception, it is not applied to any of the books in the present System; though all of them, excepting the Ledger and Inventory, are real Journals. No loss is suffered by this exclusion, the term Day Book being equally significant, and entirely unequivocal.

Equally improper is the appellation of Waste Book applied by some authors to the subsidiary Day Book, which receives the accounts excluded by the other Day Books. In the old Italian method, the terms Waste Book and Journal were appropriate, the former being a general receptacle of the first rough entries, and the latter a real Day Book.

The division of Accounts into Personal, Real, and Fictitious, is one of the most ludicrous that ever enlivened the gravity of the scientific page. Are the Personal accounts unreal? or, rather, are they something neither real nor fictitious? Is the Stock, or proprietor's account, a mere fiction? Are the accounts of Profit and Loss of the same romantic nature? In cases of loss it would be some consolation to consider them in this aerial and poetical light; but when a balance of profit occurs, the pleasure of the transfer would not be much heightened by this view of the subject. The proprietor may reasonably expect to find something *substantial* in his Stock Account; but the professors of Book-keeping, faithful to the Berkleian theory, gravely assure him that it is all fictitious and imaginary.

After rejecting the old classification, a new one may be expected; and we will therefore sketch a substitute in the following tabular view of

ACCOUNTS.

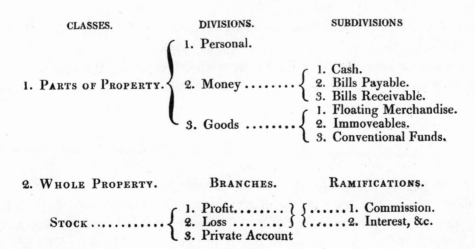

It will be observed that the second class admits no divisions, but ramifications only; its subordinate Accounts not exhausting the higher, as in the first class. The Accounts of Profit and Loss are simply branches of the Stock, their object being to prevent numerous petty entries in the latter, to collect together the individual augmentations and diminutions of the capital, and to transfer the general result in one entry to the Stock. In like manner, Commission, Interest, &c. are merely ramifications of the Profit and Loss Accounts, which prevent numerous petty entries in the latter, collect the aggregates of their respective departments, and transfer the results in one entry to the Profit or Loss. The Private Account is another main branch from the Stock, its use being to record all sums put into the business, or withdrawn, so as to keep them entirely distinct from the Profit or Loss. The result of the Private Account is also transferred in one entry to the Stock.

The Accounts are distributed into various Books, of which the following five will first require our consideration:

1st. The Cash, containing all cash transactions.

2d. The Bills Receivable, containing all bills, whether received or drawn by the proprietor, which he has not to pay or provide for when due.

3d. The Bills Payable, containing all bills which the proprietor has to pay or provide for when due. When the proprietor draws on a banker, this book is sometimes called the Banker's Acceptances.

4th. The Merchandise, containing purchases, sales, charges, discounts, profits, losses, &c.

5th. The Ledger, containing the personal accounts, the stock account and its ramifications, the accounts of immoveable and funded property, and occasional abstracts of merchandise accounts.

Each of these Books is divisible into two or more, according to the nature and extent of the business, and the number of clerks employed.

The first four are called Day Books, from their recording the transactions immediately as they occur. In general, these Books receive the primary entries, from which the secondary are posted to the Ledger. In some transactions, however, the entry and counter-entry are both recorded in the Day Books; and in others, both occur in the Ledger. Payments of due bills, purchases, or sales for cash, and transfers between Ledger Accounts, are the principal entries of this nature; but in all, the distinctions of primary and secondary cease to obtain.

Subordinate to the books of Cash and Merchandise are those of Wages and sundry expenses, in which are entered all payments, not belonging to any account in the Ledger, and too insignificant to appear in the principal books. The additions of these subordinate books are entered periodically in the Cash and Merchandise; an arrangement which appears preferable to a petty Cash Book kept by debtor and creditor, because the latter occasions two balances of cash.

The Book of Merchandise admits various divisions and appellations, according to the nature of the business which it records. In all concerns, where there is a continuous stock of goods, the Merchandise Account must be continuous also. If the business extend to various commodities, Merchandise will be an appropriate general appellative: if it be limited to one commodity, that commodity will supply a specific denomination. Hence, by the woolstapler this book may be termed the Wool Book; by the cotton-vender, the Cotton Book; by the wine merchant, the Wine Book, &c. &c. When the business consists of two or more very distinct branches, each may be allowed a separate Book of Merchandise, with an appropriate designation. In mercantile concerns, the Book of Merchandise is divisible into separate Accounts for each particular lot or cargo of goods. According to the extent of the business, and the number of clerks employed, these accounts may be comprised in one or more books. When a separation is required, commissions and adventures may be recommended as divisions; imports and exports, as subdivisions.

In those businesses which do not consist in buying and selling, the term Merchandise would be inappropriate; but in most of them a Book is required in perfect analogy to the Merchandise, and it may generally be distinguished by the name of the trade or profession. For example, Dying for the dyer, Dressing for the dresser, Carriage for the carrier, Farm or Produce for the agriculturist, Insurance for the underwriter, &c. &c. The Banker's business, however, consisting entirely of money accounts, has no book analogous to the Merchandise.

It must not be supposed that all the various Accounts and Books enumerated, are requisite in every concern. In businesses on a small scale, the Bill Books are frequently unnecessary, as the few bills that occur may be entered in the Cash Book.

The classification of accounts in the Ledger is more easily recommended than accomplished. New accounts are continually opened which will derange those already classed, unless sufficient spaces were left; and many blank folios interspersed among the accounts, may conduce to omissions, and cause an account to be overlooked, till the final proof of the books. It is certainly desirable, that similar accounts should not be separated; but, unless the Ledger be divided into two or more books, the accountant will find it an object of difficult attainment. Nor ought it to be too highly appreciated; the order of these accounts being quite immaterial, in respect to the principles and system of Book-keeping. In the following Books, both methods are shewn; the Ledger Accounts being promiscuously entered in Sets 2 and 3, and classed in Sets 4 and 5.

The simplicity and facility of the present system, render entirely unnecessary those rough or waste books in which some houses make the original entry of invoices, &c. previous to their record in the fair books. Not to mention the loss of time occasioned by this practice, it conduces to inaccuracy; for every repetition increases the liability to error. It is, moreover, inimical to that ready neatness and habitual precision, which a Book-keeper ought to possess. He is apt to be regardless of accuracy in a book, of which a fair and correct copy is afterwards to be made: thus, inattention and slovenliness may increase, till neatness and precision become elaborate attainments, instead of being familiar habits.

Much difference of opinion prevails in Counting Houses, as to the propriety of entering received documents in detail or in abstract: either plan may be adopted in the present system; but, in the Books which illustrate it, the detailed mode of entry is selected, for the following reason: In many works on Book-keeping, the suppression of the particulars of purchases, renders it impossible either to examine the balance of Merchandise, or to discover the commodities of which it consists. In a published system, at all events, the books ought to contain full information, because the original documents cannot be referred to, as in the Counting House. It is scarcely necessary to remark, that the first entry alone requires the details of the account, and that the counter-entry is always abstracted in a single line.

In the new method, the Ledger may be posted daily or weekly, according to convenience; but it is desirable to avoid long arrears. When the entry and counter-entry both occur in the Day Books, they arise simultaneously; so that, in this case, the posting is reduced to the mere entry of the reference figure. The entry and counter-entry must always indicate each other by this figure, and also by the name of the account, when specific, immediately after the introductory preposition To or By. The only exception is, the Merchandise of retailers, wholesale dealers, or manufacturers, which being a general account of trade, the counter-entries to this Book are rendered more clear, by referring to the specific subjects of its entries.

CHAPTER IX.

PROFIT AND LOSS.

PROFIT and Loss have been so universally united in one Account, that the object of their division in the present work, will naturally be inquired. That object is perspicuity. The combination of Profit and Loss occasions in the results of business an indistinctness which perplexes the inexperienced accountant. Whether an adventure terminates favourably or unfavourably, it is always closed by a transfer to " Profit and Loss:" the expression itself does not determine if the result be profitable or losing, and it is only after attentive reflection or habitual association, that the compound term " Profit and Loss " is perceived to signify profit on the debtor side of an adventure, and loss on the creditor side. In the " Profit and Loss " account itself, the same reflection or habit is required to understand, by the reversed signification of the entries, that those on the debtor side are losses, those on the creditor side, profits.

By allotting distinct Accounts to Profit and Loss, all this confusion is removed. Each adventure is closed by an entry, " To Profit," or " By Loss," which distinctly expresses its real result. Nor will this division prevent the general result of the business from being carried in a single entry to the Stock. The least of these two accounts being transferred to the greater, the net result of trade will be passed to the Stock with a clear and unequivocal expression, " By Profit," or " To Loss."

It is acknowledged, that by the compound term " Profit and Loss," the intelligent accountant does not apprehend a confused combination of the two opposite things, but the variations of capital generally, without the specific notions of those variations, that is, whether they be augmentations or diminutions. In this sense, the union of Profit and Loss is perfectly correct; but it is surely too abstract a signification for common use, always requiring an exertion of the mind to surmount the apparent ambiguity and contradiction of the term.

Accounts of Profit and Loss are necessary only in those businesses in which the result arises from a variety of sources. The object of these Accounts is to collect the particular results, and transmit the general result in one entry to the Stock. When the result of the business proceeds from a single Account, it must be transferred immediately to Stock, without the intervention of a Profit or Loss Account, as will be shewn in the Retailer's and Wholesale Dealer's Books in the following Sets. It is proper to observe, that there are two methods of closing the Accounts of Profit and Loss, according to the nature of the concern. When the capital is variable, as is generally the case, the net result of Profit or Loss is transferred to the Stock; but when the capital is invariable (as occurs sometimes in Banking and other Companies) the result must be transferred to the Private Accounts; for the Stock being fixed and permanent, it neither requires nor admits any entry besides its balance. See an example in the Bankers' Books, Set 5.

CHAPTER X.

GENERAL EXTRACT AND PROOF.

THE end of the year is a customary and convenient period for taking the General Extract, and proving the Books; but this operation is equally practicable at any other time. In preceding treatises on Book-keeping, the division of the transactions into several months, occasions intermissions so dissimilar from real business, that the period of the following Sets of Books is limited to one month. Their General Extracts necessarily correspond to this period, but without the least intention to recommend it for regular practice.

When an Account is added, the two sides either will be equal without further entry, or must be rendered equal by transferring the difference or balance to the opposite column. In the former case, the Account is closed; in the latter, it is merely equilibrated, but continues open. Much confusion has arisen in Accounts, from applying the term " Closed " indiscriminately to both cases: and it is, therefore, particularly impressed on the student's attention, that an Account is never closed, till there remains no balance to carry down or transfer.

Preparatory to the General Extract, all the accounts must be equilibrated; and, in those which are unclosed, the balances must be transferred to the opposite column; for it is solely on condition and by virtue of this equilibrating transfer that the balance can be entered at all. After valuing and carrying down the balance of goods on hand, the Merchandise Accounts must be equilibrated by an entry of Profit or Loss; the ramifications of Profit and Loss must be closed by transfers to those accounts; and the Profit and Loss themselves by transferring the less to the greater, and the net result to Stock. The Private Account must also be closed by a transfer to Stock.

The case of a fixed, invariable capital is an exception to these directions, the transfer of Profit or Loss being then made to the Private Account, which carries down and retains its own balance.

Every Account being equilibrated, and exhibiting either its close, or its result in the balance carried down, the Books will be in the following state:

1st. The Stock Balance shews the whole capital, and the other balances shew its component parts. If, therefore, an extract be made of the latter, their sum must be equal to the Stock Balance: and in this equality consists the great proof of Book-keeping. If the result of the inventory do not correspond with the Stock, the Books are incorrect, and must be revised till the error be discovered and rectified by a suitable counter-entry.

2ndly. By the great law of Equilibrium, the sum of the Debtors in the General Extract will be equal to the sum of the Creditors; for, if they do not equilibrate, some latent inaccuracy must occasion the violation of this fundamental principle.

These two descriptions are but different views of the same thing; and the best plan of the Inventory or General Extract is to combine them, by entering the Stock last in order, as the Balance of the Estate, in the manner exemplified in the following Sets of Books.

As this General Extract belongs neither to the Day Books nor to the Ledger, it must be recorded in a separate book, called the Inventory, in which may also be entered the Valuation of goods on hand requisite to obtain the Balance of the Merchandise Account in all businesses excepting the Merchant's.

In the Italian system, the General Extract is recorded in the Ledger under the title of Balance Account; but this attempt to include the Inventory in the system of the Books, is founded on wrong principles, and involves manifold inconsistency. Prior to the extract of the Balances, the Books record in their several Accounts, the entire capital, and each of its component parts. If we require them to exhibit in another account an enumeration of the component parts, we ask a mere repetition, which will occasion the following irregularities.

1stly. Accounts that remain open are apparently closed. There is no principle that can justify the abstraction of a Balance from the account to which it belongs. It is a feeble apology to say that the privation is only transient, for the purpose of proving the Books, and that the Balances are correctly restored when they are re-opened : but,

2ndly. This restitution is accomplished by a very troublesome and circuitous process, involving no less than three repetitions : the miserable Balance, after being persecuted through the Balance Account, the Waste Book and the Journal, returns at last to its own account, not in its own right or in its own name, but by favour of Stock. Of all the accounts, however, the Stock itself is most unfortunate, its balance being conveyed away, never to be restored; so that it is obliged to compound with Sundries for an equivalent, by allowing them free access to its Debtor and Creditor columns. The following example may convey a clearer idea of this compensative arrangement in the Stock Account.

Dr.					STOCK.		Cr.		
1817.					1817.				
Jan. 1	To Sundries	10,500	0	0	Jan. 1	By Sundries	20,000	0	0
Dec. 31	To Private Account	500	0	0	Dec. 31	By Profit	1,000	0	0
31	To Balance	10, 00	0	0					
	£	21,000	0	0		£	21,000	0	0
1818.					1818.				
Jan. 1	To Sundries	13,000	0	0	Jan. 1	By Sundries	23,000	0	0

It is true that no incorrectness results from this arrangement, the difference between the Debtor and Creditor entries on the 1st of January, 1818, being exactly equal to the Balance, 31 December, 1817, namely:

Cr. £23,000

Dr.   13,000

Balance £10,000

But, not to mention the tedious process by which the Account is thus regained, there is an obvious want of harmony and immediate correspondence in the entries; and it is probably the consciousness of this impropriety that has induced some writers to carry down the Balances to the opposite columns of their respective Accounts, without passing the operations of the Waste Book and Journal. This plan is so far unobjectionable: but, unfortunately, retaining the Balance Account in the Ledger, it incurs the irregularity of making two counter-transfers for one original transfer, as will be seen in the following example.

Dr.					STOCK.		Cr.		
1817.					1817.				
Dec. 31	To Private Account	500	0	0	Jan. 1	By Balance.......	9,500	0	0
31	To Balance	10,000	0	0	Dec. 31	By Profit	1,000	0	0
	£	10,500	0	0			10,500	0	0
					Dec. 31	By Balance	10,000	0	0

Dr.					BALANCE.		Cr.		
					1817.				
					Dec. 31	By Stock .. ....£	10,000	0	0

The Balance, being once transferred to the opposite column of its Account, is fully disposed of; and it is contrary to all rule and method to make a second transfer of it to the Balance Account: or, being first deposited in the latter, it cannot be methodically restored to its Account, excepting by the circuitous route previously described.

The inelegant result of the legal process, and the illegal contrivance by which that inelegance is evaded, afford a double proof that the Balance Account does not belong to the Ledger, in as much as its insertion occasions inevitable inconsistencies.

Besides the reason of propriety which requires a distinct Book for the Inventory, there is another of expediency, which deserves to be mentioned. In extensive concerns, there may be several hundreds of Balances, and when we add the Valuations of goods necessary to obtain the Merchandise Balance in many businesses, we shall find ample materials for a separate Book. Even if admissible into the Ledger, these voluminous Inventories would be extremely inconvenient, and have an appearance very different from the trim, nut-shell Balance Accounts which are to be seen in treatises on Book-keeping.

From the arguments and examples adduced, we may safely conclude that the Balance of every Account ought immediately to be carried to its opposite column; and that the Inventory, or General Extract of the Balances, being extraneous to the system of the Accounts, ought to be entered in a separate Book. It must also be observed that the entries in the Inventory are not transfers from other accounts, but simply copies or extracts: the Inventory harmonizes with the other Books, but it is not in dependent connexion with them.

Preparatory to the equilibration of the Accounts, and the entry of the Balances in the Inventory, it is recommended to sketch the General Extract on a loose sheet, in order that all errors may be rectified, before the Balances are finally entered and carried down.

CHAPTER XI.

PARTNERSHIP LEDGER.

In the case of a single proprietor, the Stock is that proprietor's Account, and shews his net capital. In the case of two or more proprietors, the Stock becomes their Joint Account, and records their collective capital. This is so far satisfactory; but additional information is required. Each Partner ought to have a distinct Account to record systematically his share of the capital. His Private Account, in which are entered the sums put into the concern, or withdrawn, is no more adequate to this purpose, than the Private Account of a single proprietor. He requires a particular Stock Account which may shew his share of capital, and to which the result of his Private Account may be transferable.

There is some difficulty in accomplishing this object, for we cannot open particular Stock Accounts in the same Ledger with the General Stock. The latter contains the whole capital, and equilibrates the other Accounts which contain the component parts. To open, besides, Accounts for the shares of the property, would amount to a repetition of the whole capital, and destroy the conformity of Debtors and Creditors.

The confined and erroneous opinion that all Accounts must come into the Ledger, has, in this instance, reduced writers on Book-keeping to a dilemma between the miserable expedients of abolishing either the Joint Stock Account, or the Accounts of the proprietors' shares. In the first case, the general Stock is to be ascertained by adding the particular shares : in the second, the Shares are stated by a memorandum in the blank space of the Joint Stock Account. It is needless to expatiate on these immethodical contrivances.

Accounts of Shares can be properly kept only by means of a separate Book, which may be distinguished as the " Partnership Ledger." This Book resembles the Inventory in its relation to the other Accounts. Its entries are not posted or transferred from them ; and, therefore, it is not in dependent connexion with them: but it is nevertheless in perfect harmony with the other Books, and it includes within itself a complete System of Equilibration. It contains the Account of Joint Capital, all Accounts from which transfers are made to Joint Capital, and a particular Account of each partner's share.

The Account of Joint Capital is constructed by reversing the entries of the Stock Account, the Debtors becoming Creditors, and the Creditors, Debtors. Thus, in case of positive property, Stock is Creditor for the net amount ; but in the Partnership Ledger Joint Capital is Debtor for the net amount, and each proprietor is Creditor for his share. The reason of this reversion is, that Stock is the proprietors' Account, whilst Joint Capital is merely an Account of the property. Both Accounts shew the whole amount of the property, but in opposite relations. Stock is the Account of the persons possessing ; Joint Capital, of the thing possessed : Stock equilibrates all the component parts of the property ; Joint Capital equilibrates the shares of the several partners.

The same reversion occurs in the subordinate Accounts. Profit is credited by Joint Capital for the whole gain, and debited to each partner for his proportion : the balances of the Private Accounts are transferred from Joint Capital to the respective partners : and, the Accounts being then equilibrated, Joint Capital will shew the whole property, and the proprietors' Accounts their particular shares.

By means of this Book the conditions and shares of a partnership may be reserved, as exemplified in the Merchants' Books, Set 4.

CHAPTER XII.

PRIVATE LEDGERS.

IT is an erroneous objection to systematic Books, that they cannot be kept without making known the entire capital of the proprietor. If he desire privacy on this point, he has merely to exclude from the Books all Accounts not belonging to the floating Stock ; as Estates, Buildings, Funded Property, Loans on Security, Private Accounts with Bankers, &c. &c. If his business be divisible into distinct parts, he may allot separate offices and books to each, and by this partition reserve even his entire floating Stock. A Private Ledger, with a few annual entries, will enable him to systematize all the branches of his property into one capital, as may be seen in the following scheme.

Exclusive of this method of privacy, in large concerns where many clerks are employed, the floating capital itself may be reserved, by dividing the Ledger into two or more Books, and by entering the Stock Account with its ramifications in a private Ledger, kept by the proprietor or confidential clerk. In the same Book may also be entered the Financial Accounts, and any others which it may be desirable to remove from common access. By means of a Cash Account in this Ledger, the particular entries of the Private Accounts, the amount of salaries paid to clerks, &c. may be completely reserved.

THE PRIVATE LEDGER OF JOHN SMITH, ESQ.

(1) *Dr.*   GENERAL STOCK.   *Cr.*

1817.						1817.				
Dec. 31	9	To Cash, Expenditure this year	9,825	0	0	Jan. 1	By Balance, my Net Capital	174,500	0	0
31		To Balance.............	181,000	0	0	Dec. 31	10 By Profit this year	16,325	0	0
		£	190,825	0	0		£	190,825	0	0
						Dec. 31	By Balance, my Net Capital £	181,000	0	0

(2) *Dr.*   COTTON STOCK, LONDON   *Cr.*

1817.						1817.					
Jan. 1		To Balance.............	37,500	0	0	Ap. 30	9	By Cash withdrawn. ...	4,000	0	0
Dec. 31	10	To Profit	6,500	0	0	Dec. 31		By Balance...........	40,000	0	0
		£	44,000	0	0			£	44,000	0	0
Dec. 31		To Balance........... £	40,000	0	0						

(3) *Dr.*   WINE STOCK, BRISTOL.   *Cr.*

1817.						1817.					
Jan. 1		To Balance.............	21,500	0	0	Aug. 31	9	By Cash withdrawn.....	6,500	0	0
Dec. 31	10	To Profit..........	5,000	0	0	Dec. 31		By Balance........... ..	20,000	0	0
		£	26,500	0	0			£	26,500	0	0
Dec. 31		To Balance............ £	20,000	0	0						

(4) *Dr.*   RAVENDALE BANK, $\frac{1}{3}$ Permanent Stock.   *Cr.*

1817.					
Jan. 1		To Balance............ £	8,000	0	0

(5) *Dr.*   FIVE-PER-CENT. FUNDS.   *Cr.*

1817.			Funds.					1817.		Funds.			
Jan. 1		To Balance	10,000	95	9,500	0	0	Dec. 31	By Balance £	15,000	14,300	0	0
July 6	9	To Cash, purchased	5,000	96	4,800	0	0						
		£	15,000		14,300	0	0						
Dec. 31		To Balance .. £	15,000		14,300	0	0						

COTTON MERCHANT, WINE MERCHANT, AND BANKER.

(6) *Dr.*   RAVENDALE ESTATE.   *Cr.*

1817. Jan. 1	To Balance .... £	80,000	0	0								

(7) *Dr.*   HOUSE AT LAMBETH.   *Cr*

1817. Jan. 1	To Balance .... £	7,500	0	0								

(8) *Drs.*   WILLIAMSON & CO. LONDON, BANKERS, Private Account.   *Crs.*

1817.						1817.					
Jan. 1		To Balance..............	10,000	0	0	June 30	9	By Cash	6,500	0	0
Oct. 31	9	To Cash	4,000	0	0	Dec. 31		By Balance	7,900	0	0
Dec. 31	10	To Profit, Interest	400	0	0						
		£	14,400	0	0			£	14,400	0	0
Dec. 31		To Balance..............	7,900	0	0						

(9) *Dr.*   CASH.   *Cr.*

1817.						1817.					
Jan. 1		To Balance.............	500	0	0	July 6	5	By 5 per Cent. Funds purchased £5000 at 96	4,800	0	0
April 30	2	To Cotton Stock, withdrawn	4,000	0	0						
June 30	8	To Williamson & Co.	6,500	0	0	Oct. 31	8	By Williamson & Co. ...	4,000	0	0
Aug. 31	3	To Wine Stock, withdrawn	6,500	0	0	Dec. 31	10	By General Stock, this year's Expenditure...	9,825	0	0
Dec. 31	10	To Profit, ⅕th Gain Ravendale Bank............	800	0	0						
31	10	To Ditto, Net Rents of Ravendale Farms	3,000	0	0	Dec. 31		By Balance...........	3,300	0	0
31	10	To Ditto, Dividends on 5 per Cent. Funds	625	0	0						
			21,925	0	0			£	21,925	0	0
Dec. 31		To Balance.............	3,300	0	0						

(10) *Dr.*   PROFIT.   *Cr.*

1817.						1817.					
Dec. 31	1	To General Stock........	16,325	0	0	Dec. 31	2	By Cotton Stock	6,500	0	0
						31	3	By Wine Stock	5,000	0	0
						31	9	By Cash, ⅕th Gain Ravendale Bank.......	800	0	0
						31	9	By Cash, Net Rental of Ravendale Farms....	3,000	0	0
						31	9	By Cash, Dividends on 5 per Cent Funds ...	625	0	0
						31	8	By Williamson & Co. Interest	400	0	0
		£	16,325	0	0			£	16,325	0	0

CHAPTER XIII.

ERRORS AND FRAUDS.

THE equality of the parts to the whole, or the equilibration of Debtors and Creditors in the general extract, is the great systematic proof of Book-keeping. It sufficiently protects the Accounts from accidental error; and it affords to all supplementary checks against intentional error, a basis without which they would be entirely ineffectual.

This proof, however, is of a negative nature: *without it*, the Books cannot be correct; but *with it*, they may be incorrect. It merely shews the general correspondence of the secondary or post entries with the original, and the general accuracy of the additions; or, in other words, that there is no uncompensated error in the counter-entries, or in the additions. It affords no check whatever on the primary entries, nor against compensated errors in the secondary. By compensated errors we mean such as are neutralized by counter-errors, so as not to disturb the equilibrium of Debtors and Creditors; and this neutralization of errors, being a very remote chance, generally originates in design and fraud. The following are the cases of compensated errors in the secondary or counter-entries:

1. One Debtor entry may be short-posted, and another over-posted the same amount.

2. One Creditor entry may be short-posted, and another over-posted the same amount.

3. A Debtor and a Creditor entry may be equally short-posted.

4. A Debtor and a Creditor entry may be equally over-posted.

5. to 8. Four similar cases of compensated error may occur in the additions of Accounts.

9. to 12. Four similar cases may occur in the transfer of Accounts to new folios.

13. to 16. Four similar cases may occur in the entry and carrying down of balances.

17. to 20. Four similar cases may occur in the general extract of balances in the Inventory, that is, in the very Audit of the Books itself.

We have here enumerated twenty simple cases in which Books may be vitiated in the secondary entries without the cognizance of the systematic proof: two or more of these cases may be united in one compensation; and, including only the single cases and their dual combinations, the varieties would amount to four hundred.

All these cases may occur in the new method of Accounts, which is the shortest and most simple possible, containing only two entries of each transaction, a primary and a secondary. In the Italian method, the possibilities of error and fraud are multiplied in the exact ratio of the repetitions: and in the same proportion are increased the difficulty and labour of detection.

The common guard against these fraudulent compensations of error in the secondary entries, consists in calling over and checking the Books by two persons, neither of whom posted the entries; and, besides the calling over, all the Additions and Transfers must be revised, as well as the General Extract itself. This check appears at first satisfactory, yet a perverse ingenuity may render it unavailing, by the erasure and vitiation of two or more *verified* entries, so as to produce one of the simple or compound cases of compensated errors, already enumerated.

There is another species of error in secondary entries, which does not affect the equilibrium of Debtors and Creditors, and therefore requires no compensation. It consists in posting the secondary entry correctly in its amount, and correctly to the debit or credit column, but to a different Account from that to which it belongs. The nature of posting renders this an error of frequent and innocent occurrence; but it is also very adaptable to sinister purposes, and can be detected only by calling over the name of the Account, as well as the folio of reference, and the amount. The opening of many Accounts in the same folio of the Ledger, conduces to the innocent commission of this error; and it would, therefore, be some preventive, to have but one Account in a folio.

We have hitherto considered Errors only in the secondary entries; but in the original entries they have a far wider range, and their detection is much more difficult. Whatever mistake or falsification be committed in an original entry, if the same wrong amount be posted in the secondary entry, neither the equilibrium of Debtors and Creditors, nor the call of the Books, has the least power to detect it. The whole system of the Accounts consists in the correspondence between the secondary and primary entries; its control, therefore, extends to the secondary entries alone; and over the primary it can exercise no jurisdiction.

The species of error to which original entries are liable, are so various, that it would be difficult, if not impossible, to enumerate them all: they may, however, be reduced to three general classes :—

    1st. The falsification of a legal entry;
    2d. The suppression of a legal entry;
    3d. The admission of an illegal entry.

Errors in primary entries that relate to Personal Accounts, may be detected by the comparison of Balances, or the interchange of Accounts Current; but fraudulent errors will not thus be discovered, if the Account Current be drawn out or examined by the contriver of the error.

Erroneous primary entries that do not relate to Personal Accounts, such as those between Cash, Bills, and Merchandise, not possessing any external check, are still less liable to detection; and no method has hitherto been suggested for this purpose, but a careful revision of every primary entry, by the document or voucher from which it was made.

In treating on errors and frauds, it is necessary to distinguish between the internal and the external. The internal include all that do not originate in received vouchers; and these alone are the subject of the present, and of the following chapter. As to the external, or those which are occasioned by incorrect documents, the only guard against them, is a vigilant examination of received Accounts, in every particular of quantity, quality, price, date, terms, and amount.

CHAPTER XIV.

SYSTEMATIC PREVENTIVE OF ERRORS AND FRAUDS.

THE facility and simplicity of the New Method, as a system of entries and counter-entries, admit a particular arrangement in the routine of the Books, which precludes the liability to error and fraud. In concerns of any magnitude, let it be an inviolable rule, that the entry and counter-entry be never both made by the same Clerk. To this division of the entries, must be united the abolition of posting, by which is understood, that no entry must come into the Books by derivation from another entry. The entry and counter-entry must be made simultaneously, and independently of each other, from the same voucher, the figures of reference being filled up hereafter by calling over. By this means, the two entries become mutual checks, not merely on their relative correspondence, but also on their absolute validity. Each clerk ought, moreover, to affix his distinctive check-mark to the Additions, Balances, and Transfers of the other.

Upon this plan it will be scarcely possible that any erroneous or fraudulent entry should escape detection by the final proof of the General Extract, excepting, indeed, in the highly improbable case of a conspiracy. Even this remote possibility may be counteracted, by the employment of a third party as Auditor of the Accounts.

Audits will be most effectually accomplished in the following manner. Let each of the clerks write the letter and folio of his entry on the original voucher, which must then be passed to the Auditor's unexamined file. The Audit will consist in comparing the voucher with the entry and counter-entry, and in certifying their accuracy, by filling up the figures of reference. To all Additions, Balances, Transfers and Extracts, the Auditor must affix his distinctive check-mark, to denote their accuracy.

It is, perhaps, impossible to contrive a more complete set of checks against internal fraud; yet it may be rendered inefficient by the erasure and vitiation of verified entries. Against this refinement of perverted ingenuity, there remains the single, but effectual check,—to defer till the general equilibration, the audit of all entries from the preceding Balances inclusive. This periodical audit of the Accounts will be facilitated by the frequency of the General Extracts. The manner in which it counteracts erasures, is as follows : the alteration of any entry *above* the addition of an Account, can have no effect, unless the Balance carried down be also altered ; and this Balance cannot be altered without detection, because it will be checked at the next examination by the General Extract, which is itself preserved from vitiation, by remaining in the Auditor's exclusive possession.

This system of Checks is perfectly applicable to the Accounts of Chartered Companies, and to the Finances of the State. Its simplicity and evidence, combined with the great final proof of Equilibrium, render it far more satisfactory than any method of repetitions. In each department of those stupendous concerns, there ought to be distinct offices for Entries, Counter entries, and Audits ; an arrangement, by which the very magnitude of the business would be made subservient to its increased security from error and fraud.

Absolute infallibility in Accounts, is a thing which has been arrogated, but which never has been, nor ever will be, attained. The present system of Checks may, however, justly pretend to what it accomplishes : it removes the possibility of internal fraud, from the proximity in which other systems left it, to such a degree of remoteness, that it can occur only by a conspiracy of the Accountants, involving the Auditor himself.

CHAPTER XV.

WAREHOUSE LEDGERS.

IT has been shewn in the first chapter that Book-keeping, as a science, results from the record of all species of property in their common symbol or representative, money : and the preceding elucidations of Accounts relate entirely to this view of the subject. All Merchandise, however, requires Accounts of two different descriptions; firstly, Accounts of its Value, which have been treated at large ; secondly, Accounts of its Quantity, which remain to be considered. The latter have received comparatively little attention ; but they are equally important : for of what avail is it to keep accurate Accounts of the cost and proceeds of goods, if the quantities bought and sold are not also systematically recorded, so as to shew by their comparison the quantity remaining on hand? What difference is there between the loss of £100 by a fraudulent entry in the Books, or the loss of £100 by the embezzlement of goods in the warehouse?

In a Merchant's business, where there is no continuity of stocks, and where the commodities occur in detached masses, the record of their quantity is very simple and easy, more especially so in the present system, which, by framing all Accounts to the form of Debtor and Creditor, combines in one view the history of each lot of goods.

In other businesses there is less facility in recording the quantities of Merchandise, and in Retail concerns it is impracticable from the minuteness of the sales.

In the Wholesale line, the general quantity may be recorded in the Book of Merchandise, by means of distinct columns for purchases and sales ; but, for the particular quantities of the several sorts, a Warehouse Book must be kept by Debtor and Creditor, ruled with numerous columns for the various sorts, and a head column for the totality. This total column is extremely useful, answering the object of a Stock Account, and bearing the same relation to the other columns as the Stock bears to the other Accounts; for, being always equal to the sum of the other columns, its entries, additions and balances, are a constant check on their operations : and, moreover, its correspondence with the general quantity recorded in the Merchandise Account, affords a mutual check on both. An example of this kind is exhibited in the Cotton Merchant's Books, Set 2d, where the quantity of Cotton is proved, to a bag and to a pound, both in the whole number of bags and the whole weight, and in the bags and weight of each particular quality. A similar record of quantity is applicable to all wholesale businesses.

In Manufactories there is more difficulty in obtaining this object, on account of the numerous stages through which the commodities pass, and the various forms which they assume between the raw material and the completion of the manufacture. In consequence of these changes, a series of Accounts becomes necessary, which must contain at least the following three :

1st. An Account of the Raw Material ;

2d. An Account of the Goods in process of Manufacture ;

3d. An Account of the Manufactured Goods.

Each of these Accounts must be ruled with total and particular columns in the manner described : they may be kept either in one Book or in separate Books, according to the system of the Manufactory, and the number of overlookers employed. These things premised, we proceed to consider the respective uses and offices of the Accounts.

1stly, The Account of Raw Materials must be debited with all purchases, and credited with all applications to the manufactory. The Balance of this Account will shew the quantity of Raw Materials on hand, unapplied.

2dly. The Account of Goods in process must be debited with the applications of the raw material ; not, however, in the quantity of that material, but in the quantity of manufactures which it ought to produce, according to those rules and proportions which are established in all regular and well managed concerns. This Account being credited with all manufactured goods, its Balance shews the quantity of goods in process of manufacture.

3dly. The Account of Manufactured Goods must be debited with all manufactures, and credited with all sales and consignments ; its Balance shewing the quantity of Manufactured Goods on hand.

The entries in these Accounts may be made daily, weekly, or monthly, according to convenience. If weekly or monthly entries are preferred, all the Warehouse Books which record the particulars of goods received and delivered, must be added for correspondent periods, and recapitulated in the various sorts that compose the total addition, preparatory to the entries in the Warehouse Ledger.

Some difficulty may be found in drawing the lines that fix the limit of commencement and termination to the process of Manufacture. This must depend entirely upon the system of the Manufactory, and the judgment of the Book-keeper. In many cases it may be expedient to take the line a little within the real termination of the process. Thus in a Woollen Manufactory, the delivery of the piece by the Weaver is undoubtedly the most convenient and definite line for separating the goods in process from the manufactures, notwithstanding the milling and other operations still requisite for the completion of the fabric. The reason for selecting this line, is that the Weaver's Book, in which are entered the pieces delivered from the looms, is a more certain record than any subsequent one that can be obtained; and as the piece has already acquired its final form (though not its final finish), no inconvenience or error can result from thence dating the manufacture.

In the Manufacturer's Books, a Warehouse Ledger is exhibited, containing three Accounts for a Woollen Manufactory, similar to those described. These are the principal Accounts, but others may be added, if necessary or convenient. Thus, if wool be not bought ready sorted for application to different qualities of cloth, an account of Sorted Wool may intervene between that of the Raw Material, and of Goods in Process; and, if desirable, an Account of Finished Goods may be added after the Account of Manufactured Goods. Similar Accounts may be opened for Oil, and the other subordinate materials.

It is scarcely necessary to observe, that when the Manufacturer sells the raw material, or buys manufactured goods, the transaction must be entered to the credit or debit of the respective Account, among the applications, or the manufactures.

A little consideration will enable any Manufacturer to strike an analogy to this system. In the case of liquids, as Beer, Oil, &c. the Process Account will be recorded in appropriate measures; in minute fabrics, as Hardware, Glass, &c. by the tale; in dry goods, as Flour, &c. by weight or measure.

The Books of an Agriculturist bear some analogy to those of a Manufacturer. A columnar Account of Live Stock may be debited with births and purchases, and credited with deaths, sales and consumption. An Account of Produce may be debited with the result of the harvest, and credited with comsumption and sales.

By means of the Warehouse Ledger, the Manufacturer's goods are controlled throughout their multifarious situations, so that merely the very petty embezzlements can escape discovery. To instance again the Woollen Manufactory, any deficiency in the quantity of Wool, that exceeds the due allowance for waste; any deficiency in the quantity of Goods in process, that is not accounted for by the greater waste of wool, or the greater weight of pieces; any deficiency in the number of Manufactured Pieces, would be immediately detected. This security from gross embezzlements, is all that can be expected. Against the peccadillos of the sorter, the spinner, the weaver, or the packer, no system can be devised: the protection of the pound of wool, and the yard of cloth, must for ever remain with the vigilance of the overlooker.

PART II.—EXEMPLIFICATIONS.

SET I.

RETAILER'S BOOKS.

***

CONCERN . . . . INDIVIDUAL.

CAPITAL . . . . VARIABLE.

BUSINESS . . . . COMMENCED.

RESULT . . . . PROFITABLE.

***

OBSERVATIONS.

THIS Set exhibits the business of John Evans, Woollen-Draper at Halifax, during the month of January 1817. The concern is supposed to commence on the 1st of that month, without any prior stock of Goods or Debts; so that there is no Inventory at this date, and the Books are opened by debiting Cash to Stock for the money in hand brought into trade.

The Financial System of John Evans is extremely simple. Receiving his returns in ready-money, he deposits in the Bank the surplus of Cash, and takes out Bills for remittance to the Wholesale Dealers who supply his shop. In this mode of business there is no occasion for a Bill-Book, the few Bills that occur being entered in the Cash. In Retail concerns on a more extensive scale, Bill-Books may be requisite, and appropriate specimens may be found in the following Sets of Books.

This Concern requires four principal Books, the Merchandise, Cash, Ledger, and Inventory; and a Memorandum-Book to record the daily amount of Ready-Money Sales and Petty Expenses, the weekly additions of which are entered in the Cash and Merchandise.

Even in a small business like this, a Private Account is very necessary, to keep distinct from the result of trade all monies put into it, or withdrawn. It will be seen, that this result is systematically ascertained, and that this humble Draper preserves in his Accounts as perfect an equilibrium of Debtors and Creditors, as can be shewn in any Merchant's or Banker's.   He enjoys, therefore, precisely the same proof of his Books, and keeps them on the same accurate principles.

He has, however, no adequate means of checking or proving his Goods, the minuteness of his sales rendering it impracticable to keep an Account of their quantities : and, for this reason, the master's vigilant eye is more required in Retail concerns, than in any other.

Analogous to these Books, are those of all Retailers, including petty manufacturers, as Shoemakers, Coopers, Tinners, &c. &c.

SET I.

THE BOOKS

OF

JOHN EVANS, WOOLLEN-DRAPER, HALIFAX.

---

1. MERCHANDISE.
2. CASH.
3. MEMORANDUM BOOK.
4. LEDGER.
5. INVENTORY.

Dr.   MERCHANDISE.   (1)

1817.		PURCHASES, &c.			
Jan. 2	1	**To Johnson and Co. Leeds.**			
		1 Piece Black Cloth .....28 yds..at 8s..11 4 0			
		1 Piece Brown Ditto .....30 yds..at 9s..13 10 0			
		1 Piece Green Ditto ......27 yds..at 10s..13 10 0			
		2 Pieces Blue Ditto, 31.28.59 yds..at 12s..35 8 0			
		1 Piece Scarlet Ditto .....26 yds..at 15s..19 10 0			
	6 m. Credit	Papers and Wrapper 0 5 0			
	or 5 p. Ct. P.B.		93	7	0
Jan. 3	2	**To Fraser and Son, Huddersfield.**			
		4 Pieces Drab Casimir			
		25. 23. 24. 24—96 yds. ....at 5s..24 0 0			
		4 Pieces Toilinette			
	3 Ms. Credit	16. 15. 15. 16—62 yds. ....at 4s..12 8 0			
		Wrapper 0 2 0			
			36	10	0
Jan. 4	1	To Cash, Petty Expenses this week as per Memorandum Book. Fol. 2	3	6	9
Jan. 8	2	**To James Smith, Frome.**			
		6 Pieces Superfine Broad Cloth.			
		Black ....25 yds..at 20s..25 0 0			
		Brown ....27 yds..at 21s..28 7 0			
		Green ....26 yds. at 22s..28 12 0			
		Blue...28.25.....53 yds..at 25s..66 5 0			
		Scarlet..........22 yds..at 28s..30 16 0			
		4 Pieces Superfine Drab Casimir			
		14. 17. 15. 18—64 yds. .at 10s. 32 0 0			
	6 m. Credit	Paper and Wrapper 0 6 0			
	or 5 p. Ct. P.B.		211	6	0
Jan. 11	1	To Cash, Petty Expenses this Week, as per Memorandum Book. Fol. 2	4	7	6
Jan. 13	2	**To Fraser and Son, Huddersfield.**			
		8 Pieces Toilinette.			
		13. 17. 16. 12 ....58 yds..at 4s..11 12 0			
		15. 14. 18. 13 ......60 yds..at 5s..15 0 0			
		6 Pieces Drab Casimir			
		22. 24. 21 ....67 yds..at 5s..16 15 0			
	3 m. Credit	23. 22. 24 ....69 yds..at 6s..20 14 0			
		Wrapper 0 3 6			
			64	4	6
Jan. 18	1	To Cash, Petty Expenses this Week, as per Memorandum Book. Fol. 2	0	14	1
		Amount carried forwards	£413	15	10

		PER CONTRA. *Cr.*			
1817.	(1)	SALES, &C.			
Jan. 4	1	By Cash, Ready Money Sales this Week, as per Memorandum Book, Fol. 1	27	16	10
Jan. 10	2	By Charles Green, Shopkeeper, Ripponden.			
		14 yds. Blue Cloth ....at 13*s.* 0*d.*........9 2 0			
		6 yds. Scarlet Ditto. ....at 16*s.* 6*d.*.......4 19 0			
		10 yds. Green Ditto.......at 11*s.* 0*d.*.......5 10 0			
		10 yds. Drab Casimir.......at 5*s.* 6*d.*.......2 15 0			
		8 yds. Toilinette ....at 4*s.* 6*d.*........1 16 0			
			24	2	0
Jan. 11	1	By Cash, Ready Money Sales this Week, as per Memorandum Book, Fol. 1	37	5	8
Jan. 11	1	By Johnson and Co., 5 per Cent. Discount on Goods, 8th January.			
		Amount...........93 7 0	4	13	4
Jan. 15	2	By William Brown, Luddenden, Shopkeeper.			
		12 yds. Toilinette ....at 4*s.* 6*d.*.. 2 14 0			
		12 yds. Casimir ....at 6*s.* 6*d.*. 3 18 0			
		16 yds. Blue Cloth............ ..at 13*s.* 0*d.*.10 8 0			
			17	0	0
Jan. 18	1	By Cash, Ready Money Sales this Week, as per Memorandum Book, Fol. 1	32	18	6
		Amount carried forwards	£143	16	4

Dr.   MERCHANDISE.   (2)

		PURCHASES, &c. Amount brought forwards	413	15	10
1817.					
Jan. 20	1	To Johnson and Co. Leeds:			
		10 Pieces of Blue Cloth,			
		25. 27. 30. 31. 32 ⎫ 285 yds. at 7*s*. 6*d*... 106 17 6			
		26. 24. 33. 28. 29 ⎭			
		Wrapper and Papers 0 6 0			
			107	3	6
Jan. 25	1	To Cash, Petty Expenses this week, as per Memorandum ⎱ Book, fo. 1 ⎰	1	18	10
Jan. 31	1	To Cash, ... Ditto .... Ditto .... Ditto........	0	17	9
Jan. 31	1	To Stock, gained this Month	38	16	4
		£	562	12	3
Jan. 31		To Balance, Goods on hand	312	3	10

(2) PER CONTRA. *Cr.*

		SALES, &c. Amount brought forwards	143	16	4
1817. Jan. 20	2	By James Smith, 5 per Cent. Discount on Goods, 8 January, Amount £211 6 0	10	11	4
Jan. 23	2	By Charles Green, Ripponden, 63 yds. Blue Cloth, at 8s. per yd.	25	4	0
Jan. 25	1	By Cash, Ready Money Sales this week, as per Memorandum Book, fo. 1	29	5	11
Jan. 31	1	By Cash, Ready Money Sales........ Ditto ...... Ditto	41	10	10
Jan. 31		By Balance, Goods on hand, as per Valuation, Inventory fo. 1 ..	312	3	10
		£	562	12	3

Dr.   CASH.   (1)

		RECEIPTS, &c.	£	s.	d.
1817.					
Jan. 1	1	To Stock .... Capital brought into Trade...........	500	0	0
4	1	To Merchandise .... Ready Money Sales this week, as per Mᵐ B.1	27	16	10
11	1	To Wilson and Co. .. Bill at 2 months on Jones and Co.	88	13	8
11	1	To Merchandise .... Ready Money Sales this week, as per Mᵐ B.1	37	5	8
15	1	To Private Account .. Aunt Baker's Legacy, Net	38	0	0
18	1	To Merchandise .... Ready Money Sales this week, as per Mᵐ B.1	32	18	6
20	1	To Wilson and Co... Bill at 2 months on Jones and Co.	200	14	8
25	2	To Merchandise .... Ready Money Sales this week, as per Mᵐ B.1	29	5	11
27	2	To Charles Green .. for Goods sold 10th Jan.	24	2	0
31	2	To Merchandise .... Ready Money Sales this week, as per Mᵐ B.1	41	10	10
		£	1,020	8	1
Jan. 31		To Balance	60	17	4

(1)   PER CONTRA.   *Cr.*

		PAYMENTS, &c.			
1817.					
Jan. 1	1	By Wilson and Co... Bankers, Halifax, deposited	450	0	0
2	1	By Private Account.. taken for Pocket Money	1	1	0
4	1	By Merchandise .... Sundry Expenses this week, as per M^m B. 2	3	6	9
11	1	By Johnson and Co. . Bill at 2 months on Jones remitted	88	13	8
11	1	By Merchandise .... Sundry Expenses this week, as per M^m B. 2	4	7	6
13	1	By Wilson and Co... deposited	100	0	0
18	1	By Merchandise .... Sundry Expenses this week, as per M^m B. 2	0	14	1
20	2	By James Smith .... Bill at 2 months on Jones remitted	200	14	8
23	1	By Private Account.. James Bell, Shoemaker, as per Receipt ..	3	12	6
25	2	By Merchandise .... Sundry Expenses this week, as per M^m B. 2	1	18	10
28	1	By Wilson and Co... deposited	100	0	0
31	2	By Merchandise .... Sundry Expenses this week, as per M^m B. 2	0	17	9
31	1	By Private Account .. paid for Board and Lodging this month	4	4	0
31		By Balance	60	17	4
		£	1,020	8	1

READY MONEY SALES.   (1)

1817.				
January 2	Amount of Receipts this Day	4	19	2
3	Ditto...... Ditto...... Ditto	10	2	0
4	Ditto...... Ditto...... Ditto	12	15	8
	Entered Cash.. .... Fol. 1 } and Merchandise, Fol. 1 } ..£	27	16	10
January 6	Amount of Receipts this Day	3	2	11
7	Ditto..... .Ditto...... Ditto	5	17	6
8	Ditto..... Ditto..... Ditto	4	10	7
9	Ditto ..... Ditto..... .Ditto	3	15	9
10	Ditto..... Ditto...... Ditto	8	0	2
11	Ditto..... Ditto..... Ditto	11	18	9
	Entered Cash...... Fol. 1 } and Merchandise, Fol. 1 } ..£	37	5	8
January 13	Amount of Receipts this Day	2	1	6
14	Ditto..... Ditto..... Ditto	4	17	1
15	Ditto..... Ditto..... Ditto	3	8	4
16	Ditto..... Ditto..... .Ditto	5	10	10
17	Ditto ..... Ditto..... Ditto	3	3	4
18	Ditto..... Ditto.. .... Ditto	13	17	5
	Entered Cash..... Fol. 1 } and Merchandise, Fol. 1 } ..£	32	18	6
January 20	Amount of Receipts this Day	1	17	4
21	Ditto..... Ditto..... Ditto	6	0	7
22	Ditto..... Ditto ..... Ditto	3	5	8
23	Ditto..... Ditto..... Ditto	3	10	6
24	Ditto..... Ditto.. .... Ditto	2	14	11
25	Ditto..... Ditto..... Ditto	11	16	11
	Entered Cash.. .... Fol. 1 } and Merchandise, Fol. 2 } ..£	29	5	11
January 27	Amount of Receipts this Day	10	17	6
28	Ditto...... Ditto...... Ditto	6	13	4
29	Ditto..... .Ditto...... Ditto	7	18	2
30	Ditto...... Ditto...... Ditto	12	4	10
31	Ditto...... Ditto..... .Ditto	3	17	0
	Entered Cash...... Fol. 1 } and Merchandise, Fol. 2 } ..£	41	10	10

(2) SUNDRY EXPENSES.

1817.				
January 1	Paid R. Brown, Stationer, for Acct. Books, &c. as per Note	2	17	6
2	Ditto S. Green, Carrier, 1 Truss from Leeds	0	5	8
3	Ditto W. Hirst, Ditto, 1 Ditto from Huddersfield	0	2	3
4	Ditto Postage......................	0	1	4
	Entered Cash ...... Fol. 1 and Merchandise, Fol. 1 ..£	3	6	9
January 8	Paid W. Hirst, Carrier, 1 Bale from Frome	1	9	0
10	Ditto T. Jones, for Parcelling Paper, as per Note......	2	18	6
11	...................Entered Cash ...... Fol. 1 and Merchandise, Fol. 1 ..£	4	7	6
January 13	Paid W. Hirst, Carrier, 1 Truss from Huddersfield	0	4	0
15	Ditto Postage............................	0	2	7
17	Ditto J. Hill, for Twine...........................	0	7	6
18	.... Entered Cash ...... Fol. 1 and Merchandise, Fol. 1 ..£	0	14	1
January 20	Paid S. Green, Carrier, 1 Truss from Leeds	0	7	0
22	Ditto R. Pole, Agent for York Insurance Company Premium and Duty on Policy 32147 for £500	1	10	0
24	Ditto Postage................................	0	1	10
25	....Entered Cash, ... Fol. 1 and Merchandise, Fol. 2 ..£	1	18	10
January 28	Paid T. White, Joiner, for Alterations in Shop........	0	15	0
30	Ditto Postage...........	0	2	9
31	....Entered Cash ...... Fol. 1 and Merchandise, Fol. 2 ..£	0	17	9

INDEX TO THE LEDGER.

A	I & J	R
	Johnson and Co. fo. 1.	
B	**K**	**S**
Brown, William, fo. 2.		Stock, .. fo. 1.
		Smith, James, 2.
C	**L**	**T**
D	**M**	**U & V**
E	**N**	**W**
		Wilson and Co. fo. 1
F	**O**	**X**
Fraser & Son, fo. 2.		
G	**P**	**Y**
Green, Charles, fo. 2.	Private Account, fo. 1.	
H	**Q**	**Z**

Dr.   ȘTOCK.   (1)

1817.				
January 31	To Balance..	567	18	10
		567	18	10

Dr.   PRIVATE ACCOUNT.

1817.					
January 2	1	To Cash, Pocket Money	1	1	0
23	1	To Cash, James Bell	3	12	6
31	1	To Cash, Board and Lodging............................	4	4	0
31	1	To Stock, Transfer....................................	29	2	6
			38	0	0

Drs.   WILSON AND CO. BANKERS,

1817.					
January 1	1	To Cash, deposited	450	0	0
13	1	To Cash, ditto.......................................	100	0	0
28	1	To Cash, ditto.......................................	100	0	0
			650	0	0
January 31		To Balance...	360	11	8

Drs.   JOHNSON AND CO.

1817.					
January 11	1	To Bill 2 months	88	13	8
11	1	To Discount 5 per Cent................................	4	13	4
31	1	To Balance...	107	3	6
			200	10	6

(1)   PER CONTRA.   *Cr.*

1817.					
January 1	1	By Cash, brought into Trade	500	0	0
31	2	By Merchandise, gained this month	38	16	4
31	1	By Private Account, Transfer	29	2	6
			567	18	10
January 31		By Balance	567	18	10

PER CONTRA.   *Cr.*

1817.					
January 15	1	By Cash, Aunt Baker's Legacy	38	0	0
			38	0	0

HALIFAX.   *Crs.*

1817.					
January 11	1	By Bill 2 months	88	13	8
20	1	By Bill 2 months	200	14	8
31		By Balance	360	11	8
			650	0	0

LEEDS.   *Crs.*

1817.					
January 2	1	By Goods	93	7	0
20	2	By Goods	107	3	6
			200	10	6
January 31		By Balance	107	3	6

Drs.   FRASER AND SON,   (2)

1817. January 31		To Balance.. ,...	100	14	6
			100	14	6

Dr.   JAMES SMITH,

1817. January 20	1	To Bill	200	14	8
20	2	To Discount..	10	11	4
			211	6	0

Dr.   CHARLES GREEN, SHOPKEEPER,

1817. January 10	1	To Goods...	24	2	0
23	2	To Goods..............................	25	4	0
			49	6	0
January 31		To Balance	25	4	0

Dr.   WILLIAM BROWN, SHOPKEEPER,

1817. January 15	1	To Goods	17	0	0

(2)   HUDDERSFIELD.   *Crs.*

1817.						
January 3	1	By Goods		36	10	0
13	1	By Goods		64	4	6
				100	14	6
January 31		By Balance		100	14	6

FROME.   *Cr.*

1817.						
January 8	1	By Goods...		211	6	0
				211	6	0

RIPPONDEN.   *Cr.*

1817.						
January 27	1	By Cash		24	2	0
31		By Balance..		25	4	0
				49	6	0

LUDDENDEN.   *Cr.*

VALUATION OF GOODS ON HAND, 31 JANUARY 1817.

193 yards Blue Cloth ....at 7s. 7d.	73	3	7
12 yards Black Ditto.............................at 8s 1d.	4	17	0
16 yards Brown Ditto...........................at 9s. 1d.	7	5	4
5 yards Green Ditto............................at 10s. 1d.	2	10	5
18 yards Blue Ditto ....at 12s. 1d.	10	17	6
14 yards Scarlet Ditto............................at 15s. 1d.	10	11	2
14 yards Black Ditto........................ ....at 20s. 2d.	14	2	4
23 yards Brown Ditto...........................at 21s. 2d.	24	6	10
20 yards Green Ditto ....at 22s. 2d.	22	3	4
30 yards Blue Ditto...........................at 25s. 2d.	37	15	0
18 yards Scarlet Ditto..................... ....at 28s. 2d.	25	7	0
72 yards Toilinette ....at 4s. 1d.	14	14	0
40 yards Ditto .... at 5s. 1d.	10	3	4
82 yards Drab Casimir ... .at 5s. 1d.	20	16	10
50 yards Ditto Ditto ....at 6s. 1d.	15	4	2
36 yards Ditto Ditto ....at 10s. 2d.	18	6	0
Entered Merchandise, Fol. 2 £	312	3	10

(1)   *Dr.*   THE ESTATE OF JOHN EVANS, WOOLLEN-DRAPER, HALIFAX,   *Cr.*

31st January 1817.

L 1	To Johnson and Co. Balance due to them..............	107	3	6	M 2	By Merchandise, Balance as per Valuation..............	312	3	10
L 2	To Fraser and Son, Balance due to them........	100	14	6	C 1	By Cash, Balance in hand	60	17	4
		207	18	0	L 1	By Wilson and Co. Balance due from them.............	360	11	8
L 1	To Stock, my net Capital......	567	18	10	2	By Charles Green, Balance due from him..............	25	4	0
					2	By William Brown, Balance due from him..............	17	0	0
	£	775	16	10		£	775	16	10

K

SET II.

WHOLESALE DEALER'S BOOKS.

———

CONCERN . . . . INDIVIDUAL.
CAPITAL . . . . VARIABLE.
BUSINESS . . . . CONTINUED.
RESULT . . . . LOSS.

———

OBSERVATIONS.

———

THE Business of a Cotton-Vender at Manchester is here exhibited for the month of February 1817; and, being a continued concern, two Inventories are given, one for the beginning, and the other for the termination of the period.

Five Principal Books are required, namely, the Cotton, Cash, Bills Receivable, Ledger, and Inventory; with a subordinate Memorandum Book to collect the amount of Postages and Sundry Expenses, for periodical entry in the Cash and Cotton. The form and use of such Memorandum Books having been sufficiently shewn in Set I. it is unnecessary to give their details in this and the following Sets; and, accordingly, we shall notice merely their weekly or monthly additions.

The Financial System of the Cotton-Dealer is nearly as simple as that of the Draper. He pays the Importers chiefly with Bills received from the Manufacturers, so that his Account with the Banker is limited to occasional discounts, and he requires no book for Bills Payable. Wholesale Concerns, however, frequently make their payments by their own Promissory Notes or Drafts, in which case a Book of Bills Payable is requisite, and appropriate forms may be seen in the following Sets.

The business being confined to a single article, the Book of Merchandise is appropriately called the Cotton Book. The acceptance of a lot of Indigo for a bad debt, gives accidental occurrence to another commodity, but the entries of this transaction come into the Cotton Book without any derangement of its system. Should a Wholesale Dealer, however, frequently speculate in articles foreign to his immediate and constant business, he ought to keep a distinct book, similar to the Mercantile Adventures attached to the Manufacturer's Set.

The Wholesale Dealer has a great advantage over the Retailer, in possessing a systematic check upon the quantities of his commodities. The particulars of every purchase and sale of Cotton being entered in appropriate columns in the Cotton Book, the general Balance of Quantity is ascertained as fully as that of Value; and, by means of the Warehouse Ledger, (a distinct book for Quantities alone, as described, Chap. XV.) the particular balances of each sort are also obtained. Thus the general balance of Quantity is proved by its correspondence to the sum of the particular balances. A *third check* is obtained, by affixing a mark [✓] against the number of each bag in the purchases when sold off: the numbers unmarked shew the individual bags that compose the particular and general balances: and, by this simple contrivance, the Cotton Book is made to answer every purpose of a separate Number Book, exclusive of its proper and more immediate offices.

The result of this set of transactions is a heavy loss, occasioned by one of those rapid depreciations which are not unfrequent in the cotton-market; but, the capital at the commencement exceeding the losses, the proprietor continues solvent.

Analogous to these books, are those of Woolstaplers, Dry-Salters, Corn-Factors, Wine Merchants, and all Wholesale Dealers whatever, who keep a continuous stock of goods.

SET II.

THE BOOKS

OF

SAMUEL MANSLEY, COTTON-VENDER, MANCHESTER.

------

1. WAREHOUSE LEDGER.
2. COTTON.
3. CASH.
4. BILLS RECEIVABLE.
5. LEDGER.
6. INVENTORY.

Dr.   COTTON.   (1)

PURCHASES.	Total.		West Indian.		Orleans.		Bahias.		Pernams.		Georgia.	
	Bags.	Net lbs.	Bags.	Net lbs.	Bags.	Net lbs.	Bags.	Net lbs.	Bags.	Net lbs.	Bags.	Net lbs.
1817.												
Jan. 31 To Balance....	120	17,994	10	1,444	23	3,363	35	5,207	41	6,050	11	1,930
Feb. 3 To Pratt & Co.	65	10,175	..	....	..	....	30	4,708	35	5,467	—	—
5 To B. Milne ...	38	6,110	10	1,595	20	3,206	..	....	..	....	8	1,309
7 To Wells & Co.	40	6,380	15	2,364	15	2,418	..	....	..	....	10	1,598
8 To T. Grant ...	46	7,533	..	....	..	....	15	2,428	31	5,105	—	—
10 To Pratt & Co.	70	11,193	..	....	..	....	30	4,966	40	6,227	—	—
	379	59,385	35	5,403	58	8,987	110	17,309	147	22,849	29	4,837
Feb. 28 To Balance	55	8,770	6	931	9	1,437	16	2,708	20	3,049	4	645

(1)   PER CONTRA.   *Cr.*

	SALES.	Total.		West Indian.		Orleans.		Bahias.		Pernams.		Georgia.	
		Bags.	Net lbs.	Bags.	Net lbs.	Bags.	Net lbs.	Bags.	Net lbs.	Bags.	Net lbs.	Bags.	Net lbs.
1817.													
Feb. 3	By Holt & Co..	12	1,792	..	....	..	....	..	....	12	1,792	—	—
3	By S. Lord	8	1,191	..	....	8	1,191	—	—	—	—	—	—
4	By B. Carr	14	2,077	..	....	..	....	14	2,077	—	—	—	—
6	By Binns & Co.	10	1,625	5	741	..	....	..	....	..	....	5	884
8	By T. Hinde...	16	2,470	5	703	5	721	..	....	..	....	6	1,046
10	By West & Co.	10	1,451	..	....	10	1,451	—	—	—	—	—	—
12	By North & Co.	15	2,198	..	....	..	....	..	....	15	2,198	—	—
13	By Holt & Co..	11	1,627	..	....	..	....	11	1,627	—	—	—	—
15	By Binns & Co.	24	3,563	..	....	..	....	10	1,503	14	2,060	—	—
17	By S. Lord	18	2,720	..	....	..	....	10	1,532	8	1,188	—	—
19	By West & Co.	32	5,159	8	1,264	16	2,586	..	....	..	....	8	1,309
20	By B. Carr	25	3,845	..	....	..	....	10	1,517	15	2,328	—	—
20	By Newton & Co.	1	131	..	....	..	....	..	....	1	131	—	—
22	By Holt & Co..	36	5,872	..	....	..	....	16	2,617	20	3,255	—	—
24	By North & Co.	27	4,318	11	1,764	10	1,601	..	....	..	....	6	953
26	By Binns & Co.	32	5,327	..	....	..	....	13	2,209	19	3,118	—	—
27	By S. Lord	33	5,249	..	....	..	....	10	1,519	23	3,730	—	—
28	By Balance....	55	8,770	6	931	9	1,437	16	2,708	20	3,049	4	645
		379	59,385	35	5,403	58	8,987	110	17,309	147	22,849	29	4,837

Dr.   COTTON.   (1)

1817.		Bags		Net lbs.	Price.	£.	s.	d.	£.	s.	d.
Jan. 31		To Balance......	120	Sundry as per Valuation......	17.994	.....	....	...	2,161	19	2
Feb. 3	5	To Pratt and Co..	....	....Liverpool.							
			30	Bahia.							
				No. Gross. Tare. Drft.							
				cwt. qr. lb. lb. lb.							
				√ 1..... 1 0 21...5..1							
				√ 2..... 1 1 9...7..1							
				√ 3.... 1 2 14...6..1							
				√ 4..... 1 1 15...6..1							
				√ 5..... 1 1 18...6..1							
				√ 6.... 1 1 25...6..1							
				√ 7..... 1 2 23...6..1							
				√ 8..... 1 2 25...5..1							
				√ 9.... 1 1 18...5..1							
				√ 10.... 1 0 27...6..1							
				√ 11..... 1 2 26...6..1							
(Present Bill at 3 Months.)				√ 12..... 1 1 9...7..1							
				√ 13.... 1 1 18...7. 1							
				√ 14..... 1 2 15...5..1							
				√ 15..... 1 2 27. .7..1							
				√ 16..... 1 2 23...6..1							
				√ 17..... 1 1 6...6..1							
				√ 18.... 1 2 1...6..1							
				√ 19..... 1 1 28...5..1							
				√ 20..... 1 1 25...5..1							
				√ 21..... 1 0 19...7..1							
				√ 22..... 1 1 23...6..1							
				√ 23..... 1 1 25...5..1							
				√ 24..... 1 2 27...5..1							
				√ 25..... 1 1 27...5..1							
				√ 26..... 1 0 26...6..1							
				√ 27.... 1 2 22...6..1							
				√ 28..... 1 1 19...7..1							
				√ 29..... 1 1 15. .7..1							
				√ 30..... 1 0 1...7..1							
				Gross ...43 3 17. 179. 30							
				Tare & } 1 3 · 13							
				Draft }							
		(continued)		Net ....42 0 4...Or...	4,708	at 2s. 2d.	510	0	8			
			150	Carried forwards	22,702	......	510	0	8	2,161	19	2

(1)   PER CONTRA.   *Cr.*

			Bags		Net lbs.	Price.	£.	s.	d.	£.	s.	d.
1817.												
Feb. 3	3	By Holt and Co..	....	.... Manchester.								
			12	Pernams.								
				No. cwt. qr. lb. Tare.Drft.								
				193.... 1 2 6..7..1								
				158.... 1 1 27..6..1								
				146.... 1 1 25 .6..1								
				218.... 1 1 9..6..1								
		(Present Bill at 3 Months)		144.... 1 2 4..7..1								
				209.... 1 2 17..6..1								
				152.... 1 0 15..4..1								
				198.... 1 0 24..4..1								
				215.... 1 0 17..6..1								
				157.... 1 1 17..6..1								
				163.... 1 1 13..6..1								
				116.... 1 1 20..6..1								
				Gross....16 2 26.70.12								
				T. & D. . 0 2 26								
				Net.....16 0 0...Or..	1,792	at 2s.8d.	....	..	..	238	18	8
Feb. 3	4	By S. Lord......	....	....Stockport.								
			8	Orleans.								
				199.... 1 2 7..6..1								
				145.... 1 0 27..5..1								
				100.... 1 1 7..6..1								
				156.... 1 1 16..5..1								
		(Present Bill at 3 Months)		211.... 1 1 23..5..1								
				121.... 1 1 2..5..1								
				141.... 1 2 0..6..1								
				195.... 1 1 12..5..1								
				Gross .. 11 0 10.43 8								
				T. & D.. 0 1 23								
				Net.... 10 2 15...Or..	1,191	at 2s.4d.	....	..	..	138	19	0
			20	Carried forwards	2,983	......	....	..	..	377	17	8

Dr.   COTTON.   (2)

			Bags		Net lbs.	Price.	£.	s.	d	£.	s.	d.
1817.			150	Brought forwards........	22,702	......	510	0	8	2,161	19	2
Feb. 3	5	To Pratt and Co..	35	Pernams.								
		(continued)										
				No. cwt. qr. lb. Tare. Drft.								
				✓ 31.... 1 0 21...5..1								
				✓ 32.... 1 1 25...5..1								
				✓ 33.... 1 1 26...6..1								
				✓ 34.... 1 1 25...7..1								
				✓ 35.... 1 2 23...7..1								
				✓ 36.... 1 0 27...7..1								
				✓ 37.... 1 1 4...6..1								
				✓ 38.... 1 1 5...5..1								
				✓ 39.... 1 2 7...6..1								
				✓ 40.... 1 0 19...6..1								
				✓ 41.... 1 2 22...5..1								
				✓ 42.... 1 2 23...6..1								
				✓ 43.... 1 0 27...7..1								
		(Present Bill at 3 Months.)		✓ 44.... 1 0 26...7..1								
				✓ 45.... 1 2 19...6..1								
				✓ 46.... 1 1 22...5..1								
				✓ 47.... 1 1 15...7..1								
				✓ 48.... 1 1 11...5..1								
				✓ 49.... 1 2 14...5..1								
				✓ 50.... 1 2 13...5..1								
				✓ 51.... 1 1 17...7..1								
				✓ 52.... 1 2 16...6..1								
				✓ 53.... 1 1 13...5..1								
				✓ 54.... 1 0 21...5..1								
				✓ 55.... 1 1 7...6..1								
				✓ 56.... 1 2 16...7..1								
				✓ 57.... 1 1 19...7..1								
				✓ 58.... 1 0 20...6..1								
				✓ 59.... 1 1 27...6..1								
				✓ 60.... 1 2 25...5..1								
				✓ 61.... 1 2 23...5..1								
				✓ 62.... 1 2 14...7..1								
				✓ 63.... 1 2 15...6..1								
				✓ 64.... 1 1 18...5..1								
				✓ 65.... 1 1 17...7..1								
				Gross.. 50 3 26.208.35								
				T. & D.. 2 0 19								
				Net ....48 3 7...Or ..	5,467	at 2s.4d.	637	16	4	1,147	17	0
			185	Carried forwards	28,169	......	....	..	..	3,309	16	2

(2)			PER CONTRA.							*Cr.*		

1817.			Bags.		Net lbs.	Price.	£.	s.	d.	£.	s.	d.
			20	Brought forwards........	2,983	......	....	..	..	377	17	8
Feb. 4	2	By B. Carr ... .Manchester.										
			14	Bahia.								
				No.　cwt. qr.　lb. Tare. Drft.								
				129... 1　2　26...7..1								
				133... 1　1　12...5..1								
				213... 1　1　 7...5..1								
				119... 1　1　26...6..1								
				166... 1　0　14...5..1								
		(Present Bill at 3 Months.)		104... 1　2　23...7..1								
				203... 1　1　14...6..1								
				115... 1　1　20...6..1								
				184... 1　2　 1...7..1								
				176... 1 ·1　15...6..1								
				216... 1　0　16...5..1								
				220... 1　1　 0...5..1								
				202... 1　1　16...6..1								
				161... 1　0　22...5..1								
				Gross...19　1　16..81.14								
				T. & D. 0　3　11								
				Net....18　2　 5....Or..	2,077	at 2s. 6d.	....	..	..	259	12	6
Feb. 6	2	By Binns and Co. ......Bury.										
			5	West Indian.								
				175... 1　1　14...5　1								
				111... 1　2　 3...6　1								
		(Present Bill at 3 Months.)		157... 1　0　25...4　1								
				125... 1　1　 5...5..1								
				180... 1　1　24...5..1								
				Gross.. 6　3　15..25..5								
				T. & D. 0　1　 2								
				Net.... 6　2　13....Or..	741	at 2s. 2d.	80	5	6			
			5	Georgia.								
				126... 1　2　22...7..1								
				160... 1　2　20 ..7..1								
				168... 1　2　 8...7..1								
				150.. 1 ·2　16...7..1								
				174... 1　2　18...7..1								
				Gross... 8　1　 0..35..5								
				T. & D. 0　1　12								
				Net.... 7　3　16....Or..	884	at 3s. 3d.	143	13	0	223	18	6
			44	Carried forwards	6,685	....	..	..	..	861	8	8

Dr.   COTTON.   (3)

			Bags.		Net lbs.	Price.	£.	s.	d.	£.	s.	d.
1817.			185	Brought forward	28,169	....	....	...	..	3,309	16	2
Feb. 5	4	To B. Milne.....	....	.... Liverpool.								
			10	West Indian.								

```
         No.    cwt. qr. lb.  Tare. Drft.
      √ 70....   1  0  21...5..1
      √ 71....   1  2  21...7..1
      √ 72. ...  1  2  19...6 .1
      √ 73....   1  1  17..6..1
      √ 74....   1  2  21...7..1
      √ 75....   1  0  21...5..1
      √ 76....   1  1  17...7..1
      √ 77....   1  1  13...5..1
      √ 78....   1  2  19...6..1
      √ 79....   1  2  12...6..1

      Gross...14  3  13...60.10
      T. & D.  0  2  14

      Net...  14  0  27.... Or..
```

| | | | | Net... 14 0 27.... Or.. | 1,595 at 1s. 10d. | | 146 | 4 | 2 | | | |
| | | | 20 | Orleans. | | | | | | | | |

```
      √ 80....   1  0  21...5..1
      √ 81....   1  1  19...7..1
      √ 82....   1  2  22...6..1
      √ 83....   1  1  17...6..1
      √ 84....   1  0  27...5..1
      √ 85....   1  2  23...7..1
      √ 86. ..   1  2  27...5..1
      √ 87....   1  1  19...6..1
      √ 88....   1  1  13. .7..1
      √ 89....   1  2  14...5..1
      √ 90....   1  2  17...6..1
      √ 91....   1  1  16...7..1
      √ 92....   1  1  15 ..7..1
      √ 93....   1  0  27...6..1
      √ 94....   1  1  27...5..1
      √ 95....   1  2  15...5..1
      √ 96....   1  2  21...6..1
      √ 97....   1  1  21...7..1
      √ 98....   1  1  27...7..1
      √ 99....   1  2  19...6..1

      Gross .. 29  3  15. 121. 20
      T. & D.  1  1   1

      Net.... 28  2  14.... Or..
```

(Present Bill at 3 Months.)

| | | | | Net.... 28 2 14.... Or.. | 3,206 at 2s. 1d. | | 333 | 19 | 2 | | | |
| *(continued)* | | | 215 | Carried forwards .... | 32,970 | .... | 480 | 3 | 4 | 3,309 | 16 | 2 |

| (3) | | PER CONTRA. | | | | | | | | | | Cr. | | |

1817.		Bags.		Net lbs.	Price.	£.	s.	d.	£.	s.	d.
		44	Brought forward	6,685	......	....	..	..	861	8	8
Feb. 8	3		By T. Hinde ....Blackburn.								
		5	West Indian.								

No.   cwt.   qr.   lb. Tare. Drft.
138... 1   0   7...4..1
20l... 1   1   8...4..1
169... 1   0   15...4..1
191... 1   1   10...5..1
217... 1   2   19...6..1

Gross... 6   2   3..23..5
T. & D. 0   1   0

Net.... 6   1   3...Or..   703 at 2s. 1d.   73   4   7

5   Orleans.
117... 1   1   24...5..1
172... 1   0   22...4..1
114... 1   2   4...6..1
106... 1   0   19...4..1
206... 1   1   10...6..1

Gross... 6   2   23..25   5
T & D. 0   1   2

Net.... 6   1   21...Or..   721 at 2s. 3d.   81   2   3

(Present Bill at 3 Months.)

6   Georgia.
192... 1   2   15...7..1
212... 1   2   2...7..1
189... 1   2   17...7..1
210... 1   2   26...7..1
167... 1   2   12...7..1
181... 1   2   14...7..1

Gross... 9   3   2..42..6
T. & D. 0   1   20

Net.... 9   1   10...Or..   1,046 at 3s. 1d.   161   5   2   315   12   0

| | | 60 | Carried forward .... | 9,155 | ...... | .... | .. | .. | 1,177 | 0 | 8 |

Dr.   COTTON.   (4)

			Bags.		Net lbs.	Price.	£.	s.	d.	£.	s.	d.
1817.			215	Brought forward	32,970	....	480	3	4	3,309	16	2
Feb. 5	4	To B. Milne	8	Georgia.								
		(continued)		No. cwt. qr. lb. Tare. Drft.								
				✓ 221... 1 1 21...5..1								
				✓ 222... 1 2 15...7..1								
				✓ 223... 1 0 19...6..1								
				✓ 224... 1 1 16...7..1								
		(Present Bill) (at 3 Months.)		✓ 225... 1 2 17...5..1								
				✓ 226... 1 2 27...5..1								
				✓ 227... 1 1 27...6..1								
				✓ 228... 1 2 19...7..1								
				Gross.. 12 0 21..48..8								
				T & D.. 0 2 0								
				Net... 11 2 21... Or..	1,309	at 2s. 10d.	185	8	10	665	12	2
Feb. 6	1	To Cash, paid ...	....	Phœnix Office, Insurance against Fire	.....	....	....	..	..	15	5	6
Feb. 7	1	To Cash, paid ...	....	Petty Expenses this week ...	.....	....	....	..	..	8	13	4
			223	Carried forward	34,279	....	....	..	..	3,999	7	2

(4) PER CONTRA. *Cr.*

			Bags.		Net lbs.	Price.	£.	s.	d.	£.	s.	d.
1817.			60	Brought forward	9,155	....	....	..	..	1,177	0	8
Feb. 10	5	By West and Co..	....	.... Manchester.								
			10	Orleans.								

No.   cwt. qr.   lb. Tare. Drft.
188... 1 1   5...5..1
153... 1 0 20...6..1
132... 1 2   0...6..1
149... 1 2   2...6..1
165... 1 1 18...5..1
107... 1 0 25...5..1
183... 1 1 17...5..1
208... 1 1 13...5..1
147... 1 0 24...4..1
214... 1 1 17...5..1

Gross.. 13 2   1..52. 10
T. & D.. 0 2   6

(*Present Bill at 3 Months.*)

				Net... 12 3 23...Or..	1,451	at 2s. 3d.	....	..	..	163	4	9
Feb. 12	4	By North and Co.	....	.... Manchester.								
			15	Pernams.								

108... 1 0 23...6..1
204... 1 0 15...5..1
164... 1 1 14...6..1
113... 1 1 14...6..1
131... 1 2   0...6..1
103... 1 1 15...5..1
124... 1 0 19...5..1
139... 1 1 12...5..1
101... 1 1 16...5..1
118... 1 1 14...5..1
186... 1 1 22...7..1
140... 1 1 21...5..1
187... 1 1 19...6..1
128... 1 1 22...6..1
190... 1 2   0...7..1

Gross.. 20 2   2..85. 15
T. & D. 0 3 16

(*Present Bill at 3 Months.*)

				Net... 19 2 14...Or..	2,198	at 2s. 7d.	....	..	..	283	18	2
			85	Carried forward	12,804	....	....	..	..	1,624	3	7

Dr.   COTTON.   (5)

			Bags.		Net lbs.	Price.	£.	s.	d.	£.	s.	d.
			223	Brought forward	34,279	......	....	..	..	3,999	7	2
1817.												
Feb. 7	5	To Wells and Co.	....	.... Liverpool.								
			15	West Indian.								

No.   cwt.   qr.   lb.   Tare.   Drft.
✓ 270...   1   1   21...7..1
✓ 271...   1   0   19...5..1
272...   1   2   21...6..1
✓ 273...   1   1   17...5..1
274...   1   1   16...7..1
275...   1   0   17...6..1
✓ 276...   1   2   23...6..1
✓ 277...   1   2   25...5..1
278...   1   2   19...5..1
279...   1   1   17...7..1
✓ 280...   1   1   25...5..1
✓ 281...   1   1   26...6..1
✓ 282...   1   0   27...6..1
✓ 283...   1   2   23...7..1
284...   1   1   15...5..1

Gross..   22   0   3.   88.15
T & D.   0   3   19

				Net.... 21 0 12.....Or..	2,364	at 1s. 9d.	206	17	0			
			15	Orleans.								

240...   1   1   17...7..1
✓ 241...   1   1   25...5..1
242...   1   2   27...5..1
✓ 243...   1   1   26...6..1
244...   1   0   27...7..1
✓ 245...   1   1   25...7..1
246...   1   2   13...6..1
✓ 247...   1   2   18...5..1
248...   1   1   11...5..1
249...   1   2   17...7..1
✓ 250...   1   1   6...6..1
251...   1   0   18...5..1
252...   1   1   26...5..1
✓ 253...   1   2   25...5..1
254...   1   2   27...6..1

(Present Bill at 3 Months.)

Gross ..22   2   0.. 87.15
T. & D.   0   3   18

		(continued.)		Net.... 21 2 10.... Or..	2,418	at 1s. 11d.	231	14	6			
			253	Carried forward..........	39,061	......	438	11	6	3,999	7	2

(5) PER CONTRA. *Cr.*

			Bags.		Net lbs.	Price.	£.	s.	d.	£.	s.	d.
1817.			85	Brought forward	12,804	....	....	..	..	1,624	3	7
Feb. 13	3	By Holt & Co....	....	.... Manchester.								
			11	Bahia.								

No.   cwt. qr.   lb. Tare. Drft.
177... 1 2 22...6..1
102... 1 1 14...6..1
154... 1 1   8...5..1
143.. 1 0 28...5..1
197... 1 1 18...6..1
122... 1 0 26...5..1
179... 1 1 17...6..1
135... 1 1 10...6..1
162... 1 0 22...6..1
110... 1 2   0...7..1
134... 1 1 25...6..1

Gross.. 15 0 22..64.11
T. & D. 0 2 19

(Present Bill at 3 Months.)

				Net ... 14 2 3...Or..	1,627 at 2s. 5d.	....	..	..	196	11	11

15	2	By Binns & Co...	....	.... Bury.					
			10	Bahia.					

159... 1 0 21...5..1
112... 1 2   2...7..1
171... 1 1 15...6..1
127... 1 2   6...7..1
200... 1 1 14...6..1
123... 1 0 26...5..1
219... 1 1 20...6..1
148... 1 1 22...6..1
137... 1 2   4...7..1
173... 1 1 16...6..1

Gross.. 14 0   6..61.10
T. & D. 0 2 15

(Present Bill at 3 Months.)

(continued)

				Net ... 13 1 19...Or..	1,503 at 2s. 4d.	175	7	0		

			106	Carried forward	15,934	....	175	7	0	1,820	15	6

M

Dr.   COTTON.   (6)

			Bags.			Net lbs.	Price.	£.	s.	d.	£.	s.	d.
1817.			253	Brought forward		39,061	....	438	11	6	3,999	7	2
Feb. 7	5	To Wells & Co...	10	Georgia.									
		(continued)											
				No. cwt. qr. lb. Tare. Drft.									
				✓ 229... 1 2 23...5..1									
				230... 1 1 19...6..1									
				231... 1 2 16...7..1									
		(Present Bill) (at 3 Months.)		✓ 232... 1 0 27...5..1									
				✓ 233... 1 1 26...7..1									
				✓ 234... 1 1 25...7..1									
				235... 1 0 27...6..1									
				✓ 236... 1 1 25...5..1									
				✓ 237... 1 1 27...5..1									
				238... 1 2 25...7..1									
				Gross.. 14 3 16..60.10									
				T. & D. 0 2 14									
				Net... 14 1 2 ..Or..		1,598	at 2s. 9d.	219	14	6			
											658	6	0
			263	Carried forward		40,659	....	....	...	..	4,657	13	2

(6)   PER CONTRA.   *Cr.*

		Bags.		Net lbs.	Price.	£	s.	d.	£	s.	d.
1817.		106	Brought forward	15,934	......	175	7	0	1,820	15	6
Feb.15	2	14	By Binns & Co... *(continued)*								

Pernams.

No.	cwt.	qr.	lb.	Tare.	Drft.
207...	1	0	25...	5..	1
182...	1	0	25.	.5..	1
136..	1	0	4..	.5..	1
185...	1	1	24...	6..	1
120...	1	1	25...	6..	1
130...	1	1	20...	6..	1
142...	1	1	13...	5..	1
178...	1	2	7...	7..	1
109...	1	1	8...	5..	1
196 ..	1	1	25...	6..	1
194...	1	1	15...	6..	1
205...	1	1	10 ..	5..	1
170...	1	2	6...	7..	1
105...	1	1	15...	6..	1

Gross.. 19 0 26.. 80. 14
T & D. 0 3 10
Net ... 18 1 10 .. Or..   2,060 at 2s. 6d.   257 10 0   432 17 0

17   4   By S. Lord ....Stockport.

10   Bahia.

	cwt.	qr.	lb.	Tare.	Drft.
1....	1	0	21...	5..	1
3....	1	2	14...	6..	1
2....	1	1	9...	7..	1
6....	1	1	25...	6..	1
8....	1	2	25...	5..	1
10....	1	0	27...	6..	1
19....	1	1	28...	5..	1
22....	1	1	23...	6..	1
24....	1	2	27...	5..	1
30....	1	0	1..	.7..	1

Gross.. 14 1 4.. 58. 10
T. & D. 0 2 12
Net ... 13 2 20... Or..   1,532 at 2s. 2d.   165 19 4

8   Pernams.

	cwt.	qr.	lb.	Tare.	Drft.
32....	1	1	25...	5..	1
34....	1	1	25...	7..	1
40....	1	0	19...	6..	1
43....	1	0	27...	7..	1
46....	1	1	22...	5..	1
50....	1	2	13...	5..	1
31....	1	0	21...	5..	1
33....	1	1	26...	6..	1

Gross.. 11 0 10.. 46.. 8
T. & D. 0 1 26
Net ... 10 2 12... Or..   1,188 at 2s. 4d.   138 12 0   304 11 4

138   Carried forward ....   20,714 ....   2,558 3 10

(Present Bill at 3 Months.)

Dr.   COTTON.   (7)

			Bags		Net lbs.	Price.	£.	s.	d.	£.	s.	d.
1817.			263	Brought forward	40,659	......	....	...	..	4,657	13	2
Feb. 8	3	To T. Grant	....	.... Liverpool.								
			15	Bahia.								

No.   cwt.   qr.   lb. Tare. Drft.
✓ 255...   1   0   27...5..1
✓ 256 ..   1   1   26...7..1
✓ 257...   1   2   22...6..1
✓ 258...   1   2   23...6..1

(Present Bill)
(at 3 Months.)

✓ 259...   1   1   27...7..1
✓ 260...   1   1   19...5..1
✓ 261...   1   2   19...5..1
✓ 262...   1   2   27...5..1
✓ 263...   1   0   27...7..1
✓ 264...   1   1   11...6..1
✓ 265...   1   2   15...6..1
✓ 266...   1   2   17...5..1
✓ 267...   1   2   14...7..1
✓ 268...   1   1   19...6..1
✓ 269...   1   0   26...5..1

Gross..   22   2   11..88. 15
T. & D.   0   3   19

(continued)

				Net ... 21 2 20... Or..	2,428 at 2s. 1d.	252	18	4			

| | | | 278 | Carried forward .... | 43,087 | ...... | 252 | 18 | 4 | 4,657 | 13 | 2 |

(7) PER CONTRA. *Cr.*

		Bags.		Net lbs.	Price.	£.	s.	d.	£.	s.	d.
1817.		138	Brought forward	20,714	......	....	..	..	2,558	3	10
Feb.19	5		By West and Co.. ....|.... Manchester.								

8	West Indian.

No.	cwt.	qr.	lb.	Tare.	Drft.
70....	1	0	21...	5..	1
72....	1	2	19...	6..	1
74....	1	2	21...	7..	1
79....	1	2	12...	6..	1
76....	1	1	17...	7..	1
75....	1	0	21...	5..	1
78....	1	2	19...	6..	1
77....	1	1	13...	5..	1
Gross..	11	3	3..	47..	8
T. & D.	0	1	27		
Net....	11	1	4 ... Or..		

1,264 at 1s.9d. 110 12 0

(Present Bill)
(at 3 Months.)

16	Orleans

81....	1	1	19...	7..	1
83....	1	1	17...	6..	1
85....	1	2	23...	7..	1
88....	1	1	13...	7..	1
86....	1	2	27...	5..	1
90....	1	2	17...	6..	1
94....	1	1	27...	5..	1
92....	1	1	15...	7..	1
96....	1	2	21...	6..	1
80....	1	0	21...	5..	1
93....	1	0	27...	6..	1
97....	1	1	21...	7..	1
82....	1	2	22...	6..	1
91....	1	1	16...	7..	1
95....	1	2	15...	5..	1
99....	1	2	19...	6..	1
Gross..	24	0	12..	98.	16
T. & D.	1	0	2		
Net...	23	0	10... Or...		

2,586 at 1s.11d. 247 16 6

8	Georgia.

227...	1	1	27...	6..	1
221...	1	1	21...	5..	1
223...	1	0	19...	6..	1
225...	1	2	17...	5..	1
224...	1	1	16...	7..	1
222...	1	2	15...	7..	1
226...	1	2	27...	5..	1
228...	1	2	19...	7..	1
Gross..	12	0	21..	48..	8
T. & D.	0	2	0		
Net...	11	2	21... Or...		

1,309 at 2s. 9d. 179 19 9

538 8 3

		170	Carried forward...... ...	25,873	......	....	..	..	3,096	12	1

Dr.   COTTON.   (8)

			Bags		Net lbs.	Price.	£.	s.	d.	£.	s.	d.
1817.			278	Brought forward	43,087	.....	252	18	4	4,657	13	2
Feb. 8	3	To T. Grant	31	Pernams.								
		(continued)		No. cwt. qr. lb. Tare. Drft.								
				√ 300... 1 2 21...5..1								
				√ 301... 1 0 27...7..1								
				√ 302... 1 2 23...6..1								
				√ 303... 1 1 15...6..1								
				√ 304... 1 1 27...7..1								
				√ 305... 1 0 19...5..1								
				√ 306... 1 2 26...5..1								
				√ 307... 1 1 19...7..1								
				√ 308... 1 2 22...6..1								
		(Present Bill)		√ 309... 1 2 21...5..1								
		(at 3 Months.)		√ 310... 1 2 22...5..1								
				√ 311... 1 0 19...6..1								
				√ 312... 1 1 16...7..1								
				√ 313... 1 2 15...7..1								
				√ 314... 1 1 19...5..1								
				√ 315... 1 1 17...6..1								
				√ 316... 1 1 15...7..1								
				√ 317... 1 2 26...6..1								
				√ 318... 1 1 22...5..1								
				√ 319... 1 2 17...6..1								
				√ 320... 1 2 17...5. 1								
				√ 321... 1 2 22...5..1								
				√ 322... 1 2 16...7..1								
				√ 323... 1 1 19...5..1								
				√ 324... 1 1 17...6..1								
				√ 325... 1 2 19...5..1								
				√ 326... 1 2 22...5..1								
				√ 327... 1 2 27...7..1								
				√ 328... 1 0 26...6..1								
				√ 329... 1 2 21...5..1								
				√ 330... 1 1 26...5..1								
				Gross ..47 1 24. 180. 31								
				T. & D. 1 3 15								
				Net ... 45 2 9... Or...	5,105 at 2s.3d.		574	6	3			
										827	4	7
			309	Carried forward..........	48,192	......	....	...	...	5,484	17	9

(8)   PER CONTRA.   *Cr.*

	Bags.		Net lbs.	Price.	£.	s.	d.	£.	s.	d.
	170	Brought forward	25,873	....	....	..	..	3,096	12	1
1817.										
Feb.20 2 By B. Carr .... Manchester.										
	10	Bahia.								

No.	cwt.	qr.	lb.	Tare.	Drft.
4....	1	1	15...	6..	1
5....	1	1	18...	6..	1
26....	1	0	26...	6..	1
17....	1	1	6...	6..	1
12....	1	1	9...	7..	1
11....	1	2	26...	6..	1
18....	1	2	1...	6..	1
21....	1	0	19.	.7..	1
28....	1	1	19...	7..	1
7....	1	2	23...	6..	1
Gross..	14	0	22..	63.	10
T.&D..	0	2	17		
Net...	13	2	5...Or..		

(Present Bill at 3 Months.)

			Net lbs.	Price.	£.	s.	d.	£.	s.	d.
Net... 13 2 5...Or..			1,517	at 2s. 0d.	151	14	0			
	15	Pernams.								

No.	cwt.	qr.	lb.	Tare.	Drft.
35....	1	2	23...	7..	1
45....	1	2	19...	6..	1
41....	1	2	22..	5..	1
37....	1	1	4...	6..	1
44....	1	0	26...	7..	1
52....	1	2	16...	6..	1
48....	1	1	11...	5..	1
55. ..	1	1	7...	6..	1
58....	1	0	20...	6..	1
36....	1	0	27...	7..	1
54....	1	0	21...	5..	1
60....	1	2	25...	5..	1
47....	1	1	15...	7..	1
42....	1	2	23...	6..	1
57....	1	1	19.	.7..	1
Gross..	21	2	26..	91.	15
T. & D.	0	3	22		
Net...	20	3	4...Or..		

			Net lbs.	Price.	£.	s.	d.	£.	s.	d.
Net... 20 3 4...Or..			2,328	at 2s. 2d.	252	4	0			
								403	18	0
	195	Carried forward	29,718	......	....	..	..	3,500	10	1

Dr.   COTTON.   (9)

			Bags		Net lbs.	Price.	£.	s.	d	£.	s.	d.
1817.			309	Brought forward	48,192	......	....	..	..	5,484	17	9.
Feb. 10	5	To Pratt and Co..	....	....Liverpool.								
			30	Bahia.								
				No. cwt. qr. lb. Tare. Drft.								
				✓ 340... 1 2 21...5..1								
				341... 1 1 19...7..1								
				✓ 342... 1 1 17...6..1								
				343... 1 2 26...6..1								
				✓ 344... 1 0 19...5..1								
				345... 1 1 14...7..1								
				346... 1 1 11...5..1								
				347... 1 2 12...6..1								
	(Present Bill at 3 Months.)			✓ 348... 1 1 5...7..1								
				349... 1 1 18...5..1								
				✓ 350... 1 2 6...6..1								
				351... 1 2 17...5..1								
				352... 1 2 19...5..1								
				353... 1 2 21...6..1								
				✓ 354... 1 2 25...7..1								
				355... 1 1 27...5..1								
				✓ 356... 1 2 26...5..1								
				✓ 357... 1 1 19...6..1								
				358... 1 2 26...7..1								
				✓ 359... 1 2 27...7..1								
				360... 1 1 15...6..1								
				✓ 361... 1 1 19...5..1								
				362... 1 2 17...5..1								
				363... 1 2 19...7..1								
				✓ 364... 1 2 21...5..1								
				365... 1 2 17...6..1								
				✓ 366... 1 1 19...7..1								
				✓ 367... 1 0 17...5..1								
				368... 1 2 21...7..1								
				✓ 369... 1 2 13...6..1								
				Gross.. 46 0 21.177.30								
				T. & D.. 1 3 11								
	(continued)			Net ....44 1 10...Or ..	4,966	at 2s. 1d.	517	5	10			
			339	Carried forward..........	53,158	......	517	5	10	5,484	17	9

(9)   PER CONTRA.   *Cr.*

				Bags		Net lbs.	Price.	£.	s.	d.	£.	s.	d.
1817.				195	Brought forward	29,718	......	....	..	..	3,500	10	1
Feb.20	4	By Newton & Co.	....		.... Liverpool, Carriers.								
				1	Pernam lost.								
					No. cwt. qr. lb. Tare.Drft.								
					301....1 0 27...7..1								
					T. & D. 0 0 8								
					Net.... 1 0 19...Or..	131 at	2s. 3d.	....	..	..	14	14	9
Feb.20	2	By Best and Co. ..	....		.... Bankers, Manchester.								
					Balance of Interest as per } their Account .... (	......	......	....	..	.	7	8	8
Feb.22	5	By Pratt and Co. ..	....		.... Liverpool.								
					Short Weights on Invoice, Feb. 3								
					36 lb. Pernams	....at	2s. 4d.	....	..	..	4	4	0
Feb.22	5	By Holt and Co. ..	...		.... Manchester.								
				16	Bahia.								
					No. cwt. qr. lb. Tare. Drft.								
					9... 1 1 18...5..1								
					14... 1 2 15...5..1								
					20... 1 1 25 ..5..1								
					23... 1 1 25...5..1								
					27... 1 2 22...6..1								
					29... 1 1 15...7..1								
					13... 1 1 18...7..1								
					15... 1 2 27...7.1								
	(Present Bill at 3 Months)				16... 1 2 23...6..1								
					25... 1 1 27...5..1								
					255... 1 0 27...5..1								
					259... 1 1 27...7..1								
					261... 1 2 19...5..1								
					266... 1 2 17. ..5..1								
					269... 1 0 26..5..1								
					267... 1 2 14...7..1								
					Gross...24 1 9..92. 16								
					T. & D. 0 3 24								
					Net....23 1 13...Or ..	2,617 at	1s.10d.	239	17	10			
		(continued)		212	Carried forwards	32,466	......	239	17	10	3,526	17	6

Dr.   COTTON.   (10)

1817.			Bags.		Net lbs.	Price.	£.	s.	d.	£.	s.	d.
			339	Brought forward	53,158	......	517	5	10	5,484	17	9
Feb.10	5	To Pratt and Co..	40	Pernams.								
		(continued)		No. cwt. qr. lb. Tare. Drft.								
				✓ 370... 1 2 21...5..1								
				✓ 371... 1 1 9...7..1								
				✓ 372... 1 0 19...6..1								
				373... 1 1 22...7..1								
				✓ 374... 1 1 23...5..1								
				✓ 375... 1 1 15...5..1								
				✓ 376... 1 1 17...7..1								
				✓ 377... 1 1 19...6..1								
				✓ 378... 1 2 23...5..1								
				379... 1 0 26...7..1								
				✓ 380... 1 1 17...6..1								
				✓ 381... 1 2 22...5..1								
				✓ 382... 1 2 23...7..1								
				✓ 383... 1 2 27...5..1								
				✓ 384... 1 1 15...6..1								
				385... 1 1 17...7..1								
				✓ 386... 1 1 15...6..1								
				✓ 387... 1 1 17...5..1								
				✓ 388... 1 0 19...5..1								
				✓ 389... 1 1 21...6..1								
				✓ 390... 1 2 22...6..1								
				✓ 391... 1 2 19...7..1								
				✓ 392... 1 1 11...6..1								
				393... 1 0 17...5..1								
				394... 1 1 22...5..1								
				395... 1 1 19...5..1								
				396... 1 1 5...7..1								
				397... 1 2 7...5..1								
				398... 1 2 19...6..1								
				399... 1 1 26...7..1								
				400... 1 0 27...7..1								
				401... 1 0 25...6..1								
				402... 1 1 15...6..1								
				403... 1 0 17...5..1								
				404... 1 1 26...5..1								
				405... 1 2 22...7..1								
				406... 1 1 12...5..1								
				407... 1 1 19...6..1								
				408... 1 2 23...7..1								
				409... 1 2 24...6..1								
				Gross...58 0 8. 237.40								
				T. & D. 2 1 25								
				Net....55 2 11....Or..	6,227 at 2s. 3d.	700	10	9			
										1,217	16	7
			379	Carried forwards	59,385	......	....	..	..	6,702	14	4

(Present Bill
at 3 Months.)

(10)   PER CONTRA.   *Cr.*

			Bags.		Net lbs.	Price.	£.	s.	d.	£.	s.	d.
1817.			212	Brought forward	32,466	......	239	17	10	3,526	17	6
Feb.22	5	By Holt and Co..	20	Pernams.								
		(continued.)										

No.   cwt. qr. lb.   Tare. Drft.

No.	cwt.	qr.	lb.	Tare.	Drft.
39...	1	2	7..	.6..	1
49...	1	2	14..	.5..	1
56...	1	2	16..	.7..	1
59...	1	1	27..	.6..	1
51...	1	1	17..	.7..	1
53...	1	1	13..	.5..	1
38...	1	1	5..	.5..	1
65...	1	1	17..	.7..	1
62...	1	2	14..	.7..	1
64...	1	1	18..	.5..	1
61...	1	2	23..	.5..	1
63...	1	2	15..	.6..	1
302...	1	2	23..	.6..	1
304...	1	1	27..	.7..	1
311...	1	0	19..	.6..	1
316...	1	1	15..	.7..	1
322...	1	2	16..	.7..	1
300...	1	2	21..	.5..	1
303...	1	1	15..	.6..	1
308...	1	2	22..	.6..	1

(Present Bill at 3 Months.)

Gross ..30   1   8 . 121. 20
T. & D.. 1   1   1

Net.... 29   0   7 ...Or..

					Net lbs.	Price.	£.	s.	d.	£.	s.	d.
				Net.... 29 0 7 ...Or..	3,255 at 2s. 0d.		325	10	0			
										565	7	10
Feb.22	2	By Black and Co..	......	......Manchester.								

3 Bags Indigo.

	lbs.
No. 1.....	197
2.....	188
3.....	198

					Net lbs.	Price.	£.	s.	d.	£.	s.	d.
				583......... .....at		8s. 0d.	....	..	..	233	4	0
			232	Carried forward..........	35,721	......	....	..	..	4,325	9	4

_Dr._   COTTON.   (11)

			Bags.		Net lbs.	Price.	£.	s.	d.	£.	s.	d.
1817.			379	Brought forward	59,385	......	....	...	..	6,702	14	4
Feb. 10	3	To R. Hill	....	.... Manchester.								
				Loss by Composition, 50 per Cent. on his debt, £.356. 12.	......	....	....	...	..	178	6	0
Feb. 10	5	To West & Co. ...	....	.... Manchester.								
				Discount for Cash 3 per Cent. on £.163. 4. 9...	......	....	....	...	..	4	17	11
Feb. 14	1	To Cash	....	Paid Petty Expenses this week	.....	......	....	...	..	5	14	1
Feb. 15	5	To J. Scott	....	.... Manchester, for Indigo, accepted in Balance lbs. No. 1 ... 197 2 ... 188 3 ... 198 583 lbs.	......	at 10s.	....	...	..	291	10	0
Feb. 20	5	To West & Co. ...	....	.... Manchester.								
				3 per Cent. Discount on £.538. 8. 3.	......	....	....	...	..	16	3	0
Feb. 21	1	To Cash	....	Paid Petty Expenses this week	.....	....	....	...	..	10	5	9
			379	Carried forward	59,385	....	....	...	..	7,209	11	1

			Bags.		Net lbs.	Price.	£.	s.	d.	£.	s.	d.
1817.			232	Brought forward	35,721	....	....	...	..	4,325	9	4
Feb.24	4	By North and Co.	....	.... Manchester.								
			11	West Indian.								

No. cwt. qr. lb. Tare. Drft.
71... 1 2 21...7..1
73 .. 1 1 17...6..1
270... 1 1 21...7..1
273... 1 1 17...5..1
280... 1 1 25...5..1
282... 1 0 27...6..1
281... 1 1 26...6..1
283... 1 2 23..7..1
276... 1 2 23...6..1
271... 1 0 19...5..1
277... 1 2 25...5..1
Gross...16 1 20..65.11
T. & D. 0 2 20
Net....15 3 0 ..Or ..

| | | | | | 1,764 at 1s. 6d. | | 132 | 6 | 0 | | | |

(Present Bill at 3 Months.)

| | | | 10 | Orleans. | | | | | | | | |

84... 1 0 27...5..1
87... 1 1 19...6..1
98... 1 1 27...7..1
89... 1 2 14. .5..1
245... 1 1 25...7..1
250... 1 1 6...6..1
241... 1 1 25...5..1
243... 1 1 26...6..1
247... 1 2 18...5..1
253. .. 1 2 25...5..1
Gross .. 14 3 16..57.10
T. & D. 0 2 11
Net....14 1 5....Or..

| | | | | | 1,601 at 1s. 8d. | | 133 | 8 | 4 | | | |

| | | | 6 | Georgia. | | | | | | | | |

229... 1 2 23...5..1
232... 1 0 27...5..1
234... 1 1 25...7..1
237... 1 1 27...5..1
233... 1 1 26...7..1
236... 1 1 25...5..1
Gross .. 8 3 13..34. 6
T. & D. 0 1 12
Net.... 8 2 1....Or..

					953 at 2s. 6d.		119	2	6			
										384	16	10
			259	Carried forwards	40,039	....	....	..	..	4,710	6	2

Dr. COTTON. (12)

			Bags.		Net lbs.	Price.	£.	s.	d.	£.	s.	d.
1817.			379	Brought forward	59,385	......	....	...	..	7,209	11	1
Feb.22	4	To S. Lord......	....	.... Stockport.								
				Short Weights on Invoice, 17th February, 36 lb. of Pernams	....	at 2s. 0d.	....	...	..	3	12	0
Feb. 27	5	To Pratt and Co..	....	.... Liverpool.								
				Expenses on Returned Bill, No. 51.............	.....	......	....	..	..	0	15	6
Feb. 28	4	To Newton & Co.	....	.... Liverpool.								
				Carriage this Month, as per Account........	.....	....	....	..	..	36	15	0
Feb. 28	1	To Cash........	....	Paid Petty Expenses this Week	.....	......	.....	..	..	6	5	8
			379	Carried forward	59,385	.....	.....	..	..	7,256	19	3

(12)   PER CONTRA.   *Cr.*

		Bags.		Net lbs.	Price.	£.	s.	d.	£.	s.	d.
1817.		259	Brought forward	40,039	....	....	..	..	4,710	6	2
Feb. 26	2		By Binns & Co... .... Bury.								
		13	Bahia.								

No.   cwt. qr.   lb. Tare. Drft.
257... 1   2   22...6..1
264... 1   1   11...6..1
260... 1   1   19...5..1
263... 1   0   27...7..1
256... 1   1   26...7..1
265... 1   2   15...6..1
262... 1   2   27...5..1
258... 1   2   23...6..1
268... 1   1   19...6..1
340... 1   2   21...5..1
354... 1   2   25...7..1
356... 1   2   26...5..1
364... 1   2   21...5..1

Gross...20   2   2..76.13
T. & D.   0   3   5

Net....19   2   25...Or..   2,209 at 1s. 10d.   202   9   10

(Present Bill at 3 Months.)

19   Pernams.

305... 1   0   19...5..1
314... 1   1   19...5..1
313... 1   2   15...7..1
320... 1   2   17...5..1
325... 1   2   19...5..1
328... 1   0   26...6..1
323... 1   1   19...5..1
324... 1   1   17...7..1
312... 1   1   16...6..1
306... 1   2   26...5..1
309... 1   2   21...5..1
307... 1   1   19...7..1
318... 1   1   22...5..1
315... 1   1   17...6..1
319... 1   2   17...6..1
317... 1   2   26...6..1
327... 1   2   27...7..1
330... 1   1   26...5..1
329... 1   2   21...5..1

Gross...28   3   25.108.19
T. & D.   1   0   15

Net....27   3   10...Or..   3,118 at 2s. 0d.   311   16   0

514   5   10

		Bags.		Net lbs.		£.	s.	d.	£.	s.	d.
		291	Carried forward.........	45,366	....	....	..	..	5,224	12	0

Dr.   COTTON.   (13)

1817.		Bags		Net lbs.		£.	s.	d	£.	s.	d.
Feb. 28	. . . .	379	Brought forward	59,385	. . . .	. . . .	. .	. .	7,256	19	3
		379	Bags	59,385	. . . .	. . . .	. .	. .	7,256	19	3
1817.											
Feb. 28	To Balance	55	as per Valuation	8,770	. . . .	. . . .	. .	. .	823	6	8

			Bags.		Net lbs.	Price.	£.	s.	d.	£.	s.	d.
1817.			291	Brought forward	45,366	. . . . . .	. . .	. .	. .	5,224	12	0
Feb.27	4	By S. Lord	. . . .	. . . . Stockport.								
			10	Bahia.								

No.   cwt. qr. lb. Tare. Drft.
342. . 1 1 17 . . . 6 . . 1
344 . . . 1 0 19 . . . 5 . . 1
357 . . . 1 1 19 . . . 6 . . 1
359 . . . 1 2 27 . . . 7 . . 1
361 . . . 1 1 19 . . . 5 . . 1
366 . . . 1 1 19 . . . 7 . . 1
369 . . . 1 2 13 . . . 6 . . 1
348 . . . 1 1 5 . . . 7 . . 1
367 . . . 1 0 17 . . . 5 . . 1
350 . . . 1 2 6 . . 6 . 1
Gross. . 14 0 21 . .00.10
T. & D. .0 2 14
Net . . . . 13 2 7 . . . Or . .

| | | | | | 1,519 | at 1s. 10d. | 139 | 4 | 10 | | | |
| | | | 23 | Pernams. | | | | | | | | |

310. . 1 2 22 . . . 5 . 1
321 . . . 1 2 22 . . . 5 . . 1
326 . . . 1 2 22 . . . 5 . . 1
370 . . . 1 2 21 . . . 5 . . 1
374 . . . 1 1 23 . . . 5 . . 1
376 . . . 1 1 17 . . 7 . 1
384 . . . 1 1 15 . . . 6 . . 1
386 . . . 1 1 15 . . . 6 . . 1
392 . . . 1 1 11 . . . 6 . . 1
389 . . . 1 1 21 . . . 6 . . 1
380 . . . 1 1 17 . . . 6 . . 1
378 . . . 1 2 23 . . . 5 . . 1
371 . . . 1 1 9 . . . 7 . . 1
372 . . . 1 0 19 . . . 6 . . 1
383 . . . 1 2 27 . . . 5 . . 1
387 . . . 1 1 17 . . . 5 . . 1
391 . . . 1 2 19 . . . 7 . . 1
390 . . . 1 2 22 . . . 6 . . 1
375 . . . 1 1 15 . . . 5 . . 1
388 . . . 1 0 19 . . . 5 . . 1
381 . . . 1 2 22 . . . 5 . . 1
382 . . . 1 2 23 . . . 7 . . 1
377 . . . 1 1 19 . . . 6 . . 1
Gross. . 34 2 20. 131.23
T. & D. 1 1 14
Net . . . 33 1 6 . . . Or . .

(Present Bill at 3 Months.)

					3,730	at 2s. 0d	373	0	0			
Feb.27	3	By Holt and Co.		. . . . Manchester.						512	4	10
				Exp[s] on return[d] Bill, No. 51 . .	. . . . . .	. . . . . .	. . .	. .	. .	0	17	0
28	4	By B. Milne	. . . .	. . . . Liverpool, abated.	. . . . . .	. . . . . .	. . .	. .	. .	0	0	2
28	1	By Stock	. . . .	Loss this Month	. . . . . .	. . . . . .	. . .	. .	. .	695	18	7
28		By Balance	55	as per Valuation	8,770	. . . . . .	. . .	. .	. .	823	6	8
			379	Bags	59,385	. . . .	. . .	. .	. .	7,256	19	3

Dr.   CASH.   (1)

1817.		RECEIPTS.	£.	s.	d.
February 1		To Balance...	89	15	6
10	5	To West and Co. Manchester	158	6	10
20	5	To West and Co. Manchester	522	5	3
			770	7	7
February 28	...	To Balance...	91	17	6

(1)   PER CONTRA.   *Cr.*

1817.		PAYMENTS.	£.	s.	d.
February 3	1	By Private Account...... Donation to the Infirmary	2	2	0
5	1	By Private Account..... Bentham and Co., Wine..............	17	10	0
6	4	By Cotton .... Phœnix Office, Insurance against Fire	15	5	6
7	4	By Cotton .... Petty Expenses this Week	8	13	4
10	2	By Best and Co. Bankers	150	0	0
12	1	By Private Account...... P. Pindar, Taylor	7	12	6
14	1	By Private Account..... Gill and Co. Brewers	12	5	0
14	11	By Cotton .... Petty Expenses this Week	5	14	1
15	1	By Private Account..... L. Rogers, Butcher	10	6	0
20	2	By Best and Co. Bankers	400	0	0
21	11	By Cotton .... Petty Expenses this Week	10	5	9
25	1	By Private Account...... Subscription to the Poor	10	10	0
28	6	By Newton and Co...... Carriers, Balance	22	0	3
28	12	By Cotton .... Petty Expenses this Week	6	5	8
28		By Balance	91	17	6
		£	770	7	7

Dr.   BILLS RECEIVABLE.   (1)

When received.	Folio.	From whom received.	No.	By whom drawn.	Date.	Term.	To whose Order.	On whom Drawn.
1817.					1817.			
Feb. 1		To Balance	36	....		...	....	....
4	2	To Best and Co..	41	Best and Co. Manchester .	Feb. 4	3 m.	Myself	Jones and Co. .. London.
5	3	To Holt and Co..	42	J. King ... Leeds	Jan. 27	3 m.	T. Rogers ...	Chaloner and Co. Ditto.
			43	T. Ball .... Rochdale ..	Feb. 1	3 m.	Holt and Co. .	Milton and Co... Ditto.
5	2	To Best and Co..	44	Best and Co. Manchester .	5	3 m.	Myself	Jones and Co. .. Ditto.
6	4	To S. Lord	45	Simeon & Co. Hull	2	3 m.	S. Lord	Kitson and Co... Ditto.
7	2	To B. Carr	46	Allen and Co. Liverpool ..	Jan. 1	4 m.	L. West	R. Manks and Co. Ditto.
7	2	To Binns and Co.	47	Carr and Co. Bury	Feb. 7	3 m.	Binns and Co..	Robarts and Co. . Ditto.
8	2	To Best and Co..	48	Best and Co. Manchester .	8	3 m.	Myself	Jones and Co. .. Ditto.
10	3	To R. Hill	49	Best and Co. Manchester .	10	2 m.	R. Hill	Jones and Co. .. Ditto.
11	3	To Holt and Co..	50	S. Goodall .. Bury	Jan. 15	5 m.	T. South	Ogle and Co. ... Ditto.
					1816.			
			51	T. Gordon .. Edinbro' ...	Dec. 20	2 m.	M. Ross	Grey and Co. .... Ditto.
					1817.			
12	4	To S. Lord	52	Mellin & Co. Perth	Jan. 20	4 m.	H. Gill	R. Graham .... Ditto.
12	2	To B. Carr	53	Peters & Co. Hull	Feb. 1	4 m.	L. Grant	Ogle and Co. ... Ditto.
			54	Souter & Co. Liverpool ..	Jan. 30	3 m.	S. Benson ..	D. Brent ...... Ditto.
			55	L. Cox .... Bury	Feb. 10	3 m.	R. Bell	J. Riley ...... Ditto.
			56	R. Birch ... Manchester .	11	3 m.	B. Carr	Jones and Co. .. Ditto.
12	2	To Best and Co. .	57	Best and Co. Manchester .	12	3 m.	Myself	Jones and Co. .. Ditto.
14	2	To Binns and Co.	58	Jaques & Co. Bristol	10	3 m.	Samson and Co.	Watts and Co. .. Ditto.
15	3	To T. Hinde ...	59	Norris & Co. Blackburn ..	14	3 m.	T. Hinde	Ogle and Co. .... Ditto.
			60	A. Ross .... Edinbro' ...	Jan. 1	5 m.	R. Wallace ...	J. Hartley ..... Ditto.
16	2	To Best and Co..	61	Best and Co. Manchester .	Feb. 16	3 m.	Myself	Jones and Co. .. Ditto.
17	4	To North and Co.	62	Evans & Co. Liverpool ..	Jan. 30	4 m.	J. Loyd	Morgan and Co. . Ditto.
			63	Johnson&Co. Manchester .	Feb. 17	3 m.	T. North	Brown and Co. .. Ditto.
17	3	To Holt and Co..	64	Best and Co. Manchester .	17	3 m.	Holt and Co. .	Jones and Co. .. Ditto.
18	2	To Binns and Co.	65	Forbes & Co. Glasgow ...	Feb. 10	4 m.	L. Murray ...	Ogle and Co. ... Ditto.
20	2	To Best and Co..	66	Best and Co. Manchester .	20	3 m.	Myself	Jones and Co. .. Ditto.
24	2	To B. Carr	67	Wilson & Co. Perth	Jan. 1	5 m.	Shield and Co.	Elmet and Co. .. Ditto.
			68	F. Laurin .. Ayr	Feb. 16	3 m.	T. Newton ...	P. Baxter ..... Ditto.
25	4	To S. Lord	69	Muir and Co. Edinbro' ...	6	4 m.	L. Murray ...	J. Kames ..... Ditto.
26	3	To Holt and Co..	70	Best and Co. Manchester .	26	3 m.	Holt and Co. .	Jones and Co. .. Ditto.
27	5	To Pratt and Co.	51	Returned	....	...	....	....
28	4	To North and Co.	71	D. Conyers . Inverness ..	Jan. 31	4 m.	T. Muir	Ray and Co. ... Ditto.
			72	West and Co. Leeds	Feb. 10	4 m.	D. Firth	Raymond and Co. Ditto.
28		To Balance .... {71}{72}		....	......	...	....	....

(1)   PER CONTRA.   *Cr.*

When due.	£	s.	d.	£	s.	d.
1817	£.	s.	d.	£.	s.	d.
April 26	...	..	..	350	0	0
May 7	...	..	..	125	16	8
April 30	100	0	0			
May 4	65	13	4	165	13	4
8	...	..	..	73	13	5
5	...	..	..	118	4	7
4	...	..	..	92	17	10
10	...	..	..	285	12	6
11	...	..	..	157	10	1
April 13	...	..	..	178	6	0
June 18	150	0	0			
Feb. 23	75	0	0	225	0	0
May 23	...	..	..	130	0	0
June 4	100	0	0			
May 3	50	0	0			
13	50	0	0			
14	50	0	0	250	0	0
15	...	..	..	363	11	0
13	...	..	..	200	0	0
17	165	12	0			
June 4	150	0	0	315	12	0
May 19	...	..	..	150	0	0
June 2	186	15	6			
May 20	97	2	8	283	18	2
20	...	..	..	200	0	0
June 13	...	..	..	350	0	0
May 23	...	..	..	500	0	0
June 4	187	5	9			
May 19	146	12	6	333	18	3
June 9	...	..	..	250	0	0
May 29	...	..	..	500	0	0
.....	...	..	..	75	0	0
June 3	127	16	8			
13	93	10	0	221	6	8
			£	5896	0	6
...	...	..	..	221	6	8

	Folio.	How disposed of.	No.	£	s.	d.	£	s.	d.
1817.				£.	s.	d.	£.	s.	d.
Feb. 4	5	By Pratt and Co..	36	350	0	0			
			41	125	16	8	475	16	8
5	5	By Wells and Co.	42	100	0	0			
			43	65	13	4			
			44	73	13	5	239	6	9
8	2	By Best and Co..	47	...	..	..	285	12	6
8	4	By B. Milne ...	45	118	4	7			
			46	92	17	10			
			48	157	10	1	368	12	6
12	5	By Pratt and Co..	49	178	6	0			
			50	150	0	0			
			51	75	0	0			
			52	130	0	0			
			53	100	0	0			
			54	50	0	0			
			55	50	0	0			
			56	50	0	0			
			57	363	11	0	1146	17	0
16	4	By B. Milne ...	58	200	0	0			
			59	165	12	0			
			60	150	0	0			
			61	150	0	0	665	12	0
18	5	By Wells and Co.	63	97	2	8			
			64	200	0	0			
			65	350	0	0	647	2	8
20	3	By T. Grant ...	62	186	15	6			
			66	500	0	0	686	15	6
25	5	By Pratt and Co.	67	187	5	9			
			68	146	12	6			
			69	250	0	0	583	18	3
26	5	By Pratt and Co.	70	...	..	..	500	0	0
27	3	By Holt and Co..	51	Returned			75	0	0
28		By Balance	{71 72}	...	..	..	221	6	8
						£	5896	0	6

INDEX TO THE

A	Folio	E	Folio

B		F	
Binns and Co. Bury	2	Furniture	1
Best and Co. Manchester	2		
Black and Co. Manchester	2		

C		G	
Carr, B. Manchester	2	Grant, T. Liverpool	3

D		H	
		Hinde, T. Blackburn	3
		Hill, R. Manchester	3
		Holt and Co. Manchester	3

LEDGER.

	Folio		Folio
I		**N**	
		North and Co. Manchester	4
		Newton and Co. Liverpool	4
K		**P**	
		Pratt and Co. Liverpool	5
		Private Account	1
L		**S**	
Lord, S. Stockport 4		Scott, J. Manchester	5
		Stock	1
M		**W**	
Milne, B. Liverpool 4		Wells and Co. Liverpool	5
		West and Co. Manchester	5

Dr.   STOCK.   (1)

1817.					
Feb. 28	1	To Private Account, Transfer	60	5	6
28	13	To Cotton, Loss this month	695	18	7
28		To Balance	3,099	14	11
			3,855	19	0

Dr.   FURNITURE.

1817.					
Jan. 31		To Balance	500	0	0

Dr.   PRIVATE

1817.					
Feb. 3	1	To Cash, Donation	2	2	0
5	1	To Cash, Wine	17	10	0
12	1	To Cash, Pindar	7	12	6
14	1	To Cash, Gill and Co.	12	5	0
15	1	To Cash, L. Rogers	10	6	0
25	1	To Cash, Donation	10	10	0
			60	5	6

(1)		PER CONTRA.		Cr.		
1817. January 31		By Balance		3,855	19	0
				3,855	19	0
February 28		By Balance ....£		3,099	14	11

		PER CONTRA.		Cr.		

		ACCOUNT.		Cr.		
1817. February 28	1	By Stock, Transfer		60	5	6
				60	5	6

P

Drs.			BEST AND CO. BANKERS,		(2)			
					£.	s.	d.
1817.							
January 31			To Balance		527	10	0
February 8	1		To Bill		285	12	6
10	1		To Cash		150	0	0
20	1		To Cash		400	0	0
20	9		To Interest		7	8	8
				£	1,370	11	2

Drs.			BINNS AND CO.					
1817.							
January 31			To Balance		285	12	6
February 6	2		To Cotton		223	18	6
15	6		To Cotton		432	17	0
26	12		To Cotton		514	5	10
				£	1,456	13	10
February 28			To Balance		621	1	4

Drs.			BLACK AND CO.					
1817.							
February 22	10		To Indigo	£	233	4	0

Dr.			B. CARR,					
1817.							
January 31			To Balance		92	17	10
February 4	2		To Cotton		259	12	6
20	8		To Cotton		403	18	0
				£	756	8	4
February 28			To Balance		79	12	3

(2)   MANCHESTER.   *Crs.*

1817.				£.	s.	d.
February 4	1	By Bill		125	16	8
5	1	By Bill		73	13	5
8	1	By Bill		157	10	1
12	1	By Bill		363	11	0
16	1	By Bill		150	0	0
20	1	By Bill		£00	0	0
			£	1,370	11	2

BURY.   *Crs.*

1817.						
February 7	1	By Bill		285	12	6
14	1	By Bill		200	0	0
18	1	By Bill		350	0	0
28		By Balance		621	1	4
			£	1,456	13	10

MANCHESTER.   *Crs.*

MANCHESTER.   *Cr.*

1817.						
February 7	1	By Bill		92	17	10
12	1	By Bill		250	0	0
24	1	By Bills		333	18	3
28		By Balance		79	12	3
			£	756	8	4

P 2

Dr.   T. GRANT,   (3)

1817.				£.	s.	d.
February 20	1	To Bills		686	15	6
28		To Balance		151	12	5
			£	838	7	11

Dr.   T. HINDE,

1817.						
February 8	3	To Cotton .... £		315	12	0

Dr.   R. HILL,

1817.			
January 31	To Balance .... £	356	12	0

Drs.   HOLT AND CO.

1817.						
January 31		To Balance		165	13	4
February 3	1	To Cotton		238	18	8
13	5	To Cotton		196	11	11
22	10	To Cotton		565	7	10
27	1	To Returned Bill		75	0	0
27	13	To Expenses on Returned Bill		0	17	0
			£	1,242	8	9
February 28		To Balance		151	15	5

(3)   LIVERPOOL.   *Cr.*

1817..				£.	s.	d.
February 8	8	By Cotton		827	4	7
24	5	By Wells and Co. .... Transfer............................		11	3	4
			£	838	7	11
February 28		By Balance		151	12	5

BLACKBURN.   *Cr.*

1817.						
February 15	1	By Bills ....£		315	12	0

MANCHESTER.   *Cr.*

1817.						
February 10	11	By Composition.... Loss 50 per Cent.....................		178	6	0
10	1	By Bill		178	6	0
			£	356	12	0

MANCHESTER.   *Crs.*

1817.						
February 5	1	By Bills		165	13	4
11	1	By Bill		225	0	0
17	1	By Bill		200	0	0
26	1	By Bill		500	0	0
28		By Balance		151	15	5
			£	1,242	8	9

Dr.   S. LORD,   (4)

1817.				£.	s.	d.
January 31		To Balance..		118	4	7
February 3	1	To Cotton...		138	19	0
17	6	To Cotton...		304	11	4
27	13	To Cotton...		512	4	10
			£	1,073	19	9
February 28		To Balance		572	3	2

Dr.   B. MILNE,

1817.				£.	s.	d.
February 8	1	To Bills		368	12	6
16	1	To Bills		665	12	0
28	13	To Abatement		0	0	2
			£	1,034	4	8

Drs.   NORTH AND CO.

1817.				£.	s.	d.
February 12	4	To Cotton		283	18	2
24	11	To Cotton		384	16	10
				668	15	0
February 28		To Balance...		163	10	2

Drs.   NEWTON AND CO.

1817.				£.	s.	d.
February 20	9	To Cotton, lost 1 Bag		14	14	9
28	1	To Cash		22	0	3
			£	36	15	0

(4) **STOCKPORT.** *Cr.*

1817.				£.	s.	d.
February 6	1	By Bill		118	4	7
12	1	By Bill		130	0	0
22	12	By Short Weights		3	12	0
25	1	By Bill		250	0	0
28		By Balance		572	3	2
			£	1,073	19	9

LIVERPOOL. *Cr.*

1817.						
January 31		By Balance		368	12	6
February 5	4	By Cotton.		665	12	2
			£	1,034	4	8

MANCHESTER. *Crs.*

1817.						
February 17	1	By Bills		283	18	2
28	1	By Bills		221	6	8
28		By Balance		163	10	2
			£	668	15	0

LIVERPOOL. *Crs.*

1817.						
February 28	12	By Carriage .... £		36	15	0

Drs.   PRATT AND CO.   (5)

1817.				£.	s.	d.
February 4	1	To Bills		475	16	8
12	1	To Bills .. , ...		1,146	17	0
22	9	To Short Weights		4	4	0
25	1	To Bills..		583	18	3
26	1	To Bills		500	0	0
28		To Balance		206	9	10
			£	2,917	5	9

Dr.   J SCOTT,

1817.						
January 31		To Balance		291	10	0

Drs.   WELLS AND CO.

1817.						
February 5	1	To Bills		239	6	9
18	1	To Bills		647	2	8
24	3	To T. Grant, Transfer		11	3	4
			£	897	12	9

Drs.   WEST AND CO.

1817.						
February 10	4	To Cotton		163	4	9
19	7	To Cotton		538	8	3
			£	701	13	0

| | (5) | LIVERPOOL. | Crs. |

1817.			£.	s.	d.
January 31		By Balance	475	16	8
February 3	2	By Cotton	1,147	17	0
10	10	By Cotton	1,217	16	7
27	1	By Returned Bill	75	0	0
27	12	By Expences on Returned Bill	0	15	6
		£	2,917	5	9
February 28		By Balance	206	9	10

| | | MANCHESTER. | Cr. |

1817.					
February 15	11	By Indigo .... £	291	10	0

| | | LIVERPOOL. | Crs. |

1817.					
January 31		By Balance................................	239	6	9
February 7	6	By Cotton	658	6	0
		£	897	12	9

| | | MANCHESTER. | Crs. |

1817.					
February 10	11	By Discount	4	17	11
10	1	By Cash	158	6	10
20	11	By Discount	16	3	0
20	1	By Cash	522	5	3
		£	701	13	0

Q

INVENTORY. (1)

1817.			Bags.			Net lbs.	Price.	£.	s.	d.
Jan. 31	Valuation........	....	....	.... Cotton on hand.						
			10	West Indian.						
				No.	cwt. qr. lb. Tare. Drft.					
				✓ 175...	1 1 14...5..1					
				✓ 138...	1 0 7...4..1					
				✓ 111...	1 2 3...6..1					
				✓ 201...	1 1 8...4..1					
				✓ 157...	1 0 25...4..1					
				✓ 169...	1 0 15...4..1					
				✓ 125...	1 1 5...5..1					
				✓ 191...	1 1 10...5..1					
				✓ 217...	1 2 19...6..1					
				✓ 180...	1 1 24...5..1					
				Gross.. 13 1	18..48.10					
				T. & D. 0 2	2					
				Net... 12 3	16...Or..	1,444 at 2s.		144	8	0
			23	New Orleans.						
				✓ 199...	1 2 7...6..1					
				✓ 117...	1 1 24...5..1					
				✓ 145...	1 0 27...5..1					
				✓ 172...	1 0 22...4..1					
				✓ 100...	1 1 7...6..1					
				✓ 114...	1 2 4...6..1					
				✓ 156...	1 1 16...5..1					
				✓ 188...	1 1 5...5..1					
				✓ 211...	1 1 23...5..1					
				✓ 106...	1 0 19...4..1					
				✓ 121...	1 1 2...5..1					
				✓ 141...	1 2 0...6..1					
				✓ 206...	1 1 10...6..1					
				✓ 153...	1 0 20...6..1					
				✓ 195...	1 1 12...5..1					
				✓ 132...	1 2 0...6..1					
				✓ 214...	1 1 17...5..1					
				✓ 149...	1 2 2...6..1					
				✓ 208...	1 1 13...5..1					
				✓ 107...	1 0 25...5..1					
				✓ 147...	1 0 24...4..1					
				✓ 183...	1 1 17...5..1					
				✓ 165...	1 1 18...5..1					
				Gross.. 31 1	6.120.23					
				T. & D. 1 1	3					
				Net... 30 0	3...Or..	3,363 at 2s. 2d.		364	6	6
			33	Carried forward		4,807	....	508	14	6

(2)   INVENTORY.

1817.			Bags		Net lbs.	Price.	£.	s.	d.
Jan. 31	Valuation........		33	Brought forward..........	4,807	......	508	14	6
			35	Bahia.					
				No. cwt. qr. lb. Tare. Drft.					
				✓ 129... 1 2 26...7..1					
				✓ 177... 1 2 22...6..1					
				✓ 133... 1 1 12...5..1					
				✓ 102... 1 1 14...6..1					
				✓ 213... 1 1 7...5..1					
				✓ 154... 1 1 8...5..1					
				✓ 119... 1 1 26...6..1					
				✓ 143... 1 0 28...5..1					
				✓ 166... 1 0 14...5..1					
				✓ 197... 1 1 18...6..1					
				✓ 161... 1 0 22...5..1					
				✓ 122... 1 0 26...5..1					
				✓ 104... 1 2 23...7..1					
				✓ 179... 1 1 17...6..1					
				✓ 203... 1 1 14..6..1					
				✓ 135... 1 1 10...6..1					
				✓ 115... 1 1 20...6..1					
				✓ 162... 1 0 22...6..1					
				✓ 184... 1 2 1. .7..1					
				✓ 110... 1 2 0...7..1					
				✓ 176... 1 1 15...6. 1					
				✓ 134... 1 1 25..6..1					
				✓ 216... 1 0 16...5..1					
				✓ 159... 1 0 21...5..1					
				✓ 220... 1 1 0...5..1					
				✓ 112... 1 2 2...7..1					
				✓ 202... 1 1 16...6..1					
				✓ 171... 1 1 15...6..1					
				✓ 127... 1 2 6...7..1					
				✓ 173... 1 1 16...6..1					
				✓ 200... 1 1 14...6..1					
				✓ 148... 1 1 22...6..1					
				✓ 219... 1 1 20...6..1					
				✓ 123... 1 0 26...5..1					
				✓ 137... 1 2 4...7..1					
				Gross ..48 2 16. 206. 35					
				T. & D. 2 0 17					
				Net ... 46 1 27 ... Or...	5,207 at 2s.4d.	607	9	8
			68	Carried forward..........	10,014	......	1,116	4	2

INVENTORY.　　　　　　　(3)

1817.			Bags.		Net lbs.	Price.	£.	s.	d.
Jan. 31	Valuation.......		68	Brought forward	10,014	....	1,116	4	2
			41	Pernams.					

```
                    No.    cwt.  qr.  lb.  Tare. Drft.
                  ✓108...  1    0   23...6..1
                  ✓204...  1    0   15...5..1
                  ✓193...  1    2    6...7..1
                  ✓164...  1    1   14...6..1
                  ✓113...  1    1   14...6..1
                  ✓158...  1    1   27...6..1
                  ✓131...  1    2    0...6..1
                  ✓146...  1    1   25...6..1
                  ✓103...  1    1   15...5..1
                  ✓218...  1    1    9...6..1
                  ✓124...  1    0   19...5..1
                  ✓139...  1    1   12...5..1
                  ✓144...  1    2    4...7..1
                  ✓101...  1    1   16...5..1
                  ✓209...  1    2   17...6..1
                  ✓118...  1    1   14...5..1
                  ✓152...  1    0   15...4..1
                  ✓186...  1    1   22...7..1
                  ✓140...  1    1   21...5..1
                  ✓198...  1    0   24...4..1
                  ✓215...  1    0   17...6..1
                  ✓157...  1    1   17...6..1
                  ✓187...  1    1   19...6..1
                  ✓163...  1    1   13...6..1
                  ✓128...  1    1   22...6..1
                  ✓116...  1    1   20...6..1
                  ✓207...  1    0   25...5..1
                  ✓182...  1    0   25...5..1
                  ✓190...  1    2    0...7..1
                  ✓130...  1    1   20...6..1
                  ✓194...  1    1   15...6..1
                  ✓205...  1    1   10...5..1
                  ✓120...  1    1   25...6..1
                  ✓196...  1    1   25...6..1
                  ✓142...  1    1   13...5..1
                  ✓109...  1    1    8...5..1
                  ✓178...  1    2    7...7..1
                  ✓170...  1    2    6...7..1
                  ✓136...  1    0    4...5..1
                  ✓105...  1    1   15...6..1
                  ✓185...  1    1   24...6..1
                                   ─────────────
                  Gross..  56   1   26. 235. 41
                  T. & D.   2   1   24
                                   ─────────────
                  Net...   54   0    2...Or...
```

| | | | | Net... 54 0 2...Or... | 6,050 at 2s. 6d. | | 756 | 5 | 0 |
| | | | 109 | Carried forward .... | 16,064 | .... | 1,872 | 9 | 2 |

(4)   INVENTORY.

1817.			Bags.		Net lbs.	Price.	£.	s.	d.
Jan. 31		Valuation........	109	Brought forward	16,064	....	1,872	9	2
			11	Best Georgia.					
				No. cwt. qr. lb. Tare. Drft.					
				✓ 126... 1 2 22...7..1					
				✓ 192... 1 2 15...7..1					
				✓ 160... 1 2 20...7..1					
				✓ 212... 1 2 2...7..1					
				✓ 168... 1 2 8...7..1					
				✓ 189... 1 2 17...7..1					
				✓ 150... 1 2 16...7..1					
				✓ 210... 1 2 26...7..1					
				✓ 174... 1 2 18...7..1					
				✓ 167... 1 2 12...7..1					
				✓ 181... 1 2 14...7..1					
				Gross.. 18 0 2..77.11					
				T. & D. 0 3 4					
				Net... 17 0 26 ..Or..	1,930	at 3s.	289	10	0
Entered Cotton, fo. 1		Total	120	Bags on hand	17,994	.... £	2,161	19	2

Dr.   THE ESTATE OF   (5)

			£.	s.	d.
		31st January, 1817.			
L.	4	To B. Milne, ... Liverpool, Balance due to him	368	12	6
L.	5	To Pratt and Co. ... Ditto .... Ditto to them	475	16	8
L.	5	To Wells and Co. .. Ditto .... Ditto to them	239	6	9
			1,083	15	11
L.	1	To Stock, my Net Capital	3,855	19	0
		£	4,939	14	11

(5) SAMUEL MANSLEY, MANCHESTER. *Cr.*

31st January 1817.

			£.	s.	d.
C.	1	By Cash, Balance in hand	89	15	6
B. R.	1	By Bills Receivable, Balance in hand, No. 36.	350	0	0
C.	1	By Cotton, Balance in hand as per Valuation	2,161	19	2
L.	1	By Furniture	500	0	0
L.	2	By Best and Co. Bankers, Manchester, Balance due from them	527	10	0
L.	2	By Binns and Co. Bury . . . . ditto . . . . . . ditto	285	12	6
L.	2	By B. Carr, Manchester . . . . ditto . . . . . . ditto from him	92	17	10
L.	3	By R. Hill, Manchester . . . . ditto . . . . . . ditto.	356	12	0
L.	3	By Holt and Co. Manchester . . . . ditto . . . . . ditto from them	165	13	4
L.	4	By S. Lord, Stockport . . . . ditto . . . . . . ditto from him	118	4	7
L.	5	By J. Scott, Manchester . . . . ditto . . . . . . ditto . . . . ditto	291	10	0
		£	4,939	14	11

INVENTORY.   (6)

1817.			Bags.			Net lbs.	Price.	£.	s.	d.
Feb. 28		Valuation of....	....	.... Cotton on hand.						
			6	West Indian.						
				No. cwt. qr. lb. Tare. Drft.						
				272... 1 2 21...6..1						
				274... 1 1 16...7..1						
				275... 1 0 17...6..1						
				278... 1 2 19...5..1						
				279... 1 1 17...7..1						
				284... 1 1 15...5..1						
				Gross... 8 2 21..36..6						
				T. & D. 0 1 14						
				Net.... 8 1 7...Or..		931	at 1s. 6d.	69	16	6
			9	Orleans.						
				240.. 1 1 17...7..1						
				242... 1 2 27...5..1						
				244... 1 0 27...7..1						
				246... 1 2 13...6..1						
				248 .. 1 1 11...5..1						
				249... 1 2 17...7..1						
				251... 1 0 18...5..1						
				252... 1 1 26...5..1						
				254... 1 2 27...6..1						
				Gross.. 13 1 15..53..9						
				T. & D. 0 2 6						
				Net... 12 3 9...Or..		1,437	at 1s. 8d.	119	15	0
			16	Bahia.						
				341... 1 1 19...7..1						
				343... 1 2 26....6..1						
				345... 1 1 14...7..1						
				346... 1 1 11...5..1						
				347... 1 2 12...6..1						
				349... 1 1 18...5..1						
				351... 1 2 17...5..1						
				352... 1 2 19...5..1						
				353... 1 2 21...6..1						
				355.. 1 1 27...5..1						
				358... 1 2 26...7..1						
				360... 1 1 15 ..6..1						
				362... 1 2 17...5..1						
				363... 1 2 19...7..1						
				365... 1 2 17...6..1						
				368... 1 2 21...7..1						
				Gross.. 25 0 19..95.16						
				T & D. 0 3 27						
				Net... 24 0 20...Or..		2,708	at 1s.10d.	248	4	8
			31	Carried forward		5,076	......	437	16	2

(7)   INVENTORY.

1817.			Bags.		Net lbs.	Price.	£.	s.	d.
Feb. 28	Valuation		31	Brought forward	5,076	....	437	16	2
			20	Pernams.					

No.	cwt.	qr.	lb.	Tare.	Drft.	
373...	1	1	22...	7..	1	
379...	1	0	26...	7..	1	
385...	1	1	17...	7..	1	
393...	1	0	17...	5..	1	
394...	1	1	22...	5..	1	
395...	1	1	19...	5..	1	
396...	1	1	5...	7..	1	
397...	1	2	7...	5..	1	
398...	1	2	19...	6..	1	
399...	1	1	26...	7..	1	
400...	1	0	27...	7..	1	
401...	1	0	25...	6..	1	
402...	1	1	15...	6..	1	
403...	1	0	17...	5..	1	
404...	1	1	26...	5..	1	
405...	1	2	22...	7..	1	
406...	1	1	12...	5..	1	
407...	1	1	19...	6..	1	
408...	1	2	23...	7..	1	
409...	1	2	24...	6..	1	

Gross.. 28 1 26. 121. 20
T. & D. 1 1   1

| Net... 27 0 25... Or.. | 3,049 at 2s. | | 304 | 18 | 0 |

4 Georgia.

230...	1	1	19...	6..	1
231...	1	2	16...	7..	1
235...	1	0	27...	6..	1
238...	1	2	25...	7..	1

Gross... 6 0 3.. 26.. 4
T. & D.. 0 1   2

| Net.... 5 3 1... Or.. | 645 at 2s. 6d. | 80 | 12 | 6 |

Entered Cotton, fo. 13 | Total............. | 55 | Bags.... on hand........ .... | 8,770 | .... | 823 | 6 | 8 |

R

Dr.   THE ESTATE OF   (8)

		28th February 1817.	£.	s.	d.
L	3	To T. Grant, Liverpool, Balance due to him	151	12	5
L	5	To Pratt & Co. Ditto .. Ditto due to them	206	9	10
			358	2	3
L	1	To Stock, my Net Capital	3,099	14	11
		£	3,457	17	2

(8)		SAMUEL MANSLEY, MANCHESTER.	*Cr.*		

		28th February 1817.	£.	s.	d.
C	1	By Cash .... Balance on hand	91	17	6
B R	1	By Bills Receivable, Ditto..Ditto	221	6	8
C	13	By Cotton, Balance on hand, as per Valuation	823	6	8
L	1	By Furniture	500	0	0
L	2	By Binns & Co. ... Bury, ... Balance due from them	621	1	4
L	2	By Black & Co. ... Manchester, Ditto ... Ditto	233	4	0
L	2	By B. Carr, ... Ditto ..... Ditto due from him	79	12	3
L	3	By Holt & Co. ... Ditto ..... Ditto due from them	151	15	5
L	4	By S. Lord, ... Stockport, . Ditto due from him	572	3	2
L	4	By North & Co. ... Manchester, . Ditto due from them	163	10	2
		£	3,457	17	2

SET III.

MANUFACTURER'S BOOKS.

CONCERN	INDIVIDUAL.
CAPITAL	VARIABLE.
BUSINESS	CONTINUED.
RESULT	Loss, INSOLVENCY, AND COMPOSITION.

OBSERVATIONS.

THE Books of John Henderson, Woollen Manufacturer at Leeds, are here exhibited, for the month of March 1817.

It is a common prejudice that, from the very nature of his business, and the numerous processes through which his goods pass, the Manufacturer is unable to keep his Accounts on the same systematic principles as those of the Wholesale Dealer or the Merchant. The difficulty, however, applies solely to the Quantities of goods, and in no respect to the Accounts, which in all businesses are composed of expenditure and returns, receipts and payments. These particulars the Manufacturer can ascertain as easily as the Merchant; and, therefore, he may with equal facility systematize his Accounts.

In the first instance, he might prove his Books, as in Set I. without any check on the stock of goods. With the Retailer this imperfection is unavoidable, because the minuteness of his sales forbids the record of their quantities. The Manufacturer, on the contrary, buys and sells in the gross; and, though the various processes of his goods render it less easy to prove their quantities than in more simple businesses, this object may be accomplished by a Warehouse Ledger with a series of Accounts for the different states of the commodities. In an extensive Manufactory, the very difficulty of checking the goods renders it but the more desirable; for they undergo so many transformations, and lie scattered in such a variety of states, that the Proprietor is ever exposed to accidental, as well as fraudulent, losses. In the following example of the Warehouse Ledger, its jurisdiction will be found so comprehensive, that no deficiency of any magnitude in the raw material, nor the deficiency of a single piece after being once put in process, can possibly occur undetected, unless the entries be designedly falsified.

There is a Book of a different description, called the Number-Book, which is prevalently used in Manufactories of Piece-goods, as a check upon the stock of merchandise. The best method of keeping this Book, is by two series of numbers, one for the Goods put in process of manufacture, and the other for the Sales. The Manufacture-Numbers come progressively into the Book, and the Sale-Numbers being posted into a parallel column, the Manufacture-Numbers against which no Sale-Numbers appear, will shew the general stock on hand, including both the manufactured goods and those in process. By means of other columns in which the progress of the goods is marked, the uncompleted may be distinguished from the finished manufactures, and any other desirable particulars obtained. The two series of Numbers for Manufactures and Sales, afford a complete check upon the general quantity of the stock; for the difference between their extremes is equal to the total number of pieces on hand. Supposing a Book of this kind to be correctly kept, it would be a very complete record and proof of the stock, ascertaining not merely the collective quantities, but the identity and history of every individual piece. Experience, however, has amply shewn its inadequacy to this purpose, arising from the confusion to which the Numbers are liable. A wrong figure put in by the weaver, or the obliteration of a figure in the finishing process, deranges the whole system of the Number-Book. When the Sale-Numbers come to be posted, and the goods to be proved, some pieces have repetitions of the same Manufacture-Number; in others this Number is not legible, and a proportionate quantity of original Numbers has entirely disappeared. In addition to the difficulty of preserving distinct and accurate Numbers, the errors which may easily be made in posting the Sales, render the Number-Book a very inefficient check on the stock of goods.

The Manufacture-Numbers are, however, useful in identifying particular pieces, so as to ascertain the hands through which they have passed, and trace any defect or loss to its real cause. Hence, though the perfect record of quantities must be resigned to the Warehouse Ledger, it is desirable to continue the Numbers as useful auxiliaries. In the following Inventory will be shewn the general check produced by the two series of Numbers on the totality of Pieces, which must always be equal to the difference between their extremes.

In large Manufactories, the unlimited detail of the expenditure requires a number of subordinate Books, in order to disburthen the Cash and Merchandise Accounts from minute entries; and, accordingly, in this concern the Overlookers of the Woolshop, the Factory, and the Warehouse, keep distinct Books for the wages and petty expenses in their respective departments. The Overlooker frequently requires several Day Books and a Ledger, comprehending a little system of Accounts within themselves; but, in subordination to the Principal Books, they are mere Memoranda which transmit their periodical additions. It is, therefore, unnecessary to exhibit them in detail, not to mention that on this occasion they would probably be more voluminous than all the other Books together. It is usual to open with each Overlooker a Cash Account in the Ledger, and, when the expenditure is very fluctuating, this method is necessary. Otherwise, the trouble may be avoided by the constant and invariable loan of a round sum, somewhat exceeding the weekly expenditure. These loans, being invariable, require only a memorandum, and always form part of the Balance of Cash. The periodical additions of the Wages will then equilibrate in the Cash and Merchandise, without requiring any entries in the Ledger.

As Manufacturers occasionally embark in mercantile speculations, examples of foreign consignments, and of returns in foreign produce, are introduced into this Set. These transactions might be entered in the Merchandise Account, without any derangement of its system; but, as their results would thereby be blended with the success of the regular business, it is better to record them in a separate Book. In the Adventures, the result of each speculation is distinctly ascertained, whilst the merits of the Manufactory are preserved unmingled with extrinsic affairs.

In this establishment there is also a Retail business, superintended by one of the overlookers. The Account of the Shop is kept by two monthly entries, one for the goods it receives, and the other for its encashed sales.

As this concern is complicated in its business, uniting with the Manufacturer, the Retailer and the Merchant; so also in its financial department it combines the Banker, the payments being made by drafts on a Cashier in London, to whom the receipts are remitted in provision. Hence the Accounts require seven principal Books, the Merchandise, Adventures, Cash, Bills Receivable, Bills Payable, Ledger, and Inventory.

The result here exhibited is a heavy loss, occasioning insolvency. It may appear improbable that a reverse of such magnitude should be incurred in the course of a month; but it must be observed, that the two ruinous occurrences of the Liverpool Bankruptcy and the Lisbon Sales, have been pending for an indefinite period, and that there is no improbability in the concurrence of their terminations. At the time of the failure at Liverpool, a large stock of goods is supposed to have been consigned to Lisbon, with instructions for immediate sale, in order to supply the deficiency of resources. The sacrifice on this forced sale, and the loss with the Liverpool House, occasion the insolvency.

At the close of March, John Henderson takes his Inventory, when, finding himself shorn of a handsome property, and considerably indebted to his Estate, with a refusal of further discounts by his Bankers, and no adequate resources against a large amount of Bills payable afloat, he directs his Cashier in London to suspend payments, and calls a meeting of his Creditors.

Under the guarantee of his uncle, Peter Grant, to whom he transfers his Buildings, Machinery, &c. a composition of twelve shillings in the pound is adjusted. The final settlement takes place on the 10th of July, when the dishonoured acceptances are given up, and the Creditors paid off by Bills on Peter Grant.

A change must here be noticed in the entries of the Bills Payable. Whilst drawn on the Cashier, they were merely Promissory Notes, or the Drawer's own Acceptances; and were not transferred to the Cashier's Account till due. But the Drafts on Peter Grant are direct Bills, the primary responsibility of which he incurs by acceptance; and, therefore, they are immediately transferred to his credit.

In this Set there are three General Extracts, the Inventory being retaken on the 11th July, when the Proprietor finds himself again a man of capital.

Analogous to the following Books are those, not merely of Manufactories of Piece Goods, but of all others; as Oil-Mills, Breweries, Foundries, &c.; and of all businesses in which the returns proceed solely or principally from labour, as Farmers, Carriers, Dyers, Dressers, and Finishers of all descriptions.

SET III.

THE BOOKS

OF

JOHN HENDERSON, WOOLLEN-MANUFACTURER, LEEDS.

---

1. WAREHOUSE LEDGER.
2. MERCHANDISE.
3. ADVENTURES.
4. CASH.
5. BILLS RECEIVABLE.
6. BILLS PAYABLE.
7. LEDGER.
8. INVENTORY.

Dr.   WOOL.   (1)

	PURCHASES.	Total			A			B			C			D		
		Pks.	sc.	lb.	Pks.	sc.	lb.	Pks.	sc.	lb.	Pks.	sc.	lb.	Pks.	sc.	lb.
1817.																
Feb. 28	To Balance	81	2	9	22	8	15	24	3	10	18	7	16	15	6	8
Mar. 3	To S. Marsh	19	5	2	..	..	..	..	..	..	13	4	4	6	0	18
5	To Welch & Co..	13	5	12	13	5	12	—	—	—	—	—	—	—	—	—
7	To T. Bruce	17	1	7	..	..	..	17	1	7	—	—	—	—	—	—
10	To Gill & Co. ...	22	7	8	..	..	..	..	..	..	13	6	13	9	0	15
11	To D. Carew	22	7	5	..	..	..	22	7	5	—	—	—	—	—	—
12	To Holt & Co. ..	13	6	17	13	6	17	—	—	—	—	—	—	—	—	—
		190	0	0	49	9	4	64	0	2	45	6	13	30	8	1
Mar. 31	To Balance	53	4	11	12	7	10	14	8	6	17	4	4	8	8	11

(1)   PER CONTRA.   *Cr.*

	APPLICATIONS.	Total.			A			B			C			D			For Pieces.	Numbers.
		Pks.	sc.	lb.	Pks.	sc.	lb.	Pks.	sc.	lb.	Pks.	sc.	lb.	Pks.	sc.	lb.		
1817.																		
Mar. 8	By Manufactory .	35	2	15	9	3	7	12	8	6	7	11	6	5	3	16	170	1,802 to 1,971.
15	By Ditto	33	2	5	9	10	13	11	10	5	6	3	15	5	1	12	172	1,972 to 2,143.
22	By Ditto	33	6	16	8	2	10	12	7	8	7	1	10	5	7	8	167	2,144 to 2,310.
29	By Ditto	33	7	3	9	5	0	11	9	0	6	7	18	5	9	5	163	2,311 to 2,473.
		135	6	19	36	9	10	48	10	19	28	..	9	21	10	1	672	
31	By Waste.......	1	0	10	..	4	4	..	4	17	..	2	0	..	1	9		
31	By Balance	53	4	11	12	7	10	14	8	6	17	4	4	8	8	11		
		190	0	0	49	9	4	64	0	2	45	6	13	30	8	1		

Dr.   MANUFACTORY.   (2)

	APPLICATIONS.	Total Pieces.	Cloths.				Casimirs.				Numbers.
			A	B	C	D	L	M	N	O	
1817.											
Feb. 28	To Balance in process	477	78	102	60	51	39	87	39	21	
Mar. 8	To Wool	170	28	36	24	16	16	24	16	10	1,802 to 1,971.
15	To Wool	172	32	32	18	14	20	23	16	12	1,972 to 2,143.
22	To Wool	167	27	35	21	18	14	30	14	8	2,144 to 2,310.
29	To Wool	163	30	38	22	17	12	20	12	12	2,311 to 2,473.
		1,149	195	243	145	116	101	189	97	63	
Mar. 31	To Balance in process	459	86	95	52	48	39	85	34	20	

(2)   PER CONTRA.   *Cr.*

	MANUFACTURES.	Total Pieces.	Cloths.				Casimirs.			
			A	B	C	D	L	M	N	O
1817.										
Mar. 8	By Merchandise	183	32	38	26	18	14	26	17	12
15	By Merchandise	165	25	34	22	17	15	31	13	8
22	By Merchandise	174	28	38	25	15	17	23	18	10
29	By Merchandise	168	24	38	20	18	16	24	15	13
		690	109	148	93	68	62	104	63	43
31	By Balance in process	459	86	95	52	48	39	85	34	20
		1,149	195	243	145	116	101	189	97	63

Dr.   MERCHANDISE.   (3)

1817.	MANUFACTURES.	Total Pieces.	Cloths.				Casimirs.			
			A	B	C	D	L	M	N	O
Feb. 28	To Balance	524	94	110	68	52	44	72	48	36
March 8	To Manufactory	183	32	38	26	18	14	26	17	12
15	To Ditto	165	25	34	22	17	15	31	13	8
22	To Ditto	174	28	38	25	15	17	23	18	10
29	To Ditto	168	24	38	20	18	16	24	15	13
		1214	203	258	161	120	106	176	111	79
Mar. 31	To Balance	452	81	86	60	39	44	84	40	18

(3)   PER CONTRA.   *Cr.*

1817.	SALES.	Total Pieces.	Cloths.				Casimirs.			
			A	B	C	D	L	M	N	O
March 4	By Goodwin and Co.	70	20	50	—	—	—	—	—	—
6	By T. Merlin	50	..	..	..	..	..	..	30	20
8	By S. Green	70	..	..	..	..	20	50	—	—
11	By Fairfax and Co.	50	20	30	..	..	—	—	—	—
12	By Goodwin and Co.	60	..	..	40	20	—	—	—	—
13	By Consignment to B. Wilson	160	20	20	20	20	20	20	20	20
14	By S. Green	80	20	30	10	20	—	—	—	—
15	By Consignment to H. Melville .... }	100	20	20	10	10	10	10	10	10
24	By Ranger and Co.	60	20	20	..	..	10	10	—	—
26	By Fairfax and Co.	50	..	..	20	10	..	..	10	10
30	By Shop	12	2	2	1	1	2	2	1	1
		762	122	172	101	81	62	92	71	61
31	By Balance	452	81	86	60	39	44	84	40	18
		1214	203	258	161	120	106	176	111	79

Dr.		MERCHANDISE.	(1)		

		PURCHASES, &c.	£.	s.	d.
1817.					
February 28		To Balance on hand, as per Inventory, fo. 2	12,882	18	8
March 3	8	To S. Marsh...... Leeds.			
		Pks. sc. lb. £. s. d.			
		9 Sheets Wool, C....13 4 4...at £35...467 5 0			
		4 Ditto Ditto, D.... 6 0 18...at 50...303 15 0			
			771	0	0
March 3	12	To T. Rogers...... Leeds.			
		16 Casks Rape Oil, ... 1807 Gallons, ...at 3s.	271	1	0
March 4	12	To Robert Millar... London.			
		10 Casks Olive Oil, ... 1093 Gallons, ...at 8s.	437	4	0
March 4	5	To T. Merlin...... London.			
		5 per Cent. Discount on £1652 10 4	82	12	6
March 5	8	To Welch and Co... Leeds.			
		Pks. sc. lbs.			
		9 Sheets Wool, A....13 5 12...at £16 per Pack.....	215	9	4
March 5	13	To Robert Smith.... Hull.			
		40 Tons Fuller's Earth ....at £3 per Ton	120	0	0
March 6	1	To Cash.......... Subscription to the Poor................	10	10	0
March 7	9	To T. Bruce........Huddersfield			
		Pk. sc. lb.			
		11 Sheets Wool, B....17 1 7...at £24 per Pack.....	410	14	0
March 7	13	To T. Newton ...... Sherburne.			
		12 Packs Teazles ......at £9 per Pack................	108	0	0
		Amount carried forward ....£	15,309	9	6

(1)   PER CONTRA.

		SALES, &c.	£.	s.	d.

1817

March 4   5   By Goodwin and Co....... London.

        7 Bales containing 70 Cloths.

	Nos.	Yards.	£.	s.	d.
G	21..801 to 810 Blue, ..A...500 at 5s. 8d..	141	13	4
	22..811 to 820 Scarlet, A...490 at 7s. 3d..	177	12	6
	23..821 to 830 Blue, ..B. .501 at 7s. 0d..	175	7	0
	24..831 to 840 Brown, B...493 at 6s. 6d..	160	4	6
	25..841 to 850 Black, .B...495 at 6s. 4d..	156	15	0
	26..851 to 860 Scarlet, B...494 at 8s. 6d..	209	19	0
	27..861 to 870 Ditto, ..B...489 at 8s. 6d..	207	16	6
	70 Tillets ....at 2s. 6d..	8	15	0
	Packing 7 Bales .....at 21s. 0d..	7	7	0

                                 1,245   9   10

March 6   5   By T. Merlin........ London.

        5 Bales, containing 50 Casimirs.

	Nos.	Yards.	£.	s.	d.
M	1..871 to 880 Black, .N..494 at 4s. 6d..	111	3	0
	2..881 to 890 Blue, ..N..490 at 4s. 10d..	118	8	4
	3..891 to 900 Ditto, .N..492 at 4s. 10d..	118	18	0
	4..901 to 910 Brown, O..492 at 6s. 2d..	151	14	0
	5..911 to 920 Scarlet, O..491 at 7s. 3d..	177	19	9
	50 Tillets ....at 1s. 6d..	3	15	0
	Packing 5 Bales, ...at 14s. 0d..	3	10	0

                                 685   8   1

March 8   7   By S. Green........ Liverpool.

        7 Bales, containing 70 Casimirs.

	Nos.	Yards.	£.	s.	d.
S G	80..921 to 930 Brown, L ..503 at 2s. 10d..	71	5	2
	81..931 to 940 Blue, . L ..502 at 3s. 3d..	81	11	6
	82..941 to 950 Black, M..501 at 3s. 6d..	87	13	6
	83..951 to 960 Ditto, M..492 at 3s. 6d..	86	2	0
	84..961 to 970 Blue, . M..498 at 3s. 10d..	95	9	0
	85..971 to 980 Ditto, M..498 at 3s. 10d..	95	9	0
	86..981 to 990 Scarlet, M.. 493 at 4s. 8d..	115	0	8
	70 Tillets ....at 1s. 6d..	5	5	0
	Packing 7 Bales,....at 14s. 0d..	4	18	0

                                 642   13   10

        Amount carried forward.............£   2,573   11   9

Dr.   MERCHANDISE.   (2)

Date	Fol	Particulars	£	s.	d.
1817.		PURCHASES, &c............ Brought forward	15,309	9	6
March 7	13	To Marmot and Co....... London.			
		c. q. lb. £. s. d.			
		1 Chest Brown Soap........10 1 0 at 85s....43 11 3			
		1 Ditto Mottled Soap.......10 2 2 at 100s....52 11 9			
		Chests...... 0 4 10	96	7	10
March 8	13	To B. Wallis........... Leeds.			
		20 Packs Sizing.............at 90s. per pack...........	90	0	0
March 8	1	To Cash........ for Wages and Petty Expenses this Week.			
		Sorting, Carding, Spinning, &c. as per Book..A..178 15 9			
		Weaving, Milling, &c......... Ditto......B..193 15 10			
		Dressing, Pressing, Packing, &c..Ditto......C..181 4 8	553	16	3
March 10	9	To Gill and Co....... Wakefield.			
		p. sc. lb.			
		9 Sheets Wool.....C......13 6 13 at £33.:447 5 9			
		6 Ditto Ditto.....B......9 0 15 at 48..435 0 0	882	5	9
March 10	14	To Garth and Co....... Leeds.			
		50 Pieces Canvas,....at 30s.................75 0 0			
		80 Pieces Tilletting...at 25s.................100 0 0	175	0	0
March 11	11	To D. Carew...... Bradford.			
		p. s. lb.			
		15 Sheets Wool....B...22 7 5...at £22 per pack....	497	5	10
March 11	14	To J. Belson........ Leeds.			
		100 Ropes, weight 1000lbs....at 6d...........25 0 0			
		10 Dozen Tilletting Twine...at 20s...........10 0 0	35	0	0
March 12	14	To Manson and Co......Leeds.			
		10 Reams Lapping Paper....at 60s..........30 0 0			
		1000 lbs. Rope Paper.........at 6d...........25 0 0	55	0	0
		Amount carried forward ....£	17,694	5	2

(2)   PER CONTRA.   *Cr.*

				£.	s.	d.
		SALES, &c.	Brought forward	2,573	11	9

1817.

March 11 | 6 | By Fairfax and Co........ Glasgow.

5 Bales, containing 50 Cloths.

No.	Nos.	Yards	£.	s.	d.
F 7...	991 to 1000 Black A..501 at 5s.3d..		131	10	3
8...	1001 to 1010 Brown A..501 at 5s.4d..		133	12	0
9..	1011 to 1020 Blue B..501 at 7s.0d..		175	7	0
10...	1021 to 1030 Ditto B..495 at 7s.0d..		173	5	0
11...	1031 to 1040 Scarlet B..495 at 8s.6d..		210	7	6
	50 Tillets ....at 2s.6d..		6	5	0
	Packing 5 Bales at 21s.0d..		5	5	0

835 | 11 | 9

March 12 | 5 | By Goodwin and Co....... London.

6 Bales containing 60 Cloths.

No.	Nos.	Yards	£.	s.	d.
G 28..	1041 to 1050 Black C..506 at 8s.4d..		210	16	8
29..	1051 to 1060 Blue ..C..500 at 9s.0d..		225	0	0
30..	1061 to 1070 Brown C..491 at 8s.6d..		208	13	6
31..	1071 to 1080 Scarlet C..500 at 10s.6d..		262	10	0
32..	1081 to 1090 Blue ..D..502 at 12s.0d..		301	4	0
33..	1091 to 1100 Scarlet D..502 at 13s.6d..		338	17	0
	60 Tillets ......at 2s.6d..		7	10	0
	Packing 6 Bales at 21s.0d..		6	6	0

1,560 | 17 | 2

March 13 | A 5 | By Consignment to B. Wilson.... Gibraltar.

Shipped per Mary, by C. Follet, Liverpool.

8 Bales containing 80 Cloths.

No.	Nos.	Yards	£.	s.	d.
B W 1..	1101 to 1110 Brown A..497 at 5s.4d..		132	10	8
2..	1111 to 1120 Blue . A..494 at 5s.8d..		139	19	4
3..	1121 to 1130 Black . B..489 at 6s.4d..		154	17	0
4..	1131 to 1140 Ditto . B..497 at 6s.4d..		157	7	8
5..	1141 to 1150 Brown C..502 at 8s.6d..		213	7	0
6..	1151 to 1160 Blue.. C..496 at 9s.0d..		223	4	0
7..	1161 to 1170 Ditto . D..496 at 12s.0d..		297	12	0
8..	1171 to 1180 Scarlet D..499 at 13s.6d..		336	16	6
	80 Tillets .....at 2s.6d..		10	0	0
(continued)	Packing 8 Bales at 21s.0d..		8	8	0

Amount carried forward......£ 1,674 2 2 | 4,970 | 0 | 8

Dr.   MERCHANDISE.   (3)

		PURCHASES, &c.	£.	s.	a.
		Brought forward	17,694	5	2
1817.					
March 12	12	To Holt & Co. . . . . . Huddersfield.			
		p. sc. lb.			
		9 Sheets Wool A . . 13 6 17 at £15 per pack	203	11	3
13	15	To J. Plane . . . . . Leeds.			
		50 dozen Boards, at 6s. per dozen	15	0	0
15	1	To Cash, ... for Wages and Petty Expenses this week :			
		£. s. d.			
		Sorting, Carding, Spinning, &c. as per Book A. . . 173 2 4			
		Weaving, Milling, &c. as per Book B. 189 16 8			
		Dressing, Finishing, Packing, &c. as per Book C. 172 18 6	535	17	6
		Amount carried forward. . . . .£	18,448	13	11

PER CONTRA.   *Cr.*

			£.	s.	d.
SALES, &c.	Brought forward		4,970	0	8

1817.

			£.	s.	d.
March 13	A 5	By Consignment to B. Wilson, *continued* 1,674	2	2

8 Bales containing 80 Casimirs.

No.	Nos.	Yds.	£.	s.	d.
B W 9..	1181 to 1190 Brown L . 501 at 2s. 10d.		70	19	6
10..	1191 to 1200 Blue . L . 496 at 3s. 3d.		80	12	0
11..	1201 to 1210 Black M . 501 at 3s. 6d.		87	13	6
12..	1211 to 1220 Black M . 492 at 3s. 6d.		86	2	0
13..	1221 to 1230 Brown N 494 at 4s. 8d.		115	5	4
14..	1231 to 1240 Blue . N . 498 at 4s. 10d.		120	7	0
15..	1241 to 1250 Ditto O . 494 at 6s. 4d.		156	8	8
16..	1251 to 1260 Scarlet O . 500 at 7s. 3d.		181	5	0
	80 Tillets .... 1s. 6d.		6	0	0
	Packing 8 Bales .. 14s. 0d.		5	12	0

			£.	s.	d.
			2,584	7	2

March 14	7	By S. Green ..... Liverpool.

8 Bales containing 80 Cloths.

No.	Nos.	Yds.	£.	s.	d.
S G 87..	1261 to 1270 Black A 497 at 5s. 3d.		130	9	3
88..	1271 to 1280 Brown A 505 at 5s. 4d.		134	13	4
89..	1281 to 1290 Blue B 503 at 7s. 0d.		176	1	0
90..	1291 to 1300 Ditto B 496 at 7s. 0d.		173	12	0
91..	1301 to 1310 Scarlet B 495 at 8s. 6d.		210	7	6
92..	1311 to 1320 Black C 502 at 8s. 4d.		209	3	4
93..	1321 to 1330 Black D 501 at 11s. 0d.		275	11	0
94..	1331 to 1340 Blue D 504 at 12s. 0d.		302	8	0
	80 Tillets .... at 2s. 6d.		10	0	0
	Packing 8 Bales at 21s. 0d.		8	8	0

			£.	s.	d.
			1,630	13	5

		£.	s.	d.
Amount carried forward .. ..£	9,185	1	3

Dr.   MERCHANDISE.   (4)

			£.	s.	d.
		PURCHASES, &c. Brought forward	18,448	13	11
1817.					
March 22	1	To Cash, ... for Wages and Petty Expenses this Week :			
		£. s. d.			
		Sorting, Carding, Spinning, &c. as per Book A. 177 15 5			
		Weaving, Milling, &c. . . . . Ditto . . . . B. 196 17 3			
		Dressing, Pressing, Packing, &c. . . Ditto . . . . C. 179 10 3			
			554	2	11
22	1	To Cash, ... Paid Wallis and Co. for Stamps and Stationery	28	13	0
29	14	To Ranger and Co. . . . . . . Liverpool.			
		7½ per Cent. Discount on £827. 11. 8.	62	1	5
29	1	To Cash, ... for Wages and Sundry Expenses this Week :			
		£. s. d.			
		Sorting, Carding, &c. as per Book A. 171 11 8			
		Weaving, Milling, &c. Ditto . . . . B. 192 5 6			
		Dressing, Pressing, &c. Ditto . . . . C. 168 14 2			
			532	11	4
30	6	To Henry Melville, ... London.			
		Amount of Discounts, Salaries, &c. this Quarter, as advised	528	12	6
30	11	To Horton and Co. . . . . . Bankers.			
		Balance of Interest and Charges in their favour, as per Account	39	5	4
30	1	To Cash, ... for Postages this Month	10	15	9
30	1	To Cash, ... for Taxes this Month	18	11	10
30	1	To Cash, ... for Salaries this Month :			
		£. s. d.			
		J. Steadfast, Overlooker A. 6 5 0			
		T. Careful, Ditto . . . . . B. 6 5 0			
		S. Jones, Ditto . . . . . C. 6 5 0			
		R. Peters, Clerk 12 10 0			
			31	5	0
		Amount carried forward . . . . £	20,254	13	0

(4)   PER CONTRA.   *Cr.*

			£.	s.	d.
	Sales, &c. Brought forward		9,185	1	3

1817.

March 15   A 1   By Consignment to Henry Melville, London.

6 Bales, containing 60 Cloths.

No.	Nos.	Yards.	£.	s.	d.
HM 81..	1341 to 1350 Brown A..	499 at 5s.4d..	133	1	4
82..	1351 to 1360 Black A..	500 at 5s.3d..	131	5	0
83..	1361 to 1370 Blue B..	505 at 7s.0d..	176	15	0
84..	1371 to 1380 Ditto B..	508 at 7s.0d..	177	16	0
85..	1381 to 1390 Black C..	502 at 8s.4d..	209	3	4
86..	1391 to 1400 Scarlet D..	493 at 13s.6d..	332	15	6
	60 Tillets ...... at	2s.6d..	7	10	0
	Packing 6 Bales at	21s.0d..	6	6	0

4 Bales, containing 40 Casimirs.

No.	Nos.	Yards.	£.	s.	d.
87..	1401 to 1410 Brown L..	501 at 2s.10d..	70	19	6
88..	1411 to 1420 Black M..	504 at 3s.6d..	88	4	0
89..	1421 to 1430 Blue N..	503 at 4s.10d..	121	11	2
90..	1431 to 1440 Scarlet O..	501 at 7s.3d..	181	12	3
	40 Tillets...... at	1s.6d..	3	0	0
	Packing 4 Bales at	14s.0d..	2	16	0
			1,642	15	1

March 24   14   By Ranger and Co.....Liverpool.

4 Bales, containing 40 Cloths.

No.	Nos.	Yards.	£.	s.	d.
RL 1..	1441 to 1450 Blue A..	499 at 5s.8d..	141	7	8
2..	1451 to 1460 Black A..	502 at 5s.3d..	131	15	6
3..	1461 to 1470 Brown B..	502 at 6s.6d..	163	3	0
4..	1471 to 1480 Scarlet B..	500 at 8s.6d..	212	10	0
	40 Tillets ...... at	2s.6d..	5	0	0
	Packing 4 Bales at	21s.0d..	4	4	0

2 Bales, containing 20 Casimirs.

No.	Nos.	Yards.	£.	s.	d.
5..	1481 to 1490 Brown L..	496 at 2s.10d..	70	5	4
6..	1491 to 1500 Blue M..	503 at 3s.10d..	96	8	2
	20 Tillets...... at	1s.6d..	1	10	0
	Packing 2 Bales at	14s.0d..	1	8	0
			827	11	8

Amount carried forward .... £   11,655   8   0

Dr.		MERCHANDISE.	(5)		

			£.	s.	d.
		PURCHASES, &c. Brought forward £	20,254	13	0
1817.					
March 30	9	To Halset and Co. . . . . for Dying this Month, as per Account . . .	1,135	16	9
30	15	To S. Morgan, ... for Healds and Slays, as per Account	26	12	6
30	15	To Peters and Co. . . . . for Carriage this Month	57	8	8
30	10	To Bandor and Co. . . . . for Millwright's Work	227	10	0
30	10	To F. Denton . . . . for Cards this Month	136	15	0
30	16	To Field and Co. . . . . . . Huddersfield :			
		60 dozen Coals at 10s. 30 0 0			
		Freight, &c. . . . . 5s. 15 0 0			
			45	0	0
March 30	2	To Profit	2,149	1	2
		£	24,032	17	1
March 31		To Balance on hand, as per Inventory fo. 5	11,174	7	10

(5)   PER CONTRA.   *Cr.*

			£.	s.	d.
		SALES, &c. Brought forward £	11,655	8	0

1817.

March 26 | 6 | By Fairfax and Co. . . . . . Glasgow.

3 Bales, containing 30 Cloths.

	No.	Nos.	Yards.	£.	s.	d.
F	12. .	1501 to 1510 Black C. .	499 at 8s. 4d. .	207	18	4
	13. .	1511 to 1520 Blue C. .	508 at 9s. 0d. .	228	12	0
	14. .	1521 to 1530 White D. .	503 at 10s. 6d. .	264	1	6
		30 Tillets	at 2s. 6d. .	3	15	0
		Packing 3 Bales	at 21s. 0d. .	3	3	0

2 Bales, containing 20 Casimirs.

	15. .	1531 to 1540 Blue N. .	497 at 4s. 10d. .	120	2	2
	16. .	1541 to 1550 Scarlet O. .	499 at 7s. 3d. .	180	17	9
		20 Tillets	at 1s. 6d. .	1	10	0
		Packing 2 Bales	at 14s. 0d. .	1	8	0

        1,011   7   9

March 30 | 3 | By Shop, ... for 6 Cloths and 6 Casimirs.

		£.	s.	d.
1551. . 1552 Blue A. . .	101 at 5s. 8d. . . .	28	12	4
1553. . 1554 Black B. . .	103 at 6s. 4d. . . .	32	12	4
1555 Brown C. . .	51 at 8s. 6d. . . .	21	13	6
1556 Scarlet D. . .	52 at 13s. 6d. . . .	35	2	0
1557. . 1558 Blue L. . .	102 at 3s. 3d. . . .	16	11	6
1559. . 1560 Brown M. . .	102 at 3s. 8d. . . .	18	14	0
1561 Black N. . .	52 at 4s. 6d. . . .	11	14	0
1562 Scarlet O. . .	51 at 7s. 3d. . . .	18	9	9

        183   9   5

			£.	s.	d.
March 30	15	By Peters and Co. . . . . 5 per Cent. Discount on £57. 8. 8.	2	17	5
30	14	By J. Belson . . . . 5 Ditto. . . . . Ditto. . . . . . . 35. 0. 0.	1	15	0
30	15	By S. Morgan . . . . 5 Ditto. . . . . Ditto. . . . . . . 26. 12. 6.	1	6	8
30	16	By Field and Co. . . . . . 5 Ditto. . . . . Ditto. . . . . . . 45. 0. 0.	2	5	0

			£.	s.	d.
31		By Balance on hand, as per Inventory fo. 5	11,174	7	10
		£	24,032	17	1

INDEX TO THE ADVENTURES.

Dr.   CONSIGNMENT TO   (1)

1817.				£.	s.	d.
February 28		To Balance, ... 25 Bales Cloths and Casimirs		3,947	9	8
March 15	4	To Merchandise, . 10 Ditto Cloths and Casimirs		1,642	15	1
29	4	To Henry Melville, London, 5 per Cent. Discount on Sales		207	5	7
			£	5,797	10	4

(1)   HENRY MELVILLE, LONDON.   *Cr.*

1817.				£.	s.	d.
March 29	4	By Henry Melville, ... London.				
		Net Proceeds of 35 Bales as per his Account Sales.				
		£. s. d.				
		70 Pieces Cloths.. A. 3,410 yards at 4s. . 682 0 0				
		70.... Ditto..... B. 3,426 ditto at 5s. . 856 10 0				
		M 40.... Ditto..... C. 1,982 ditto at 7s. .693 14 0				
		No. 56 to 90. 30.... Ditto..... D. 1,500 ditto at 10s. .750 0 0				
		40 Pieces Casimirs L. 1,978 ditto at 2s. . 197 16 0				
		40.... Ditto..... M. 1,974 ditto at 3s. . 296 2 0				
		30.... Ditto..... N. 1,480 ditto at 4s. . 296 0 0				
		30.... Ditto..... O. 1,494 ditto at 5s. . 373 10 0				
				4,145	12	0
29	2	By Loss		1,651	18	4
				5,797	10	4

Dr. CONSIGNMENT TO (2)

			£.	s.	d.
1817.					
February 28	To Balance, 16 Bales Cloths and Casimirs		2682	10	8
		£	2682	10	8

(2) GOMES AND CO. CADIZ. *Cr.*

1817.					£.	s.	d.
March 10	4	By Gomes and Co. . . . . . Cadiz.					

Net Proceeds of 16 Bales as per their Account Sales.

	Nos.		Yds.	Rials.	Rs. Pl. Qs.
G	1 & 2. . . . 20 Pieces Cloths . . A	. . . 986 at 20	. . . . . 19,720. 0
	3 & 4. . . . 20 Pieces Ditto . . . B	. . 1010 at 25	. . . . . 25,250. 0
	5 & 6. . . . 20 Pieces Ditto . . . C	. . 1000 at 30	. . . . . 30,000. 0
	7 & 8. . . . 20 Pieces Ditto . . . D	. . 994 at 40	. . . . . 39,760. 0
	9 & 10. . . . 20 Pieces Casimirs L	. . 978 at 12	. . . . . 11,736. 0
	11 & 12. . . . 20 Pieces Ditto . . . M	. 1004 at 15	. . . . . 15,060. 0
	13 & 14. . . . 20 Pieces Ditto . . . N	. 1002 at 18	. . . . 18,036. 0
	15 & 16. . . . 20 Pieces Ditto . . . O	. 996 at 24	. . . . . 23,904. 0

183,466. 0

CHARGES.

Rs. Pl. Qs.

Duties and Custom House Charges	55,040. 7
Warehouse Rent, ½ per Cent.	917. 5
Postages and Petty Expenses, ½ per Ct.	917. 5
Commission, 4 per Cent.	7338. 10
Guarantee, 2 per Cent.	3669. 5

67,883. 0

Net Proceeds 115,583. 0

		At the Exchange of 36*d.* per Piastre of 8 Rials	2167	3	7
March 10	2	By Loss	515	7	1
		£	2682	10	8

| Dr. | CONSIGNMENT TO | (3) |

1817.		£.	s.	d.
Feb. 28	To Balance, 150 Bales Cloths and Casimirs	26,851	15	6
		26,851	15	6

(3)   BRAGA AND CO. LISBON.   *Cr.*

1817.				£.	s.	d.
March 20	4	By Braga and Co.....Lisbon.				

Net Proceeds of 150 Bales, as per their Account Sales.

		Yards.	Reas.	Mil-reas.
B 1 to 30..300 Pieces Cloths .. A..	14,926 at	1.000...	14,926.000
31 to 60..300 Pieces Ditto ... B..	14,874 at	1.200...	17,848.800
61 to 75..150 Pieces Ditto ...C..	7,428 at	1.500...	11,142.000
76 to 90..150 Pieces Ditto ...D..	7,440 at	2.000...	14,880.000
91 to 110..200 Pieces Casimirs L..	9,952 at	.600...	5,971.200
111 to 130..200 Pieces Ditto .. M..	9,926 at	.700...	6,948.200
131 to 141..100 Pieces Ditto .. N..	4,960 at	.800...	3,968.000
141 to 150..100 Pieces Ditto .. O..	4,944 at	1.000...	4,944.000

                                     80,628.200

                      CHARGES.

Duties and Custom-House Charges 9,152.500
Warehouse Rent, ½ per Cent 403.141
Postages and Petty Expenses, ¼ per Cent..... 403.141
Commission, 4 per Cent................. 3,225.128
                                       13,183.910

                  Net Proceeds 67,444.290

				£.	s.	d.
		At the Exchange of 57*d.* per Milrea		16,018	0	4
March 20	2	By Loss		10,833	15	2
				26,851	15	6

Dr.	COCHINEAL PER FERNANDO	(4)

1817.				£.	s.	d.
March 15	4	To Gomes and Co. Cadiz, 10 Bags as per Invoice.				

	No.	lbs.
W	121	202
	122	187
	123	196
	124	210
	125	179
	126	176
	127	206
	128	212
	129	199
	130	188

	Piast.	Rls. Pl. Qs.
1955 lbs...... at 8.....	125,120.	0
Duties and Shipping Charges	23,620.	0
	148,740.	0
Commission, 2 per Cent..........	2,975.	0
Cost .... Rte.	151,715.	0

At the Exchange of 36*d.* per Piastre of 8 Rials   2,844   13   1

March 17   16   To C. Follet, ... Liverpool.

Charges on the above.

	£.	s.	d.
Freight and Primage	57	16	10
Duty and Custom-House Charges	261	3	6
Insurance of £3,000, at 2 Guineas per Cent.	63	0	0
Policy, ¼ per Cent...........................	7	10	0
Del-Credere, ½ Ditto	15	0	0
Landing and Petty Charges	4	15	0
	409	5	4
Commission, 2 per Cent.	8	3	8

     417   9   0

March 27   15   To E. Merton, ... Leeds.

5 per Cent. Discount on £1,471. 10. 0..................   73   11   6

£ 3,335   13   7

(4)   FROM CADIZ.   *Cr.*

			£.	s.	d.
1817					
March 24	9	By Halset and Co.........Leeds.	•		

5 Bags, viz :

		cwt.	qr.	lbs.		lbs.
No. 121	Gross...	1	3	14	Tare	8
122	Gross...	1	2	26	Tare	7
123	Gross...	1	3	8	Tare	8
124	Gross...	1	3	22	Tare	8
125	Gross...	1	2	18	Tare	7

Gross 9 0 4 Tare 38
Tare 0 1 10

Net.. 8 2 22 ....Or 974 lbs. at 30s. | 1,461 | 0 | 0

March 25 | 15 | By E. Merton, ...Leeds.

5 Bags, viz :

		cwt.	qr.	lbs.		lbs.
No. 126	Gross...	1	2	14	Tare	6
127	Gross...	1	3	18	Tare	8
128	Gross...	1	3	24	Tare	8
129	Gross...	1	3	10	Tare	7
130	Gross...	1	2	26	Tare	6

Gross 9 0 8 Tare 35
Tare 0 1 7

Net 8 3 1.........Or 981 lbs. at 30s. | 1,471 | 10 | 0

March 30 | 2 | By Loss ....·· | 403 | 3 | 7

£ | 3,335 | 13 | 7

Dr.   CONSIGNMENT TO   (5)

1817.				£.	s.	d.	£.	s.	d.
March 13	3	To Merchandise, 16 Bales Cloths and Casimirs, per Mary....		....	..	..	2,584	7	2
March 18	16	To C. Follet, ... Liverpool.							

Charges on the above.

	£.	s.	d.						
Export Duty, ½ per Cent. on £2584. 7. 2.....	12	18	5						
Freight, 487 feet, at 2s. per foot.............	48	14	0						
Primage, 5 per Cent.....................	2	8	8						
Bills Lading............................	0	4	0						
Petty Charges	0	16	0						
Carriage, 60 Cwt. per Canal, at 2s. 6d........	7	10	0						
Cartage and Porterage	2	8	0						
Commission, 5s. per Bale.................	4	0	0						

				£.	s.	d.	£.	s.	d.
				78	19	1			
Insurance of £2800, at 2 Guineas per Cent.....	58	16	0						
Policy Duty, ¼ per Cent...................	7	0	0						
Del-Credere, ½ per Cent..................	14	0	0						
Commission, ¼ per Cent..................	7	0	0						
				86	16	0			
							165	15	1
							2,750	2	3
March 31		To Balance, 16 Bales					2,750	2	3

(5)   B. WILSON, GIBRALTAR.   *Cr.*

1817.		£.	s.	d.
March 31	By Balance, 16 Bales	2,750	2	3
		2,750	2	3

Dr.   COMPOSITION.   (6)

1817.				£.	s.	d.
July 10	2	To Profit		18,145	13	2
			£	18,145	13	2

(6)   PER CONTRA.   *Cr.*

By Sundry Creditors, for their Abatement 40 per Cent. on the following Balances; viz.

1817.				£.	s.	d.
July 10	11	Horton & Co. ..... on £14,950 0 0		5,980	0	0
	7	Hilton & Co. ..... on 2,670 16 0		1,068	6	5
	8	Taylor & Co. ..... on 2,635 6 0		1,054	2	5
	7	R. Selkirk .... on 1,980 15 9		792	6	4
	8	S. Marsh .... on 2,211 19 4		884	15	9
	8	Welch & Co. ..... on 1,761 11 10		704	12	9
	9	T. Bruce .... on 2,457 15 1		983	2	0
	9	Gill & Co. .... on 2,564 16 9		1,025	18	8
	9	Halset & Co. ..... on 3,841 17 5		1,536	15	0
	10	Bandor & Co. .... on 1,165 5 0		466	2	0
	10	F. Denton .... on 727 15 9		291	2	4
	13	T. Newton ...... on 108 0 0		43	4	0
	13	Marmot & Co. .... on 247 2 10		98	17	2
	13	B. Wallis .... on 239 5 0		95	14	0
	16	C. Follet .... on 583 4 1		233	5	7
	12	Holt & Co. ...... on 1,075 7 9		430	3	1
	12	Robert Millar .... on 765 7 6		306	3	0
	17	Benson & Co. .... on 987 8 6		394	19	4
	17	Pindar & Sons .... on 659 10 0		263	16	0
	16	L. Bruce .... on 462 11 6		185	0	7
	14	Manson & Co. .... on 55 0 0		22	0	0
	11	D. Carew .... on 497 5 10		198	18	4
	12	T. Rogers .... on 271 1 0		108	8	5
	13	Robert Smith ..... on 120 0 0		48	0	0
	14	Garth & Co. ..... on 175 0 0		70	0	0
	16	Clifford & Co. .... on 2,150 0 0		860	0	0
		£45,364 2 11 .... £		18,145	13	2

Dr.   CASH.   (1)

		RECEIPTS.	£.	s.	d.
1817.					
Feb. 28		To Balance	1,071	4	10
Mar. 4	11	To Horton & Co. Leeds, their Notes	500	0	0
11	11	To Ditto........ Ditto... Ditto...........................	600	0	0
18	11	To Ditto........ Ditto... Ditto...........................	600	0	0
24	11	To Ditto........ Ditto... Check to Grant & Co.	57	16	6
25	11	To Ditto........ Ditto... their Notes	550	0	0
30	3	To Shop, ... Receipts this Month per S. Jones.............	165	18	6
		£	3,544	19	10
Mar. 31		To Balance	880	17	0
		£	880	17	0
July 11		To Balance	603	6	6

(1)   PER CONTRA.   *Cr.*

1817.		PAYMENTS.	£.	s.	
Mar. 4	1	By Private Account, ... T. Gore, Tailor, his Note................	14	12	6
6	1	By Merchandise,....... Subscription to the Poor	10	10	0
8	2	By Merchandise,....... Wages and Petty Expenses this Week	553	16	3
10	1	By Private Account, ... S. Gill, Linen Draper	15	6	0
12	1	By.... Ditto .... Cash to Wife	10	0	0
14	1	By.... Ditto .... J. Brown, Butcher	12	13	6
15	3	By Merchandise,....... Wages and Petty Expenses this Week	535	17	6
17	1	By Private Account, ... taken for Pocket Money	5	5	0
19	1	By.... Ditto .... Hopson & Co. Brewers	14	7	4
20	1	By.... Ditto .... Bell & Co. Flour and Malt	17	12	0
22	4	By Merchandise,....... Wages and Petty Expenses this Week	554	2	11
22	15	By J. Plane, Leeds, ... Boards	15	0	0
22	4	By Merchandise, J. Wallis, for Stationary and Stamps	28	13	0
24	1	By Private Account, ... Grant & Co. Wine and Spirits, per Check on } Horton & Co.	57	16	6
29	4	By Merchandise,....... Wages and Petty Expenses this Week	532	11	4
30	4	By.... Ditto .... Postage this Month	10	15	9
30	4	By.... Ditto .... Taxes	18	11	10
30	15	By Peters & Co. Leeds,.. Balance	54	11	3
30	14	By J. Belson, .. Ditto.... Ditto...........................	33	5	0
30	15	By S. Morgan,.. Ditto.... Ditto.....................,.......	25	5	10
30	16	By Field & Co.. Ditto.... Ditto............................	42	15	0
30	4	By Merchandise, ... Salaries this Month	31	5	0
30	11	By Horton & Co. Leeds, Balance of Account	69	9	4
31		By Balance	880	17	0
		£	3,544	19	10
July 10	2	By Loss, Composition Deed, and Expenses of Meeting	55	10	6
11	14	By Manson & Co. Leeds, Return of Composition Abatement	22	0	0
11	1	By Private Account, Expenses since 31st March................	200	0	0
11		By Balance	603	6	6
		£	880	17	0

Υ

Dr.   BILLS RECEIVABLE.   (1)

When & from whom received.			No.	Drawn By		Date and Term.			Order of	Drawn on.	
1817.						1817.		. . .	. . . .	. . . .	. . . .
Mar.3	4	To Braga and Co.	167	Carvalho and Co.	Lisbon . .	Feb. 18	30 d.s.		Braga and Co.	S. Fox	London.
		Exchange at 57d.	168	Ulloa and Co. . .	Ditto . . .	Feb. 12	60 d.s.		A. Rico	Guimarraens&Co.	Ditto.
		Rs. 16,842. 105	169	Silva and Co.	Ditto . . .	Feb. 15	30 d.s.		Braga and Co.	Mira and Co. . . .	Ditto.
			170	Ulloa and Co.	Ditto . . .	Feb. 18	30 d.s.		Ditto	Ditto	Ditto.
			171	Braga and Co. . .	Ditto . . .	Feb. 18	60 d.s.		Myself	Le Maitre & Co.	Ditto.
3	5	To Goodwin & Co.	172	Giorgione & Co. . .	Leghorn .	Jan. 2	3 m.		Goodwin & Co.	J. Alfieri	Ditto.
			173	Goodwin and Co.	London .	Mar. 1	2 m.		Myself	Jones and Co. .	Ditto.
4	5	To Nield and Co.	174	Denison and Co. . .	Liverpool	Mar. 3	2 m.		Nield and Co.	Chaloner and Co.	Ditto.
4	5	To T. Merlin . . .	175	Moore and Co. . .	Bristol . .	Feb. 26	3 m.		T. Merlin . . .	Curtis and Co. .	Ditto.
			176	T. Merlin	London . .	Mar. 1	2 m.		Myself	Ditto	Ditto.
6	11	To Horton & Co.	177	Willis and Co. . .	Leeds . . .	Mar. 1	2 m.		J. Blaek . . .	Ogle and Co. . .	Ditto.
			178	Peters and Co. . .	Hull	Feb. 26	2 m.		White and Co.	Green and Co. .	Ditto.
			179	Horton and Co. . .	Leeds . . .	Mar. 5	2 m.		Myself	Mellin and Co. .	Ditto.
8	4	To Braga and Co.	180	Silva and Co.	Lisbon . .	Feb. 22	60 d.s.		Braga and Co.	Mira and Co. . . .	Ditto.
			181	Turner and Co. . . .	Ditto . . .	Feb. 20	30 d.s.		S. Brown . . .	White and Co. .	Ditto.
		Exchange at 56¾d.	182	Ulloa and Co.	Ditto . . .	Feb. 22	30 d.s.		Braga and Co.	Mira and Co. . . .	Ditto.
		Rs. 23,374. 450.	183	Le Brun and Co.	Ditto . . .	Feb. 18	60 d.s.		J. Nott	Holles and Co. .	Ditto.
			184	J. Arnold	Ditto . . .	Feb. 22	30 d.s.		Braga and Co.	S. Marriott . . .	Ditto.
11	11	To Horton & Co.	185	Baxter and Co. . .	Hull	Feb. 1	3 m.		S. Sims	Reinhard and Co.	Ditto.
			186	G. Walker	Leeds . . .	Mar. 10	2 m.		Order	Ranger and Co. .	Ditto.
			187	Horton and Co. .	Ditto . . .	Mar. 6	2 m.		Myself	Mellin and Co. .	Ditto.
			188	Montaigne & Co.	Paris . . .	Jan. 11	4 m.		Order	B. Wright	Ditto.
13	5	To Goodwin & Co.	189	Rauch and Co. . .	Hambro'	Feb. 18	2 m.		D. Carter . . .	Albert and Co. .	Ditto.
13	6	To Fairfax & Co.	190	Wall and Co.	Exeter . .	Mar. 3	3 m.		Order	Baxter and Co. .	Ditto.
15	4	To Braga and Co.	191	Abrantes and Co.	Porto . . .	Feb. 2	60 d.s.		P. Lord	Rees and Co. . . .	Ditto.
		Exch. at 57½d.	192	S. Rose	Lisbon . .	Feb. 28	60 d.s.		Order	Walker and Co.	Ditto.
		Rs. 11,458. 900									
18	11	To Horton & Co.	193	R. Williams	Leeds . . .	Feb. 10	3 m.		Horton & Co.	Rogers and Co. .	Ditto.
18	4	To Gomes & Co.	194	Almagro and Co. . .	Cadiz . . .	Mar. 2	3 m.		Gomes and Co.	Roberts and Co.	Ditto.
		Exch. at 36d.									
		R.P. 24,576. 14									
22	4	To Braga and Co.	195	B. Hoffman	Lisbon . .	Mar. 10	30 d.s.		Braga and Co.	Langle and Co. .	Ditto.
		Exch. at 56¾d.	196	Carvalho and Co.	Ditto . . .	Mar. 8	30 d.s.		Order	S. Peart	Ditto.
		Rs. 7,419. 385	197	Ditto	Ditto . . .	Mar. 6	60 d.s.		B. Hoffman . .	Ditto	Ditto.
			198	Viera and Co. . .	Ditto . . .	Mar. 8	60 d.s.		Braga and Co.	Butter and Co. .	Ditto.
		Carried forwards	. . .	. . . .	. . . . . .	. . . . .	. . .		. . . .	. . . .	. . . .

(1)   PER CONTRA.   *Cr*

Due.	£.	s.	d.	£.	s.	d.
1817.						
April 7	1000	0	0			
May 7	750	0	0			
April 7	800	0	0			
April 7	450	0	0			
May 7	1,000	0	0	4,000	0	0
April 5	327	16	0			
May 4	400	0	0	727	16	0
May 5	...	..	..	4,618	2	0
May 29	1,000	0	0			
May 4	569	17	10	1,569	17	10
May 4	500	0	0			
April 29	500	0	0			
May 8	500	0	0	1,500	0	0
May 12	1,500	0	0			
April 12	1,000	0	0			
April 12	1,500	0	0			
May 12	1,250	0	0			
April 12	750	0	0	6,000	0	0
May 4	437	12	6			
May 13	384	15	0			
May 9	500	0	0			
May 14	200	0	0	1,522	7	6
April 21	...	..	..	700	0	0
June 6	...	..	..	248	16	0
May 19	1,750	0	0			
May 19	983	8	6	2,733	8	6
May 13	...	..	..	950	0	0
June 5	...	..	..	460	16	4
April 26	500	0	0			
April 26	375	10	0			
May 26	628	17	6			
May 26	250	0	0	1,754	7	6
......	....	...	...	26,785	11	8

		When and to whom Remitted.	£.	s.	d.
1817.					
Mar. 3	6	By Henry Melville .... Nos. 167 to 173	4,727	16	0
4	6	By Ditto .... 174 to 176	6,187	19	10
6	6	By Ditto .... 177 to 179	1,500	0	0
8	6	By Ditto .... 180 to 184	6,000	0	0
11	6	By Ditto .... 185 to 188	1,522	7	6
13	6	By Ditto .... 189 to 190	948	16	0
15	6	By Ditto .... 191 to 192	2,733	8	6
18	6	By Ditto .... 193 to 194	1,410	16	4
22	6	By Ditto .... 195 to 198	1,754	7	6
		Carried forward	26,785	11	8

Dr.   BILLS RECEIVABLE.   (2)

When and from whom received.			No.	Drawn By.	Date and Term.			Order of.	Drawn on.	
		Brought forward	. .	. . . .	. . . . . .	1817.	. .	. . . .	. . . .	. . . . . .
Mar. 25	11	To Horton & Co.	199	Booth and Co.	Wakefield	Mar. 15	2 m.	L. Strange . .	R. Field	London.
27	15	To E. Merton .	200	J. Walker . .	Leeds . .	16	3 m.	Horton and Co.	T. Andrews . . .	Ditto.
			201	P. Simson . .	Ditto . .	21	3 m.	Ditto	Farmer & Co. .	Ditto.
			202	Horton and Co.	Ditto . .	26	3 m.	E. Merton . .	Mellin & Co. . .	Ditto.
29	14	To Ranger & Co.	203	Bates and Co.	Liverpl. .	25	3 m.	Ranger & Co.	R. Brown	Ditto.
			204	W. White . .	Ditto. . .	27	3 m.	Ditto	T. Black	Ditto.
29	4	To Braga & Co.	205	Abrantes & Co.	Lisbon. .	1	30d.s.	Braga and Co.	Ogle and Co. . .	Ditto.
		Exch. at 57d.	206	S. Covado . .	Ditto. . .	2	30d.s.	Crusados & Co.	Pinto and Co. .	Ditto.
		Rs. 6,549. 450	207	Alves and Co.	Ditto . .	2	30d.s.	Order	Ditto	Ditto.
July 10	12	To B. Wilson .	208	Myself	Leeds . .	July 10	2 m.	Peter Grant .	B. Wilson . . .	Gibraltar.
10	5	To Goodwin & Co.	209	Ditto	Ditto . .	10	2 m.	Ditto	Goodwin & Co.	London.
10	5	To T. Merlin .	210	Ditto	Ditto . .	10	2 m.	Ditto	T. Merlin	Ditto.
10	6	To Fairfax & Co.	211	Ditto	Ditto . .	10	2 m.	Ditto	Fairfax and Co.	Glasgow.
10	7	To S. Green . .	212	Ditto	Ditto . .	10	2 m.	Ditto	S. Green	Liverpool.

(2)

Due.	£.	s.	d.	£.	s.	d.
1817.						
....	....	..	..	26,785	11	8
May 18	....	..	..	1,000	0	0
June 19	500	0	0			
24	500	0	0			
29	397	18	6	1,397	18	6
28	365	10	3			
30	400	0	0	765	10	3
May 3	350	0	0			
3	650	0	0			
3	507	19	10	1,507	19	10
				31,457	0	3
Sept. 13	....	..	..	1,000	0	0
13	....	..	..	3,574	19	10
13	....	..	..	651	2	8
13	....	..	..	3,263	6	0
13	....	..	..	3,625	0	2
				12,114	8	8

PER CONTRA.   Cr.

When and to whom remitted.	£.	s.	d.
1817. Brought forward	26,785	11	8
Mar. 25 6 By Henry Melville.... No. 199	1,000	0	0
27 6 By Ditto .... 200 to 202	1,397	18	6
29 6 By Ditto .... 203 to 207	2.273	10	1
	31,457	0	3
July 10 17 By Peter Grant .... 208 to 212	12,114	8	8
	12,114	8	8

Dr.		BILLS PAYABLE.		(1)		
Due.	Fo.	Drawn On, Accepted, and Paid By.		£.	s.	d.
1817. Mar. 3	6	To Henry Melville, London, ... Nos. 252 to 260.............		3,726	12	6
6	6	To..... Ditto........................225 to 230.............		2,273	18	0
10	6	To..... Ditto........................287 to 296.............		3,810	5	0
13	6	To..... Ditto........................261 to 270.............		4,354	10	0
15	6	To..... Ditto........................297 to 305.............		3,583	8	0
17	6	To..... Ditto........................231 to 240.............		3,500	0	0
19	6	To..... Ditto........................271 to 280.............		3,756	2	10
22	6	To..... Ditto........................241 to 246.............		2,500	0	0
24	6	To..... Ditto........................305 to 314.............		3,750	0	0
27	6	To..... Ditto........................281 to 286.............		3,050	10	4
29	6	To..... Ditto........................247 to 251.............		1,825	10	0
31	2	To Balance outstanding..................................		37,377	13	11
			£	73,508	10	7

(1) PER CONTRA. *Cr.*

1817.	Fo.	Order of.	Date & Term.	Due.	No.	£.	s.	d.	£.	s.	d.
			1817.	1817.							
Feb. 28		By Balance outstanding ..	....	....	....	....	....	....	57,590	6	8
Mar. 4	11	By Horton & Co.	Mar. 4	2 m.	May 7	375	500	0	0			
						376	500	0	0			
						377	500	0	0			
						378	1,000	0	0	2,500	0	0
4	7	By Hilton & Co.	Mar. 4	3 m.	June 7	379	224	10	0			
5	8	By Taylor & Co.	....	....	....	380	350	0	0			
5	7	By R. Selkirk	....	....	....	381	426	17	6	1,001	7	6
11	11	By Horton & Co.	Mar. 11	2 m.	May 14	382	600	0	0			
						383	750	0	0			
						384	750	0	0	2,100	0	0
11	8	By S. Marsh	Mar. 11	3 m.	June 14	385	268	9	4			
11	8	By Welch & Co.	11	....	....	386	372	15	0			
12	9	By T. Bruce	11	....	....	387	400	0	0			
12	9	By Gill & Co.........	11	....	....	388	545	3	0	1,586	7	4
18	11	By Horton & Co.	11	2 m.	May 14	389	300	0	0			
						390	350	0	0			
						391	450	0	0			
						392	500	0	0	1,600	0	0
18	9	By Halset & Co.	Mar. 18	3 m.	June 21	393	500	0	0			
18	10	By Bandor & Co.	....	....	....	394	400	0	0			
18	10	By F. Denton	....	....	....	395	250	0	0			
18	7	By Hilton & Co.	....	....	....	396	650	0	0			
18	7	By R. Selkirk.........	....	....	....	397	341	10	0			
18	8	By Taylor & Co.	....	....	....	398	431	12	0			
18	8	By S. Marsh	....	....	....	399	200	0	0	2,773	2	0
25	11	By Horton & Co.	Mar. 25	2 m.	May 28	400	250	0	0			
						401	300	0	0			
						402	500	0	0			
						403	500	0	0	1,550	0	0
25	13	By Marmot and Co.	Mar. 25	2 m.	May 28	404	96	7	10			
25	13	By T. Newton	....	....	....	405	108	0	0			
25	13	By B. Wallis	....	....	....	406	90	0	0			
25	16	By C. Follet	....	....	....	407	417	9	0	711	16	10
25	12	By Holt & Co.	Mar. 25	3 m.	June 28	408	203	11	3			
25	12	By Robert Millar	....	....	....	409	437	4	0			
25	7	By Hilton & Co.	....	....	....	410	500	0	0			
25	8	By Taylor & Co.	....	....	....	411	500	0	0			
25	8	By Welch & Co.	....	....	....	412	454	15	0	2,095	10	3
									£ 73,508	10	7

Dr. BILLS PAYABLE. (2)

1817.			£.	s.	d.
July 10		To Sundry, for Bills unpaid, relinquished under the Deed of Composition, viz.			
	7	To Hilton & Co. ..... Leeds.	2,520	16	0
	8	Taylor & Co. ...... London	2,135	6	0
	7	R. Selkirk, ... Wakefield	1,795	17	6
	8	S. Marsh, ... Leeds	1,440	19	4
	8	Welch & Co. ......Ditto	1,546	2	6
	9	T. Bruce, ... Huddersfield	1,681	7	6
	9	Gill & Co. .... Wakefield......................	1,182	11	0
	9	Halset & Co. ...... Leeds	1,862	12	0
	10	Bandor & Co. ...... Ditto	700	0	0
	10	F. Denton, ... Ditto	450	0	0
	13	Marmot & Co. ..... London.	247	2	10
	13	T. Newton, ... Sherburne	108	0	
	13	B. Wallis, ... Leeds	239	5	0
	16	C. Follet, ... Liverpool	417	9	0
	12	Holt & Co. .... Huddersfield.................	1,075	7	9
	12	Robert Millar, ... London	765	7	6
	16	L. Bruce, ... Huddersfield	462	11	6
	17	Pindar & Sons, ... Leeds	659	10	0
	17	Benson & Co. .... Ditto	987	8	6
	16	Clifford & Co. Bankers, Wakefield	2,150	0	0
	11	Horton & Co. Ditto... Leeds	14,950	0	0
		£	37,377	13	11

(2)			PER CONTRA.			*Cr*		
						£.	s.	d.
1817.								
Mar. 31	1	By Balance	....			37,377	13	11
					£	37,377	13	11

Dr.   BILLS PAYABLE.   (3)

1817.	Fo.	Drawn On and Accepted By	£.	s.	d.
July 10	17	To Peter Grant, London, Nos. 413 to 438, due Sep. 13, 1817	27,218	9	9
		£	27,218	9	9

(3)   PER CONTRA.   *Cr.*

1817.	Fo.	Order of.	No.	Date & Term.		Due.	£.	s.	d.
July 10				1817.		1817.			
July 10	11	By Horton & Co.	413	July 10	2 m.	Sep. 13	8,970	0	0
	7	.... Hilton & Co.	414	....	....	....	1,602	9	7
	8	.... Taylor & Co.	415	....	....	....	1,581	3	7
	7	.... R Selkirk	416	....	....	....	1,188	9	5
	8	.... S. Marsh	417	....	....	....	1,327	3	7
	8	.... Welch & Co.	418	....	....	....	1,056	19	1
	9	.... T. Bruce	419	....	....	....	1,474	13	1
	9	.... Gill & Co.	420	....	....	....	1,538	18	1
	9	.... Halset & Co.	421	....	....	....	2,305	2	5
	10	.... Bandor & Co.	422	....	....	....	699	3	0
	16	... L. Bruce	423	....	....	....	277	10	11
	14	... Manson & Co.	424	....	....	....	33	0	0
	11	... D. Carew	425	....	....	....	298	7	6
	12	... T. Rogers	426	....	....	....	162	12	7
	13	... Robert Smith	427	....	....	....	72	0	0
	14	.... Garth & Co.	428	....	....	....	105	0	0
	16	.... Clifford & Co.	429	....	....	....	1.290	0	0
	10	.... F. Denton	430	....	....	....	436	13	5
	13	.... T. Newton	431	....	....	....	64	16	0
	13	.... Marmot & Co.	432	....	....	....	148	5	8
	13	... B. Wallis	433	....	....	....	143	11	0
	16	.... C. Follet	434	....	....	....	349	18	6
	12	... Holt & Co.	435	....	....	....	645	4	8
	12	... Robert Millar	436	....	....	....	459	4	6
	17	.... Benson & Co.	437	....	....	......	592	9	2
	17	.... Pindar & Sons	438	....	....	....	395	14	0
						£	27,218	9	9

LEDGER.

N

		Folio
Nield and Co. .... Liverpool	....	5
Newton, T. ...... Sherburne	....	13

U

Folio

O

V

P

Private Account	....	1
Plane, J. .... Leeds	....	15
Peters and Co. .... Leeds	....	15
Pindar and Sons, .. Leeds	....	17
Profit	....	2

W

Welch and Co. .... Leeds	....	8
Wilson, B. .... Gibraltar	....	12
Wallis, B. .... Leeds	....	13

R

Rogers, T. .... Leeds	....	12
Ranger and Co. .... Liverpool	....	14

X

S

Stock	....	1
Shop	....	3
Selkirk, R. ...... Wakefield	....	7
Smith, Robert, .. Hull	....	13

Y

T

Taylor and Co. .... London..	....	8

Z

Dr.   STOCK.   (1)

1817.				£.	s.	d.
March 31	1	To Private Account		147	12	10
31	2	To Loss		25,131	13	6
				25,279	6	4
March 31		To Balance		6,667	0	9
July 11	1	To Private Account		200	0	0
11		To Balance		10,616	2	6
				17,483	3	3

Dr.   PRIVATE ACCOUNT.

1817.						
March 4	1	To Cash, ... T. Gore		14	12	6
10	1	To Cash, ... S. Gill		15	6	0
12	1	To Cash, ... Wife...............................		10	0	0
14	1	To Cash, ... J. Brown		12	13	6
17	1	To Cash, ... Pocket Money		5	5	0
19	1	To Cash, ... Hopson and Co.		14	7	4
20	1	To Cash, ... Bell and Co.		17	12	0
24	1	To Cash, ... Grant and Co.		57	16	6
				147	12	10
July 11	1	To Cash, ... Expenses since 31 March		200	0	0

(1)		PER CONTRA.			Cr.		
1817.					£.	s.	d.
February 28		By Balance			18,612	5	7
March 31		By Balance			6,667	0	9
					25,279	6	4
July 11	2	By Profit			17,483	3	3
					17,483	3	3
July 11		By Balance			10,616	2	6

		PER CONTRA.			Cr.		
1817.							
March 30	1	By Stock			147	12	10
					147	12	10
July 11	1	By Stock			200	0	0

Dr.		PROFIT.		(2)		
1817.				£.	s.	d.
March 31	2	To Transfer to Loss		2,149	1	2
July 11	2	To Transfer from Loss		662	9	11
11	1	To Stock		17,483	3	3
				20,294	14	4

Dr.		LOSS.				
1817.						
March 10	A 2	To Consignment to Gomes and Co.		515	7	1
15	5	To Nield and Co. Composition Abatement		13,854	6	0
20	A 3	To Consignment to Braga and Co.		10,833	15	2
29	4	To Braga and Co. Difference of Exchange		22	4	6
29	A 1	To Consignment to Henry Melville		1,651	18	4
30	A 4	To Cochineal per Fernando		403	3	7
				27,280	14	8
July 10	1	To Cash, Deed of Composition, &c.		55	10	6
10	5	To Goodwin and Co. . . Discount		188	3	2
10	5	To T. Merlin .... Ditto		34	5	5
10	6	To Fairfax and Co. ... Ditto		171	15	0
10	7	To S. Green, ... Ditto		190	15	10
11	14	To Manson and Co. . . Return of Composition Abatement		22	0	0
				662	9	11

(2)			PER CONTRA.		*Cr.*		

1817.				£.	s.	d.
March 31	5	By Merchandise		2,149	1	2
July 10	A 6	By Composition		18,145	13	2
				20,294	14	4

			PER CONTRA.		*Cr.*		

1817.						
March 31	2	By Transfer from Profit		2,149	1	2
31	1	By Stock		25,131	13	6
				27,280	14	8
July 11	2	By Transfer to Profit		662	9	11
				662	9	11

Dr.   MANUFACTORY   (3)

1817.				£.	s.	d.
February 28		To Balance		6,500	0	0

Dr.   MACHINERY

1817.						
February 28		To Balance		1,500	0	0

Dr.   DWELLING HOUSE.

1817.						
February 28		To Balance		2,200	0	0

Dr.   FURNITURE.

1817.						
February 28		To Balance		800	0	0

Dr.   SHOP.

1817.						
February 28		To Balance		367	13	4
March 30	5	To Goods this Month		183	9	5
				551	2	9
March 31		To Balance		385	4	3

(3)   AND WAREHOUSES.   *Cr.*

1817.			£.	s.	d.
July 10	17	By Peter Grant, Transfer	6,500	0	0

AND UTENSILS.   *Cr.*

1817.					
July 10	17	By Peter Grant, Transfer	1,500	0	0

PER CONTRA.   *Cr.*

1817.					
July 10	17	By Peter Grant, Transfer	2,200	0	0

PER CONTRA.   *Cr.*

PER CONTRA.

1817.					
March 30	1	By Cash from S. Jones	165	18	6
31		By Balance	385	4	3
			551	2	9

Drs.   GOMES AND CO.   (4)

1817.				£.	s.	d.
			Rials Plate. Qs. Exch.			
February 28		To Balance .... 60,708 14 at 36*d.*		1,138	5	10
March 10	A 2	To Net Proceeds of 16 Bales Woollens.... 115,583 0 at 36*d.*		2,167	3	7
		Rte. . 176,291 14		3,305	9	5

Drs.   BRAGA AND CO.

1817.						
			Mil-reas. Exch.			
March 20	A 3	To Net Proceeds of 150 Bales Woollens .. 67,444. 290 at 57*d.*		16,018	0	4
		Rs... 67,444. 290		16,018	0	4

Dr.   HENRY MELVILLE, LONDON,

1817.						
February 28		To Balance		1,318	15	3
March 29	A 1	To Net Proceeds of 35 Bales Woollens		4,145	12	0
				5,464	7	3

(4) CADIZ. *Crs.*

1817.			Rials Pl.	Qs.	Exch.	£.	s.	d.
March 15	A 4	By Cochineal, per Fernando 151,715	0	at 36d.	2,844	13	1
18	1	By Bills Receivable 24,576	14	at 36d.	460	16	4
		Rte. . 176,291	14	....	3,305	9	5

LISBON. *Crs.*

1817.			Mil-Reas.	Exch.	£.	s.	d.
March 3	1	By Bills Receivable 16,842. 105	at 57 d.	4,000	0	0
8	1	By Bills Receivable 25,374. 450	at 56¾d.	6,000	0	0
15	1	By Bills Receivable 11,458.900	at 57¼d.	2,733	8	6
22	1	By Bills Receivable 7,419.385	at 56¾d.	1,754	7	6
29	2	By Bills Receivable 6,349.450	at 57 d.	1,507	19	10
29	2	By Loss, Difference of Exchange		22	4	6
		Rs. . 67,444. 290		16,018	0	4

SALES ACCOUNT. *Cr.*

1817.			£.	s.	d.
March 5	6	By Cashier's Account, Transfer	1,318	15	3
29	A 1	By Discount on Sales	207	5	7
30	6	By Cashier's Account, Transfer	3,938	6	5
			5,464	7	3

Drs.   NIELD AND CO.   (5)

1817.				£.	s.	d.
February 28		To Balance		18,472	8	0
				18,472	8	0

Drs.   GOODWIN AND CO.

1817.						
February 28			To Balance ...., ...	2,384	12	0
March 4	1		To Goods	1,245	9	10
12	2		To Goods	1,560	17	2
				5,190	19	0
March 31			To Balance	3,763	3	0

Dr.   T. MERLIN.

1817.						
February 28			To Balance	1,652	10	4
March 6	1		To Goods	685	8	1
				2,337	18	5
March 31			To Balance	685	8	1

(5)   LIVERPOOL.   *Crs.*

1817.				£.	s.	d.
March 4	1	By Bills Receivable		4,618	2	0
15	2	By Loss, abated by Composition, 75 per Cent...............		13,854	6	0
				18,472	8	0

LONDON.   *Crs.*

1817.				£.	s.	d.
March 3	1	By Bills Receivable		727	16	0
13	1	By Bills Receivable		700	0	0
31		By Balance		3,763	3	0
				5,190	19	0
July 10	2	By Discount...... Transfer to Loss		188	3	2
10	2	By Bills Receivable		3,574	19	10
				3,763	3	0

LONDON.   *Cr.*

1817.				£.	s.	d.
March 4	1	By Discount		82	12	6
4	1	By Bills Receivable		1,569	17	10
31		By Balance		685	8	1
				2,337	18	5
July 10	2	By Discount....... Transfer to Loss		34	5	5
10	2	By Bills Receivable		651	2	8
				685	8	1

Drs.   FAIRFAX AND CO.   (6)

1817.				£.	s.	d.
February 28			To Balance	1,836	17	6
March 11	2		To Goods	835	11	9
26	5		To Goods	1,011	7	9
				3,683	17	0
March 31			To Balance	3,435	1	0

Dr.   HENRY MELVILLE, LONDON.

1817.				£.	s.	d.
February 28			To Balance	752	10	0
March 3	1		To Bills Receivable	4,727	16	0
4	1		To Bills Receivable	6,187	19	10
5	4		To Sales Account, Transfer	1,318	15	3
6	1		To Bills Receivable	1,500	0	0
8	1		To Bills Receivable	6,000	0	0
11	1		To Bills Receivable	1,522	7	6
13	1		To Bills Receivable	948	16	0
15	1		To Bills Receivable	2,733	8	6
18	1		To Bills Receivable	1,410	16	4
22	1		To Bills Receivable	1,754	7	6
25	2		To Bills Receivable	1,000	0	0
27	2		To Bills Receivable	1,397	18	6
29	2		To Bills Receivable	2,273	10	1
30	4		To Sales Account, Transfer	3,938	6	5
				37,466	11	11
March 31			To Balance	807	2	9

(6)   GLASGOW.   *Crs.*

1817.			£.	s.	d.
March 13	1	By Bills Receivable	248	16	0
31		By Balance	3,435	1	0
			3,683	17	0
July 10	2	By Discount,.. ... Transfer to Loss	171	15	0
10	2	By Bills Receivable	3,263	6	0
			3,435	1	0

CASHIER'S ACCOUNT.   *Cr.*

1817.			£.	s.	d.
March 3	1	By Bills Payable..... due this day.....................	3,726	12	6
6	1	By Bills Payable........ ditto..........................	2,273	18	0
10	1	By Bills Payable........ ditto......	3,810	5	0
13	1	By Bills Payable........ ditto.........................	4,354	10	0
15	1	By Bills Payable........ ditto.........................	3,583	8	0
17	1	By Bills Payable..... ... ditto.........................	3,500	0	0
19	1	By Bills Payable........ ditto.........................	3,756	2	10
22	1	By Bills Payable........ ditto	2,500	0	0
24	1	By Bills Payable........ ditto.........................	3,750	0	0
27	1	By Bills Payable....... ditto.........................	3,050	10	4
29	1	By Bills Payable........ ditto.........................	1,825	10	0
30	4	By Discounts, &c.	528	12	6
31		By Balance	807	2	9
			37,466	11	11
July 10	17	By Peter Grant, Transfer	807	2	9

Dr.   S. GREEN,   (7)

1817.			£.	s.	d.
February 28		To Balance	1,542	8	9
March 8	1	To Goods	642	13	10
14	3	To Goods	1,630	13	5
			3,815	16	0
March 31		To Balance	3,815	16	0

Drs.   HILTON AND CO.

1817.					
March 4	1	To Bills Payable	224	10	0
18	1	To Bills Payable	650	0	0
25	1	To Bills Payable	500	0	0
31		To Balance	150	0	0
			1,524	10	0
July 10	A 6	To Composition, 40 per Cent. abated	1,068	6	5
10	3	To Bills Payable	1,602	9	7
			2,670	16	0

Dr.   R. SELKIRK,

1817.					
March 5	1	To Bills Payable	426	17	6
18	1	To Bills Payable	341	10	0
31		To Balance	184	18	3
			953	5	9
July 10	A 6	To Composition, 40 per Cent. abated	792	6	4
10	3	To Bills Payable	1,188	9	5
			1,980	15	9

(7)			LIVERPOOL.		*Cr.*	

1817. March 31		By Balance	£ 3,815	s. 16	d. 0
July 10 10	2 2	By Discount...... Transfer to Loss .... By Bills Receivable	190 3,625	15 0	10 2
			3,815	16	0

			LEEDS.		*Crs.*	

1817. February 28		By Balance	1,524	10	0
March 31 July 10	2	By Balance .... By Bills Payable, given up	150 2,520	0 16	0 0
			2,670	16	0

			WAKEFIELD.		*Cr.*	

1817. February 28		By Balance	953	5	9
March 31 July 10	2	By Balance .... By Bills Payable, given up	184 1,795	18 17	3 6
			1,980	15	9

Drs.   TAYLOR AND CO.   (8)

1817.				£.	s.	d.
March 5	1	To Bills Payable		350	0	0
18	1	To Bills Payable		431	12	0
25	1	To Bills Payable		500	0	0
31		To Balance		500	0	0
				1,781	12	0
July 10	A 6	To Composition, 40 per Cent. abated		1,054	2	5
10	3	To Bills Payable		1,581	3	7
				2,635	6	0

Dr.   S. MARSH,

1817.						
March 11	1	To Bills Payable		268	9	4
18	1	To Bills Payable		200	0	0
31		To Balance		771	0	0
				1,239	9	4
July 10	A 6	To Composition, 40 per Cent. abated		884	15	9
10	3	To Bills Payable		1,327	3	7
				2,211	19	4

Drs.   WELCH AND CO.

1817.						
March 11	1	To Bills Payable		372	15	0
25	1	To Bills Payable		454	15	0
31		To Balance		215	9	4
				1,042	19	4
July 10	A 6	To Composition, 40 per Cent. abated		704	12	9
10	3	To Bills Payable		1,056	19	1
				1,761	11	10

(8)		LONDON.			*Crs.*		

1817.				£.	s.	d.
February 28		By Balance		1,781	12	0
				1,781	12	0
March 31		By Balance		500	0	0
July 10	2	By Bills Payable, given up		2,135	6	0
				2,635	6	0

		LEEDS.			*Cr.*		

1817.						
February 28		By Balance		468	9	4
March 3	1	By Wool		771	0	0
				1,239	9	4
March 31		By Balance		771	0	0
July 10	2	By Bills Payable, given up		1,440	19	4
				2,211	19	4

		LEEDS.			*Crs.*		

1817.						
February 28		By Balance		827	10	0
March 5	1	By Wool		215	9	4
				1,042	19	4
March 31		By Balance		215	9	4
July 10	2	By Bills Payable, given up		1,546	2	6
				1,761	11	10

Dr.			T. BRUCE.		(9)	
1817.				£.	s.	d.
March 12		1	To Bills Payable	400	0	0
31			To Balance	776	7	7
				1,176	7	7
July 10		A 6	To Composition, 40 per Cent. abated	983	2	0
10		3	To Bills Payable	1,474	13	1
				2,457	15	1

Drs.			GILL AND CO.			
1817.						
March 12		1	To Bills Payable	545	3	0
31			To Balance	1,382	5	9
				1,927	8	9
July 10		A 6	To Composition, 40 per Cent. abated	1,025	18	8
10		3	To Bills Payable	1,538	18	1
				2,564	16	9

Drs.			HALSET AND CO.			
1817.						
March 18		1	To Bills Payable	500	0	0
24		A 4	To Cochineal	1,461	0	0
31			To Balance	1,979	5	5
				3,940	5	5
July 10		A 6	To Composition, 40 per Cent. abated	1,536	15	0
10		3	To Bills Payable	2,305	2	5
				3,841	17	5

(9)   HUDDERSFIELD.   *Cr.*

1817.			£.	s.	d.
February 28		By Balance	765	13	7
March 7	1	By Wool...	410	14	0
			1,176	7	7
March 31		By Balance	776	7	7
July 10	2	By Bills Payable, given up	1,681	7	6
			2,457	15	1

WAKEFIELD.   *Crs.*

1817.					
February 28		By Balance	1,045	3	0
March 10	2	By Wool	882	5	9
			1,927	8	9
March 31		By Balance	1,382	5	9
July 10	2	By Bills Payable, given up	1,182	11	0
			2,564	16	9

LEEDS.   *Crs.*

1817.					
February 28		By Balance	2,804	8	8
March 30	5	By Dying	1,135	16	9
			3,940	5	5
March 31		By Balance	1,979	5	5
July 10	2	By Bills Payable, given up	1,862	12	0
			3,841	17	5

Drs.   BANDOR AND CO.   (10)

1817.				£.	s.	d.
March 18	1	To Bills Payable		400	0	0
31		To Balance		465	5	0
				865	5	0
July 10	A 6	To Composition, 40 per Cent. abated		466	2	0
10	3	To Bills Payable		699	3	0
				1,165	5	0

Dr.   F. DENTON.

1817.						
March 18	1	To Bills Payable		250	0	0
31		To Balance		277	15	9
				527	15	9
July 10	A 6	To Composition, 40 per Cent. abated		291	2	4
10	3	To Bills Payable		436	13	5
				727	15	9

(10)		LEEDS.		_Crs._		
1817.				£.	s.	d.
February 28		By Balance		637	15	0
March 30	5	By Mill-wright's Work		227	10	0
				865	5	0
March 31		By Balance		465	5	0
July 10	2	By Bills Payable, given up		700	0	0
				1,165	5	0

		LEEDS.		_Cr._		
1817.						
February 28		By Balance		391	0	9
March 30	5	By Cards		136	15	0
				527	15	9
March 31		By Balance		277	15	9
July 10	2	By Bills Payable, given up		450	0	0
				727	15	9

Drs.   HORTON AND CO.   (11)

1817.				£.	s.	d.
March 4	1	To Bills Payable		2,500	0	0
11	1	To Bills Payable		2,100	0	0
18	1	To Bills Payable		1,600	0	0
25	1	To Bills Payable		1,550	0	0
30	1	To Cash		69	9	4
				7,819	9	4
July 10	A 6	To Composition, 40 per Cent. abated		5,980	0	0
10	3	To Bills Payable		8,970	0	0
				14,950	0	0

Dr.   D. CAREW,

1817.						
July 10	A 6	To Composition, 40 per Cent. abated		198	18	4
10	3	To Bills Payable		298	7	6
				497	5	10

(11)		BANKERS, LEEDS.				*Crs.*

1817.			*£.*	*s.*	*d.*
February 28		By Balance	500	0	0
March 4	1	By Cash	500	0	0
6	1	By Bills Receivable	1,500	0	0
11	1	By Bills Receivable	1,522	7	6
11	1	By Cash	600	0	0
18	1	By Cash	600	0	0
18	1	By Bills Receivable	950	0	0
24	1	By Cash, Check to Grant and Co.	57	16	6
25	1	By Cash	550	0	0
25	2	By Bills Receivable	1,000	0	0
30	4	By Interest and Charges	39	5	4
			7,819	9	4
July 10	2	By Bills Payable, given up	14,950	0	0

		BRADFORD.				*Cr.*

1817.					
March 11	2	By Wool	497	5	10

Dr.   T. ROGERS,   (12)

1817.				£.	s.	d.
July 10	A 6	To Composition, 40 per Cent. abated		108	8	5
10	3	To Bills Payable		162	12	7
				271	1	0

Drs.   HOLT AND CO.

1817.						
March 25	1	To Bills Payable		203	11	3
July 10	A 6	To Composition, 40 per Cent. abated		430	3	1
10	3	To Bills Payable		645	4	8
				1,075	7	9

Dr.   ROBERT MILLAR,

1817.						
March 25	1	To Bills Payable		437	4	0
July 10	3	To Bills Payable		459	4	6
10	A 6	To Composition, 40 per Cent. abated		306	3	0
				765	7	6

Dr.   B. WILSON,

(12)   LEEDS.   *Cr.*

1817.				£.	s.	d.
March 3	1	By Rape Oil		271	1	0

HUDDERSFIELD.   *Crs.*

1817.						
March 12	3	By Wool		203	11	3
July 10	2	By Bills Payable, given up		1,075	7	9

LONDON.   *Cr.*

1817.						
March 4	1	By Olive Oil		437	4	0
July 10	2	By Bills Payable, given up		765	7	6

GIBRALTAR.   *Cr.*

1817.						
July 10	2	By Bills Receivable, my Draft		1,000	0	0

Dr.   ROBERT SMITH,   (13)

1817.			£.	s.	d.
July 10	A 6	To Composition, 40 per Cent. abated	48	0	0
10	3	To Bills Payable	72	0	0
			120	0	0

Drs.   MARMOT AND CO.

1817.			£.	s.	d.
March 25	1	To Bills Payable	96	7	10
July 10	A 6	To Composition, 40 per Cent. abated	98	17	2
10	3	To Bills Payable	148	5	8
			247	2	10

Dr.   T. NEWTON,

1817.			£.	s.	d.
March 25	1	To Bills Payable	108	0	0
July 10	A 6	To Composition, 40 per Cent. abated	43	4	0
10	3	To Bills Payable	64	16	0
			108	0	0

Dr.   B. WALLIS,

1817.			£.	s.	d.
March 25	1	To Bills Payable	90	0	0
July 10	A 6	To Composition, 40 per Cent. abated	95	14	0
10	3	To Bills Payable	143	11	0
			239	5	0

(13)   HULL.   *Cr.*

1817.				£.	s.	d.
March 5	1	By Fullers' Earth		120	0	0

LONDON.   *Crs.*

1817.						
March 7	2	By Soap		96	7	10
July 10	2	By Bills Payable, given up		247	2	10

SHERBURNE.   *Cr.*

1817.						
March 7	1	By Teazles		108	0	0
July 10	2	By Bills Payable, given up		108	0	0

LEEDS.   *Cr.*

1817.						
March 8	2	By Sizing		90	0	0
July 10	2	By Bills Payable, given up		239	5	0

Drs.			RANGER AND CO.		(14)		
1817.					£.	s.	d.
March 24	4	To Goods			827	11	8

Dr.			J. BELSON,				
1817.							
March 30	5	To Discount			1	15	0
30	1	To Cash..			33	5	0
					35	0	0

Drs.			GARTH AND CO.				
1817.							
July 10	A 6	To Composition, 40 per Cent. abated			70	0	0
10	3	To Bills Payable			105	0	0
					175	0	0

Drs.			MANSON AND CO.				
1817.							
July 10	A 6	To Composition, 40 per Cent. abated			22	0	0
10	3	To Bills Payable			33	0	0
11	1	To Cash			22	0	0
					77	0	0

(14)   LIVERPOOL.   *Crs*

1817.				£.	s.	d.
March 29	4	By Discount		62	1	5
29	2	By Bills Receivable		765	10	3
				827	11	8

LEEDS.   *Cr.*

1817.						
March 11	2	By Ropes		35	0	0

LEEDS   *Crs.*

1817.						
March 10	2	By Canvas, &c.		175	0	0

LEEDS.   *Crs.*

1817.						
March 12	2	By Paper		55	0	0
July 11	2	By Loss, Return of Composition Abatement		22	0	0
				77	0	0

Dr.   J. PLANE,   (15)

1817.			£.	s.	d.
March 22	1	To Cash	15	0	0

Dr.   S. MORGAN,

1817.					
March 30	5	To Discount	1	6	8
30	1	To Cash	25	5	10
			26	12	6

Dr.   E. MERTON,

1817.					
March 25	A 4	To Cochineal	1,471	10	0

Drs.   PETERS AND CO.

1817.					
March 30	5	To Discount	2	17	5
30	1	To Cash	54	11	3
			57	8	8

(15)		LEEDS.		*Cr.*		
				£.	s.	d.
1817. March 13	3	By Boards		15	0	0

		LEEDS.		*Cr.*		
1817. March 30	5	By Healds and Slays		26	12	6

		LEEDS.		*Cr.*		
1817. March 27	A 4	By Discount		73	11	6
27	2	By Bills Receivable		1,397	18	6
				1,471	10	0

		LEEDS.		*Crs.*		
1817. March 30	5	By Carriage		57	8	8

Drs.   FIELD AND CO.   (16)

1817.				£	s.	d.
March 30	5	To Discount		2	5	0
30	1	To Cash		42	15	0
				45	0	0

Dr.   C. FOLLET,

1817						
March 25	1	To Bills Payable		417	9	0
31		To Balance		165	15	1
				583	4	1
July 10	A 6	To Composition, 40 per Cent. abated		233	5	7
10	3	To Bills Payable		349	18	6
				583	4	1

Drs.   CLIFFORD AND CO.

1817.						
July 10	A 6	To Composition, 40 per Cent. abated		860	0	0
10	3	To Bills Payable		1,290	0	0
				2,150	0	0

Dr.   L. BRUCE.

1817.						
July 10	A 6	To Composition, 40 per Cent. abated		185	0	7
10	3	To Bills Payable		277	10	11
				462	11	6

(16)   **HUDDERSFIELD.**   *Crs.*

1817.			£.	s.	d.
March 30	5	By Coals	45	0	0

LIVERPOOL.   *Cr.*

1817.					
March 17	A 4	By Charges on Cochineal per Fernando	417	9	0
18	A 5	By Charges on Woollens per Mary	165	15	1
			583	4	1
March 31		By Balance	165	15	1
July 10	2	By Bills Payable, given up	417	9	0
			583	4	1

WAKEFIELD, BANKERS.   *Crs.*

1817.					
July 10	2	By Bills Payable, given up	2,150	0	0

BRADFORD.   *Cr.*

1817.					
July 10	2	By Bills Payable, given up	462	11	6

Drs.			BENSON AND CO.		(17)		
					£.	s.	d.
1817.							
July 10	A 6		To Composition, 40 per Cent. abated		394	19	4
10	3		To Bills Payable		592	9	2
					987	8	6

Drs.			PINDAR AND SONS,				
1817.							
July 10	A 6		To Composition, 40 per Cent. abated		263	16	0
10	3		To Bills Payable		395	14	0
					659	10	0

Dr.			PETER GRANT,				
1817.							
July 10	3		To Dwelling House, ... Transfer		2,200	0	0
10	3		To Manufactory and Warehouse, Ditto		6,500	0	0
10	3		To Machinery and Utensils, ... Ditto		1,500	0	0
10	6		To Henry Melville, ... Ditto		807	2	9
10	2		To Bills Receivable		12,114	8	8
11			To Balance		4,096	18	4
					27,218	9	9

(17)   LEEDS.   *Crs.*

1817.				£.	s.	d.
July 10	2	By Bills Payable		987	8	6

LEEDS.   *Crs.*

1817.						
July 10	2	By Bills Payable		659	10	0

LONDON.   *Cr.*

1817.						
July 10	3	By Bills Payable		27,218	9	9
				27,218	9	9
July 11		By Balance, his Loan		4,096	18	4

INVENTORY.   (1)

			£.	s.	d.

1817.

February 28   Valuation of Goods on hand.

Pks. sco. lb.

					£.	s.	d.			
22	8	15	A Wool .... at £16..	363	13	4			
24	3	10	B Wool	24..	583	0	0		
18	7	16	C Wool	35..	652	15	0		
15	6	8	D Wool	50..	776	3	4	2,375	11	8

Total 81   2   9   Wool.

857 Gallons Rape Oil .... at .. 3s.	128	11	0	
472 Ditto. Olive Oil .... at .. 8s.	188	16	0	
10 Tons Fuller's Earth .... at £ 4..	40	0	0	
5 Cwt. Mottled Soap .... at 5..	25	0	0	
5 Ditto Brown Ditto .... at 4..	20	0	0	
4 Packs Teazles. .... at 10..	40	0	0	
5 Packs Sizing .... at 6..	30	0	0	472 7 0

Goods in all Stages of Process, averaged at the Middle Stage.

78	Pieces Cloths	A 50 yards each..........at £7..	546	0	0	
102	Pieces Ditto	B 50 yards each..........at 9..	918	0	0	
60	Pieces Ditto	C 50 yards each..........at 12..	720	0	0	
51	Pieces Ditto	D 50 yards each..........at 16..	816	0	0	3,000 0 0
39	Pieces Casimirs	L 50 yards each..........at £3..	117	0	0	
87	Pieces Ditto	M 50 yards each..........at 4..	348	0	0	
39	Pieces Ditto	N 50 yards each..........at 6..	234	0	0	
21	Pieces Ditto	O 50 yards each..........at 8..	168	0	0	867 0 0

477 Pieces.

Manufactured Goods.

46 Pieces Cloths	A Raw White.............. at £ 9..	414	0	0
24 Pieces Ditto	A Dark Blue... Unfinished... at 11..	264	0	0
24 Pieces Ditto	A Ditto .... Finished..... at 12..	288	0	0
38 Pieces Ditto	B Raw White............. at 11..	418	0	0
10 Pieces Ditto	B Dark Blue... Unfinished... at 13..	130	0	0
10 Pieces Ditto	B Brown ...... Ditto .... at 12..	120	0	0
10 Pieces Ditto	B Black ...... Ditto .... at 12..	120	0	0
24 Pieces Ditto	B Dark Blue... Finished .... at 14..	336	0	0
12 Pieces Ditto	B Brown ...... Ditto .... at 13..	156	0	0
6 Pieces Ditto	B Black ..... Ditto .... at 13..	78	0	0
26 Pieces Ditto	C Raw White .... at 14..	364	0	0
10 Pieces Ditto	C Dark Blue... Unfinished... at 16..	160	0	0

240 Pieces................Carried forward ....£ 2,848   0   0   6,714   18   8

(2)   INVENTORY.

		£.	s.	d.
1817.				
February 28	240 Pieces............. Brought forward........ £2,848 0 0	6,714	18	8
	12 Pieces Cloths C Brown..... Unfinished.. at £15..180 0 0			
	10 Pieces Ditto C Black...... Ditto...... at 15..150 0 0			
	10 Pieces Ditto C Scarlet..... Ditto...... at 19..190 0 0.			
	32 Pieces Ditto D Raw White............at 18..576 0 0			
	10 Pieces Ditto D Dark Blue.. Unfinished.. at 21..210 0 0			
	10 Pieces Ditto D Scarlet..... Ditto...... at 24 .240 0 0	4,394	0	0
	22 Pieces Casimirs L Raw White............ at £ 4.. 88 0 0			
	10 Pieces Ditto L Brown..... Unfinished.. at 5.. 50 0 0			
	12 Pieces Ditto L Dark Blue.. Ditto...... at 6.. 72 0 0			
	22 Pieces Ditto M Raw White........... at 5..110 0 0			
	10 Pieces Ditto M Brown..... Unfinished.. at 6.. 60 0 0			
	20 Pieces Ditto M Black...... Ditto...... at 6..120 0 0			
	10 Pieces Ditto M Dark Blue.. Ditto...... at 7.. 70 0 0			
	10 Pieces Ditto M Scarlet.... Ditto...... at 8.. 80 0 0			
	22 Pieces Ditto N Raw White........... at 7..154 0 0			
	8 Pieces Ditto N Black...... Finished.... at 9.. 72 0 0			
	8 Pieces Ditto N Brown..... Ditto...... at 9.. 72 0 0			
	8 Pieces Ditto N Dark Blue.. Ditto...... at 10.. 80 0 0			
	2 Pieces Ditto N Scarlet..... Ditto...... at 11.. 22 0 0			
	14 Pieces Ditto O Raw White........... at 9..126 0 0			
	3 Pieces Ditto O Black...... Finished.... at 11 . 33 0 0			
	6 Pieces Ditto O Dark Blue . Ditto...... at 12. 72 0 0			
	9 Pieces Ditto O Brown..... Ditto...... at 11 . 99 0 0			
	4 Pieces Ditto O Scarlet..... Ditto...... at 13.. 52 0 0			
	524 Pieces.	1,432	0	0
	60 Pieces Canvas..................... at 30s... 90 0 0			
	120 Pieces Tilleting .... at 25s...150 0 0			
	50 Ropes .... at 8s... 20 0 0			
	20 Reams Paper................... at 60s... 60 0 0			
	40 Dozen Boards .... at 6s... 12 0 0			
	10 Dozen Band .... at 20s... 10 0 0	342	0	0
	Entered Merchandise, fo. 1...... Total .... £	12,882	18	8

PROOF OF THE STOCK OF PIECES.

477 Pieces in Process.

524 Ditto.... Manufactured.

Sum 1,001 Pieces.

Extreme Manufacture Number. 1,801

Extreme Sale Number 800

Pieces 1,001 Difference.

Dr.   THE ESTATE OF   (3)

28th February 1817.

			£.	s.	d.
B P	1	To Bills Payable,. . . . . Amount outstanding	57,590	6	8
L	7	To Hilton & Co. Leeds,. . . . . . . Balance due to them	1,524	10	0
L	7	To R. Selkirk, Wakefield, ... Ditto . . due to him	953	5	9
L	8	To Taylor & Co. London, ... Ditto . . due to them	1,781	12	0
L	8	To S. Marsh, Leeds,. . . . . Ditto . . due to him	468	9	4
L	8	To Welch & Co. . . . . Ditto . . due to them	827	10	0
L	9	To T. Bruce, Huddersfield, ... Ditto . . due to him	765	13	7
L	9	To Gill & Co. Wakefield, ... Ditto . . due to them	1,045	3	0
L	9	To Halset & Co. . Leeds . . . . Ditto . . ditto	2,804	8	8
L	10	To Bandor & Co. Ditto . . . . Ditto . . ditto	637	15	0
L	10	To F. Denton,. . . Ditto . . . . Ditto . . due to him	391	0	9
L	11	To Horton & Co. Ditto . . . . Ditto . . due to them	500	0	0
			69,289	14	9
L	1	To Stock, my Net Capital	18,612	5	7
		£	87,902	0	4

JOHN HENDERSON, LEEDS. *Cr.*

28th February 1817.

			£.	s.	d.
C	1	By Cash, ... Balance in hand	1,071	4	10
M	1	By Merchandise, as per Valuation	12,882	18	8
A	1	By Consignment to Henry Melville, London	3,947	9	8
A	2	By Consignment to Gomes & Co. Cadiz	2,682	10	8
A	3	By Consignment to Braga & Co. Lisbon	26,851	15	6
L	3	By Manufactory and Warehouses, Value	6,500	0	0
L	3	By Machinery and Utensils, ... Ditto	1,500	0	0
L	3	By Shop, ... Goods and Debts	367	13	4
L	3	By Dwelling House, ... Value	2,200	0	0
L	3	By Furniture, ... Ditto	800	0	0
L	4	By Gomes and Co. Cadiz, ... Balance due from them	1,138	5	10
L	4	By Henry Melville, London,[1] ..... Balance of Sales	1,318	15	3
L	5	By Nield & Co. Liverpool, ... Balance due from them	18,472	8	0
L	5	By Goodwin & Co. London, ... Ditto.... ditto... ditto	2,384	12	0
L	5	By T. Merlin, London, ... Ditto.... ditto... him	1,652	10	4
L	6	By Fairfax & Co. Glasgow, ... Ditto.... ditto... them	1,836	17	6
L	7	By S. Green, Liverpool, ... Ditto.... ditto... him	1,542	8	9
L	6	By Henry Melville, London, ... Balance of Cash	752	10	0
		£	87,902	0	4

INVENTORY. (4)

				£.	s.	d.

1817.

March 31

Valuation of Goods on hand.

Pks.	sco.	lbs.				£.	s.	d.			
12	7	10	Wool	A	................at £15..	189	7	6			
14	8	6	Ditto	B	...............at	22..	323	4	4		
17	4	4	Ditto	C	... .at	33..572	11	0			
8	8	11	Ditto	D	..............at	48..418	4	0			

Total 53 4 11 Wool.   **1,503 6 10**

1,254	Gallons Rape Oil................at	3s...188	2	0			
783	Gallons Olive Ditto.............at	8s...313	4	0			
35	Tons Fullers' Earth..............at £4...140	0	0				
8	Cwt. Brown Soap...............at	90s...	36	0	0		
7	Ditto Mottled Soap ....at 105s.	. 36	15	0			
8	Packs Teazles..................at £9...	72	0	0			
15	Ditto Sizing...................at	5...	75	0	0		

861 1 0

Goods in all Stages of Process, averaged at the Middle Stage.

86	Pieces Cloths, each 50 yards,	A	......at £ 7...602	0	0	
95	Pieces Ditto, each 50 ditto,	B	......at	9...855	0	0
52	Pieces Ditto, each 50 ditto,	C	......at	12...624	0	0
48	Pieces Ditto, each 50 ditto,	D	......at	16...768	0	0

2,849 0 0

39	Pieces Casimirs, each 50 yards,	L	......at £ 3...117	0	0	
85	Pieces Ditto, each 50 ditto,	M	......at.	4...340	0	0
34	Pieces Ditto, each 50 ditto,	N	......at	6 ..204	0	0
20	Pieces Ditto, each 50 ditto,	O	......at	8...160	0	0

459   **821 0 0**

Manufactured Goods.

26	Pieces Cloths,	A Raw ....at £ 9...234	0	0		
15	Pieces Ditto,	A Brown.... Unfinished ...at	10...150	0	0
12	Pieces Ditto,	A Dark Blue. Ditto.......at	11...132	0	0
28	Pieces Ditto,	A Black.....Ditto........at	10...280	0	0
30	Pieces Ditto,	B Raw ....at	11..330	0	0
27	Pieces Ditto,	B Dark Blue. Unfinished ...at	13...351	0	0
29	Pieces Ditto,	B Brown....Finished.....at	13...377	0	0
18	Pieces Ditto,	C Raw..................at	14...252	0	0
15	Pieces Ditto,	C Dark Blue. Unfinished ...at	16...240	0	0
5	Pieces Ditto,	C Black.... Ditto ....at	15... 75	0	0
14	Pieces Ditto,	C Brown....Finished .....at	16...224	0	0
8	Pieces Ditto,	C Scarlet....Ditto........at	19...152	0	0
12	Pieces Ditto,	D Raw ....at	18...216	0	0
9	Pieces Ditto,	D Dark Blue. Unfinished ...at	21...189	0	0
4	Pieces Ditto,	D Black.....Ditto........at	20... 80	0	0
14	Pieces Ditto,	D Scarlet....Finished .....at	25...350	0	0

3,632 0 0

266 Pieces................Carried forward..............£   **9,666 7 10**

(5)   INVENTORY.

1817.		£.	s.	d.
March 31	266 Pieces .... Brought forward	9,666	7	10

20 Pieces Casimirs L Raw .... at £4.. 80 0 0				
12 Pieces Ditto L Dark Blue .. Finished .... at 6.. 72 0 0				
12 Pieces Ditto L Brown ..... Unfinished .. at 5.. 60 0 0				
26 Pieces Ditto M Raw .... at 5..130 0 0				
12 Pieces Ditto M Dark Blue .. Unfinished .. at 7.. 84 0 0				
14 Pieces Ditto M Brown ..... Ditto ...... at 6.. 84 0 0				
4 Pieces Ditto M Black .. .. Ditto ...... at 6.. 24 0 0				
16 Pieces Ditto M Dark Blue .. Finished .... at 8..128 0 0				
12 Pieces Ditto M Scarlet .... . Ditto .... at 10..120 0 0				
16 Pieces Ditto N Raw .... at 7..112 0 0				
11 Pieces Ditto N Black ...... Unfinished .. at 8.. 88 0 0				
6 Pieces Ditto N Scarlet ..... Ditto........ at 10.. 60 0 0				
7 Pieces Ditto N Dark Blue... Finished ... at 10.. 70 0 0				
6 Pieces Ditto O Raw .... at 9.. 54 0 0				
3 Pieces Ditto O Black ..... Unfinished .. at 10.. 30 0 0				
3 Pieces Ditto O Scarlet..... Ditto ...... at 12.. 36 0 0				
6 Pieces Ditto O Dark Blue... Finished.... at 12.. 72 0 0				
452 Pieces		1,304	0	0

40 Pieces Canvas .... at 30s.... 60 0 0				
70 Pieces Tilleting .... at 25s....87 10 0				
30 Ropes .... at 5s.... 7 10 0				
6 Dozen Band .... at 20s.... 6 0 0				
8 Reams Lapping Paper .... at 60s....24 0 0				
400 lbs. Rope Paper.................. at 6d....10 0 0				
30 Dozen Boards .... at 6s.... 9 0 0		204	0	0
Entered Merchandise, fo. 5. ..... Total.............. £		11,174	7	10

PROOF OF THE STOCK OF PIECES.

459 Pieces in Process.

452 Ditto. . . . Manufactured.

Sum 911 Pieces.

Extreme Manufacture Number. 2,473

Extreme Sale Number 1,562

Pieces 911 Difference.

Dr.   THE ESTATE OF   (6)

31st March 1817.

			£.	s.	d.
B P	2	To Bills Payable........Amount outstanding................	37,377	13	11
L	7	To Hilton & Co. Leeds..........Balance due to them...........	150	0	0
L	7	To R. Selkirk, Wakefield.........Ditto.....to him.............	184	18	3
L	8	To Taylor & Co London........Ditto.....to them...........	500	0	0
L	8	To S. Marsh,....Leeds..........Ditto.....to him.............	771	0	0
L	8	To Welch & Co. Ditto...........Ditto.....to them...........	215	9	4
L	9	To T. Bruce, Huddersfield........Ditto.....to him.............	776	7	7
L	9	To Gill & Co Wakefield.........Ditto.....to them...........	1,382	5	9
L	9	To Halset & Co. Leeds..........Ditto.....to them...........	1,979	5	5
L	10	To Bandor & Co. Ditto...........Ditto.....to them...........	465	5	0
L	10	To F. Denton, ..Ditto...........Ditto.....to him.............	277	15	9
L	11	To D. Carew, Bradford..........Ditto.....to him.............	497	5	10
L	12	To T. Rogers, Leeds............Ditto.....to him.............	271	1	0
L	13	To Robert Smith, Hull..........Ditto.....to him.............	120	0	0
L	14	To Garth & Co. Leeds..........Ditto.....to them...........	175	0	0
L	14	To Manson & Co. Ditto...........Ditto.....to them...........	55	0	0
L	16	To C. Follet, Liverpool..........Ditto.....to him.............	165	15	1
		£	45,364	2	11

Dr.   THE ESTATE OF

11th July 1817.

			£.	s.	d.
L	12	To B. Wilson, Gibraltar.......Balance due to him...............	1,000	0	0
L	17	To Peter Grant, London........Ditto.....ditto.................	4,096	18	4
			5,096	18	4
L	1	To Stock, 'my Net Capital.....................................	10,616	2	6
		£	15,713	0	10

(6) JOHN HENDERSON, LEEDS. *Cr.*

31st March 1817.

			£.	s.	d.
C	1	By Cash, ... Balance in hand.	880	17	0
M	5	By Merchandise, as per Valuation	11,174	7	10
L	3	By Manufactory and Warehouses, ... Value.	6,500	0	0
L	3	By Machinery and Utensils. .... Ditto.	1,500	0	0
L	3	By Shop .... Goods and Debts	385	4	3
L	3	By Dwelling House........... Value.	2,200	0	0
L	3	By Furniture .... Ditto.	800	0	0
A	5	By Consignment to B. Wilson, Gibraltar	2,750	2	3
L	5	By Goodwin and Co. London...... Balance due from them.	3,763	3	0
L	5	By T. Merlin, ... Ditto........ Ditto ..... from him	685	8	1
L	6	By Fairfax and Co. Glasgow....... Ditto ..... from them.	3,435	1	0
L	7	By S. Green, Liverpool........... Ditto ..... from him	3,815	16	0
L	6	By Henry Melville, London .... Cash Account.	807	2	9
			38,697	2	2
L	1	By Stock, my Deficiency	6,667	0	9
			45,364	2	11

JOHN HENDERSON, LEEDS. *Cr.*

11th July 1817.

			£.	s.	d.
C	1	By Cash, ... Balance in hand.	603	6	6
M	5	By Merchandise, as per Valuation	11,174	7	10
L	3	By Shop, ... Goods and Debts	385	4	3
L	3	By Furniture, ... Value	800	0	0
A	5	By Consignment to B. Wilson, Gibraltar	2,750	2	3
			15,713	0	10

SET IV.

MERCHANTS' BOOKS.

CONCERN . . . . A PARTNERSHIP.
CAPITAL . . . . VARIABLE.
BUSINESS . . . . CONTINUED.
RESULT . . . . PROFITABLE.

OBSERVATIONS.

THE term Merchant is applied rather indiscriminately to persons on a large scale of business; but, in a strict sense, it is limited to those who keep no continuous stock of goods. This is the real distinction between Merchants and Wholesale Dealers or Manufacturers, who equally trade in whole masses, but are always presumed to hold stocks of their peculiar articles. Hence, when an order is executed by a Manufacturer or Wholesale Dealer, no Commission appears in his Invoice; and, taking the risk of the market, his profit or loss results immediately from the price charged. But, when an order is given to a Merchant, he is presumed to charge the same prices as he pays the Dealer who furnishes the goods, and to receive his remuneration from the Commission alone. On the other hand, the Merchant differs from an Agent in not being limited to particular or general agencies, and in embarking in speculations and adventures on his own account. Whilst such concerns are pending, he frequently holds stock of various articles, but these stocks are only occasional and temporary; for a constant importer and stock-holder of any commodity becomes a Wholesale Dealer.

From this absence of a continuous stock, the Merchant is enabled to ascertain the *particular Profit or Loss* on every lot of merchandise; whereas other branches of Trade can determine only the *General Result* of business from one period to another.

On a retrospect of the preceding Sets of Books, it will be perceived that Re-tailers, Wholesale Dealers, and Manufacturers, can all systematically ascertain their Profit or Loss, and their entire capital, by two distinct processes; firstly, by the Stock Account; and, secondly, by the General Extract of the Balances; this double method of obtaining the Capital, being the great proof-check of which Accounts are susceptible, and extending alike to all descriptions of business.

But, in regard to the commodities, there is a considerable gradation of proof and certainty. The Retailer, by reason of the minuteness of his sales, can have no systematic check on his wares. The Manufacturer, by means of the Warehouse Ledger, can efficiently check his goods in every stage, from all but very minute embezzlements. The Wholesale Dealer has a still nicer check on his commodities; but the fullest and most accurate is reserved for the Merchant, who, seeing in one Account the entrance and exit of each distinct mass of merchandise, can identify the whole as well as every part, without requiring any auxiliary Book, similar to the Warehouse Ledger.

It is only, however, in the Account-Sales Book, that preceding writers have done justice to this luminous arrangement. This Book (in part of its Accounts at least) has been very appropriately kept by Debtor and Creditor, and divided into distinct Accounts for every separate lot of merchandise. Considering the beauty and advantage of this method, it is really surprising that it should not have been extended to Orders and Investments; for it is equally applicable to all Mer-chandise Accounts, as will be seen in the following Books.

There is no necessity that the different items of an Invoice or Account-Sales should come in the same order and arrangement in the Books as in the Documents transmitted. For example, though an Account-Sales be kept by Debtor and Cre-ditor in the Books, the Document is never transmitted in this form, the sales being first stated, and the charges deducted at the foot. In the Books, the different articles are necessarily entered in the order of their occurrence; but, in the docu-ments, they are combined and arranged in any way that perspicuity or custom may dictate.

When, in Commission Invoices, the Merchant does not charge the same prices as he gave for the goods provided for the order, the whole Invoice rendered must then be entered on the Creditor side, and the resulting difference be equilibrated by an entry of Profit or Loss.

When a Merchant speculates in any commodity, not for an immediate object, but in anticipation of future orders or adventures, this speculation is in itself an adventure for which a distinct Account must be opened, and from which transfers at current prices must hereafter be made to those Commissions or Adventures to which the goods are applied. The Merchandise transactions are obviously divided into Commissions and Adventures, to each of which a distinct Book should be allotted; and, in extensive concerns, these may be subdivided according to the nature of the business, and the number of clerks employed.

In this business eight principal Books are required, namely, the Commissions, Adventures, Cash, Bills Receivable, Bills Payable, Ledger, Inventory, and Partnership Ledger, besides a Memorandum Book for the sundry expenses not pertaining to any specific Account. The salaries of clerks are here supposed to be periodically paid, so that they require no Accounts in the Ledger, and are entered in the Sundry Expenses. This being a mere Memorandum Book, the addition of which is entered monthly in the Cash, it is unnecessary to give any exemplification of it.

The mercantile speculations of the Manufacturer in the preceding Set, exhibiting sufficient examples of simple Adventures, and the subject of Joint Accounts having been hitherto imperfectly treated, the following Book of Adventures is devoted to its illustration. Two general rules may be laid down for the entry of joint transactions.

1st. When you are the manager, enter the whole transaction, and, per contra, transfer to your Associates their respective shares.

2d. When you are not the manager, enter only your own share of the transaction.

According as Joint Adventures are more or less complicated, they require one or more Accounts in the Day Book, and a Merchandise Account in the Ledger, or otherwise.

The Joint Cotton Account, fo. 4, is an unmanaged transaction, requiring only one Account in the Day Book, and no Merchandise Account in the Ledger. The Joint Oil, fo. 3, is a managed transaction, but involving only the purchase and sale of one lot of merchandise, it is exhibited in one folio like the other; although the comparison of purchase and sale at the foot might have been transferred to the Ledger; and, supposing the purchase and sale to have each required a separate folio, this transfer would then have been necessary.

The Adventure Accounts, fo. 1, 2, and 3, exhibit a managed Joint Transaction of a more complicated nature, requiring, besides these three Accounts, a general Account in the Ledger to shew the result. It is a mission of goods to Buenos Ayres on equal account of three parties, one there, and two in London. The probabilities of time not permitting the origin and close of a distant adventure to be exhibited in the short compass to which a Work of the present nature is confined, two shipments are assumed exactly similar in investment; so that, the second investment being given along with the first sales and returns, the three Accounts together exhibit the complete record of the transaction from beginning to end. Fo. 1 shews the Account of Investment, and the distribution of the shares to the three parties; fo. 2 records the Sales at Buenos Ayres, and the Returns to England, the foreign participator retaining his third of the proceeds; fo. 3 contains the sale and distribution of the returns; and, in the Account of Adventure per Diana in the Ledger, the result of the speculation is ascertained.

Upon the Joint Sales at Buenos Ayres, Account fo. 2, it must be observed, that this and all other intermediate Accounts between the first investment and the final returns, must be entered in full amount, without any transfer or distribution of shares. The object of such intermediate Accounts is to shew the form and state of the property, and in whose hands it lies. In circuitous speculations which involve a succession of sales and missions from one place to another, a correspondent series of intermediate Accounts is required.

When your property is insured by others, an Account of Insurance is entirely unnecessary, and the premiums, &c. ought to be carried immediately to the Account of the Underwriters, or of the intervening Broker. But, when you insure the property of others, an Account of Insurance must be opened, to receive on the one side the premiums, and on the other the averages, &c. in order to shew the result of such speculations.

Insurance Passive is a mere charge on merchandise, and no more requires a separate Account than Freight or any other charge; but Insurance Active is a real adventure, and requires an appropriate Account. In like manner, Guarantee or Del-Credere, which is the insurance of Personal Debts, is a real adventure, and ought to be distinctly recorded, instead of being entered with Commission, as is usually done. On taking the General Extract, the Account of Insurance must always carry down as a Balance the amount of Premiums on risks pending, and be then equilibrated by a transfer to Profit or Loss. The Account of Guarantee, also, must carry down a Balance of Del-Credere on debts outstanding, and be equilibrated by a similar transfer.

Exchange Arbitrations form another species of Adventures requiring a distinct Account for their appropriate record. In the three transactions exhibited, there is a successive increase of combination in the exchanges.

In the first, by one correspondent, Three Exchanges are combined;

London on Lisbon,
London on Leghorn,
Lisbon on Leghorn.

In the second, by two correspondents, Four Exchanges are combined;

London on Lisbon,
London on Leghorn,
Cadiz on Leghorn,
Cadiz on Lisbon.

In the third, by two correspondents, Five Exchanges are combined;

London on Lisbon,
London on Leghorn,
Cadiz on Leghorn,
Cadiz on Paris,
Lisbon on Paris.

Mutual agency is here supposed to be contributed without commission by a circle of correspondents, the postages and variations of the calculated exchanges being hereafter entered from the annual Accounts Current.

The Money Accounts in this Set of Books exhibit another variation of the Financial System. The Bills Receivable are partly remitted, but chiefly retained till due. The Bills Payable are partly discounted, but chiefly paid when due. The Exchange Arbitrations and other transactions afford numerous examples of the purchase and sale of Foreign Bills. For the register of due Bills and Acceptances, a Calendar is required with distinct pages or divisions for every day of business in the year; but this being a mere Memorandum Book, it is unnecessary to exemplify it. In the Accounts with correspondents abroad, is shewn the distinction between the Sterling and the Foreign Account, and the mode of transferring from the one to the other, when a settlement takes place. In inland Accounts also, it is sometimes expedient to have two or more Accounts with the same person. Hence with the Insurance Broker two Accounts are opened; one for Insurance Passive, called the Account of Insurances, and the other for Insurance Active, called the Account of Subscriptions.

At the General Extract of the Balances, it seldom happens that every Merchandise Account is fully closed. There will generally be orders or adventures for which goods are partly provided, and importations partly sold off, or on which charges are incurred without any sales. Frequent as such circumstances must be, they appear to create considerable difficulty in the settlement of accounts; and, in proof of this, we may appeal to the awkward expedients which must have fallen within the observation of every experienced Accountant. For instance, it is a common plan on such occasions, to carry the balance of a pending commission to the Account Current of the committent, or to enter the charges on unsold goods in the Account Sales of a different consignment. But, by keeping the Merchandise Accounts by Debtor and Creditor, they shew at all times and in all stages their respective Balances, as clearly as the Personal Accounts; and there is not the least occasion to transfer them till the transactions are fully closed. See examples, Commissions, fo. 1, where Monteiro & Costa's Sugar per Roderic commences with a Balance of Insurance and Freight; Commissions fo. 4, where Sandoval & Co.'s Order for Linens is partly provided, a blank being left for the name of the vessel, to be filled up on shipment; also Adventures fo. 10, where merely Insurance is provided on a cargo at sea.

The Mercantile concern exhibited is a partnership with two unequal shares; but the minor partner having the chief conduct of the business, he receives half the profit, after allowance of interest on the capital. The reversion of the Joint Stock entries, and the systematic record of the Partners' shares, have already been treated at full in the Chapter on the Partnership Ledger, to which the reader is referred.

It is supposed that the Partnership Ledger is here a Private Book, and that the shares of capital are known to the partners alone. Hence, in the Ledger the Interest is calculated, not on the shares, but on the general Stock, and afterwards distributed in the Private Book.

SET IV.

THE BOOKS

OF

JOHN HAMILTON, AND CHARLES SIMPSON,

GENERAL MERCHANTS, LONDON.

---

1. COMMISSIONS.
2. ADVENTURES.
3. CASH.
4. BILLS RECEIVABLE.
5. BILLS PAYABLE.
6. LEDGER.
7. INVENTORY.
8. PARTNERSHIP LEDGER.

INDEX TO THE COMMISSIONS.

———

Fo. 1. Sugar per Roderic, Account Monteiro & Costa.

2. Woollens per Wellington, Account Monteiro & Costa.

3. Tallow per Neptune, Account Sandoval & Co.

4. Linens per   , Account Sandoval & Co.

(1)   *Dr.*   SUGAR PER RODERIC, CONSIGNED BY MONTEIRO AND COSTA,

1817.			£.	s.	d.
		36 Chests Brown..... M C...... No. 1 to 36 ⎱ Bonded for 24 Ditto Yellow .... 37 to 60 ⎰ Exportation. 40 Ditto White .... 61 to 100			
		100 Chests.			
April 30		To Balance, Insurance and Freight	539	16	4
May 5	1	To Cash,... London Dock Charges	67	3	6
5	3	To Promiscuous Charges, Postages, &c. ½ per Cent. on Sales	15	11	9
5	1	To Cash, ... Brokerage .... ⅛ Ditto ...... Ditto	15	11	9
5	2	To Commission, 3 per Cent. on Sales.................. £ 93 10 4			
		¼ Ditto .... Ditto ... Insurance, £ 3,000.. 7 10 0	101	0	4
5	2	To Guarantee, 2 per Cent. on Sales .... £ 62 6 10			
		½ Ditto on Underwriters ...... £ 3,000... 15 0 0	77	6	10
5	3	To Interest, 4 Months on Sales	51	19	1
			868	9	7
May 5	8	To Monteiro and Costa, Net Proceeds	2,248	13	7
		£	3,117	3	2

RIO DE JANEIRO, FOR SALE ON THEIR ACCOUNT.   *Cr.*   (1)

			£.	s.	d.

1817.

May 1 11 By Philip Wanstead, London........ (2 & 2 m^s)

	c.	q.	℔.	£.	s.	d.
20 Chests Brown ... Gross...	278	2	27			
T. & D.	34	1	20			
Net ...	244	1	7 at 40s...	488	12	6

	c.	q.	lb.			
14 Chests Yellow... Gross...	195	3	1			
T. & D.	24	1	8			
Net ...	171	1	21 at 50s...	428	11	11

	c.	q.	lb.			
15 Chests White... Gross...	213	2	6			
T. & D.	25	3	15			
Net ...	187	2	19 at 60s...	563	0	2

1,480   4   7

May 3 12 By Thomas Jackson and Son, London......... (2 & 2 m^s)

	c.	q.	lb.	£.	s.	d.
10 Chests Yellow... Gross...	140	1	12			
T. & D.	16	2	24			
Net ...	123	2	16 at 50s...	309	2	2

	c.	q.	lb.			
11 Chests White ... Gross...	160	2	20			
T. & D.	17	3	8			
Net ...	142	3	12 at 60s...	428	11	5

737   13   7

May 5 12 By David Hunter and Co. London........ (2 & 2 m^s)

	c.	q.	lb.	£.	s.	d.
16 Chests Brown... Gross...	232	1	4			
T. & D.	26	3	25			
Net ...	205	1	7 at 40s...	410	12	6

	c.	q.	lb.			
14 Chests White ... Gross...	186	2	12			
T. & D.	23	2	26			
Net ...	162	3	14 at 60s...	488	12	6

899   5   0

£   3,117   3   2

(2)   *Dr.*   WOOLLENS SHIPPED PER WELLINGTON, TO MONTEIRO

1817.				£.	s.	d.
May 2	10	To Williams & Heywood, London.....(1 & 2 mˢ)				
		Ps. No.				
		M & C..1 & 2..20 Baize, assorted Colours..1..at 230s..230 0 0				
		3 & 4..20 Ditto.......Ditto....2..at 255s..255 0 0				
		Packing 4 Bales ...at 27s.6d.. 5 10 0				
				490	10	0
3	11	To Stansfield & Nephew, London.....(1 & 2 mˢ)				
		Ps. Yds.				
		M & C..5..20 Cloths, assorted Colours..483 at 5s.0d..120 15 0				
		6..20 Ditto.....Ditto......507 at 10s.0d..253 10 0				
		7..20 Ditto.....Ditto......496 at 15s.0d..372 0 0				
		8..20 Ditto.....Ditto......489 at 20s.0d..489 0 0				
		80 Tillets........at 2s.6d.. 10 0 0				
		Packing 4 Bales ...at 30s.0d.. 6 0 0				
				1,251	5	0
3	10	To Hargreaves & Sons, London.....(1 & 2 mˢ)				
		Ps. Yds.				
		M & C..9..20 Casimirs, assorted Colours, 387 at 5s.0d.. 96 15 0				
		10..20 Ditto......Ditto.....393 at 7s.6d..147 7 6				
		11..20 Ditto......Ditto.....405 at 10s.0d..202 10 0				
		60 Tillets........at 1s.6d.. 4 10 0				
		Packing 3 Bales ...at 21s.0d.. 3 3 0				
				454	5	6
5	1	To Cash, ...Export Duty, 1 per Cent. 21 19 2		2,196	0	6
		Shipping Charges 10 17 6				
		Freight, 437½ feet, at 2s. 6d. per foot..... 54 13 9				
		Primage, 5 per Cent. on ditto 2 14 8				
				90	5	1
5	14	To Roberts & Smith, London.				
		Insurance of £2000, with Private Underwriters, } 63 0 0				
		at 3 Guineas per Cent................... }				
		Policy Duty, ¼ per Cent........................ 5 0 0				
				68	0	0
5	A 8	To Insurance, £500, by Ourselves, at 3 Guineas per Cent.. 15 15 0				
		Policy Duty, ¼ per Cent.............. 1 5 0				
				17	0	0
				2,371	5	7
5	3	To Promiscuous Charges, Postages, &c. ½ pʳ Cᵗ on £2,371.5.7		11	17	2
5	2	To Commission, 2 per Cent. on £2,371. 5. 7........... 47 8 6				
		¼ Ditto ...on Insurance £2,500. .... 6 5 0				
				53	13	6
5	2	To Guarantee, ½ per Cent. on Underwriters, £2,500		12	10	0
				2,449	6	3

AND COSTA, RIO DE JANEIRO, PER THEIR ORDER AND ACCOUNT. *Cr.* (2)

1817. May 1		ORDER.	£.	s.	d.
		40 Pieces Baize .... No. 1 and 2			
		80 Pieces Cloths......... from 5s. to 20s.			
		60 Pieces Casimirs....... from 5s. to 10s.			
		180 Pieces assorted Colours.			
May 5	3	By Interest, 3 Months on £2,196. 0. 6.	27	9	0
5	8	By Monteiro & Costa....... Amount Invoice.................	2,421	17	3
			2,449	6	3

(3)   *Dr.*   TALLOW PER NEPTUNE, CONSIGNED BY SANDOVAL

500 Serrons S No. 1 to 500.

1817.				£.	s.	d.	£.	s.	d.
May 3	14	To Roberts & Smith, Insurance of £2,000 with Private Underwriters at 4 Guineas per Cent.		84	0	0			
		Policy Duty ¼ per Cent.		5	0	0	89	0	0
3	A 8	To Insurance, £500 by Ourselves at 4 Guineas per Cent.		21	0	0			
		Policy Duty ¼ per Cent.		1	5	0	22	5	0
19	1	To Cash, ... Duty on 969 1 11 (Cwt. qr. lb.) at 3s. 2d. per Cwt. ...		153	9	7			
		Custom-House Charges, &c.		17	12	6			
		Dock Dues, Landing, Cartage, &c.		37	15	1	208	17	2
21	1	To Cash, ... Freight on 54 5 1 19 (Ts. cwt. qr. lb.) at £5 per Ton.		271	7	1			
		Primage 5 per Cent.		13	11	4	284	18	5
28	3	To Promiscuous Charges, Postages, &c. ½ per Cent. on Sales					13	11	10
28	1	To Cash, Brokerage on Sale ½ per Cent.					13	11	10
28	2	To Commission, 3 per Cent. on Sales		81	11	2			
		¼ ...., on Insurance £2,500.		6	5	0	87	16	2
28	2	To Guarantee, 2 per Cent. on Credit Sales		49	13	10			
		½ .... on Underwriters £2,500.		12	10	0	62	3	10
28	3	To Interest, 4 months on £2,484. 9. 9.					41	8	2
							823	12	5
28	9	To Sandoval & Co. Net Proceeds...............................					1,894	19	0
						£	2,718	11	5

AND CO. BUENOS AYRES, FOR SALE ON THEIR ACCOUNT.   *Cr.*   (3)

1817.					£.	s.	d.
May 22	13	By Hammond & Morley, London.					
			cwt. qr. lb.				
		200 Serrons, Gross Weight 447 2 9					
			cwt. qr. lb.				
		Tare 25 lb. per Serron, 44 2 16					
		Draft 1....Ditto.... 1 3 4					
		———— 46 1 20					
		(2 & 2 mˢ) Net...401 0 17 at 57s. 6d.			1,153	6	2
24	12	By Peter Walsingham, London.					
			cwt. qr. lb.				
		100 Serrons, Gross Weight 210 3 14					
			cwt. qr. lb.				
		Tare 25 lb. per Serron, 22 1 8					
		Draft 1....Ditto 0 3 16					
		———— 23 0 24					
		(2 & 2 mˢ) Net...187 2 18 at 57s. 6d. .. 539 10 6					
			cwt. qr. lb.				
		50 Serrons Inferior, Gross Wt. . 109 2 10					
			cwt. qr. lb.				
		Tare 25 lb. per Serron, 11 0 18					
		Draft 1....Ditto 0 1 22					
		———— 11 2 12					
		Net...97 3 26 at 50s. 244 19 1			784	9	7
26	13	By James Donald & Sons, London.					
			cwt. qr. lb.				
		100 Serrons, Gross Weight, ...218 1 24					
			cwt. qr. lb.				
		Tare 25 lb. per Serron, 22 1 8					
		Draft 1....Ditto 0 3 16					
		———— 23 0 24					
		(2 & 2 mˢ) Net...195 1 0 at 56s.			546	14	0
		Credit			2,484	9	9
28	1	By Cash.					
			cwt. qr. lb.				
		50 Serrons, Gross Weight 98 3 18					
			cwt. qr. lb.				
		Tare 25 lb. per Serron, 11 0 18					
		Draft 1....Ditto 0 1 22					
		———— 11 2 12					
		Net... 87 1 6 at 55s. ... 240 1 8					
		Less Discount 2½ per Cent. 6 0 0			234	1	8
		£			2,718	11	5

(4)	*Dr.*	LINENS SHIPPED PER	TO SANDOVAL

1817.			£.	s.	d.
May 24	11	To Macnamara & Sons, London... (P. B. 4 m³)			
		No. £. s. d.			
		S. 1 & 2.. 100 Pieces White Linen assorted No. 1 at 40s.. 200 0 0			
		3 & 4.. 100 Pieces Ditto....... ditto ...... 2 at 50s.. 250 0 0			
		5 & 6.. 100 Pieces Ditto....... ditto ...... 3 at 60s.. 300 0 0			
		7 & 8.. 100 Pieces Ditto....... ditto ...... 4 at 70s.. 350 0 0			
		9 & 10.. 100 Pieces Ditto....... ditto ...... 5 at 80s.. 400 0 0			
		Packing 10 Bales ...... at 50s.. 25 0 0			
			1,525	0	0

AND CO. BUENOS AYRES, PER THEIR ORDER AND ACCOUNT. *Cr.* (4)

1817.

ORDER.

500 Pieces White Linens, Quality No. 1 to 5

500 Pieces Printed Ditto. . Ditto. . . . . . 1 to 5.

1,000 Pieces in 20 Bales. . . . S. . . . No. 1 to 20.

INDEX TO ADVENTURES.

---

(1) *Dr.*   JOINT MISSION PER TRAFALGAR, TO SANDOVAL & CO. BUENOS AYRES;

1817.				£.	s.	d.
May 7	10	To Williams & Heywood, London. (1 & 2 mˢ)				
		No. Pieces £. s. d.				
		S..1 to 20...300 Baize, assorted Colours, at 210s...3,150 0 0				
		Packing Charges 30 0 0				
				3,180	0	0
May 10	11	To Stansfield & Nephew, London. (1 & 2 mˢ)				
		No. Pieces. Yards.				
		S..21 to 45....500 Blue Cloth..12,378..at 5s. 0d...3,094 10 0				
		46 to 50.... 100 Scarlet Ditto..2,483..at 7s. 6d... 931 2 6				
		Tillets and Packing Charges....... 120 0 0				
				4,145	12	6
May 14	10	To Campbell & Douglas, London. (2 & 2mˢ)				
		No. Pieces. No.				
		S..51 to 58....400 Printed Calicos..2...at 27s. 6d....550 0 0				
		59 to 66....400....Ditto.......4...at 37s. 6d....750 0 0				
		67 to 70....200....Ditto.......6...at 50s. 0d....500 0 0				
		Packing Charges 47 10 0				
				1,847	10	0
May 17	11	To Macnamara & Sons, London. (2 & 2 mˢ)				
		No. Pieces. No.				
		S..71 to 78...400 White Linens...3...at 45s. 0d... 900 0 0				
		79 to 86...400....Ditto......5...at 65s. 0d... 1,300 0 0				
		87 to 90...200....Ditto......7...at 80s. 0d... 800 0 0				
		91 to 98...400 Printed Linens..3...at 55s. 0d... 1,100 0 0				
		99 to 106...400....Ditto......5...at 77s. 6d... 1,550 0 0				
		107 to 110...200....Ditto......7...at 95s. 0d... 950 0 0				
		Packing Charges 100 0 0				
				6,700	0	0
				15,873	2	6
May 19	1	To Cash,... Paid for Export Duty and Shipping Charges ...158 13 0				
		Freight 117½ Tons, at £5, with 5 pʳ Cᵗ Primᵉ..616 17 6				
				775	10	6
19	14	To Roberts & Smith... Insurance of £17,000, at 3 Gˢ pʳ Cᵗ. 535 10 0				
		Policy Duty ¼ per Cent.......... 42 10 0				
				578	0	0
19	A 8	To Insurance, £1000 by Ourselves, at 3 Guineas per Cent... 31 10 0				
		Policy Duty, ¼ per Cent............ 2 10 0				
				34	0	0
				17,260	13	0
May 19	3	To Promiscuous Charges, ½ per Cent. for Postages and Sundry........		86	6	1
19	2	To Commission, 2 per Cent. on £17,260. 13. 0........345 4 3				
		¼ per Cent. on Insurance £18,000........ 45 0 0				
				390	4	3
19	2	To Guarantee, ½ per Cent. on Underwriters £18,000		90	0	0
19	3	To Interest, ..2 Months on Debentures £458. 16. 8............		3	16	6
				17,830	19	10

D. WALKER $\frac{1}{3}$; SANDOVAL & CO. $\frac{1}{3}$; OURSELVES MANAGERS $\frac{1}{3}$.   *Cr.*   (1)

1817.				£.	s.	d.
May 19	4	By Debentures, Bounty on Cottons and Linens		458	16	9
19	3	By Interest, 3 Months on Woollens ...£7,325. 12. 6... 91 11 5 *(£. s. d.)*				
		4 m. on Cottons and Linens,..8,547. 10. 0...142 9 2		234	0	7
				692	17	4
19	13	By David Walker, London, ...his $\frac{1}{3}$ Interest 5,712 14 2				
19	9	By Sandoval and Co. Buenos Ayres, their $\frac{1}{3}$ Ditto 5,712 14 2				
19	5	By Adventure per Trafalgar, ...our $\frac{1}{3}$ Ditto 5,712 14 2		17,138	2	6
				17,830	19	10

(2)   *Dr.*   JOINT PROCEEDS EX DIANA, AT BUENOS AYRES ;

			Dls.	Rs.	Exch.	£.	s.	d.
1817.								
May 1	9	To Sandoval and Co. Buenos Ayres, Cost of a Bill on Grant and Co. Remitted per Diana, £2,000 ......at 50d.	9,600	0				
		Commission, 1 per Cent.	96	0				
			9,696	0...	at 50d.	2,020	0	0
May 1	9	To Sandoval and Co. Buenos Ayres, Invoice of 15,000 Dollars per Diana	15,000	0				
		Export Duty, 7½ per Cent...Ds. 1,125						
		Shipping Charges Bags, &c..... 90						
			1,215	0				
			16,215	0				
		Commission, 2 per Cent.............	324	2				
		Cost	16,539	2...	at 50d.	3,445	13	6
May 12	9	To Sandoval and Co. Invoice of 15,523 Ox Hides per Diana						
		Marked S.. Weight 11,985$\frac{31}{35}$ Pesadas, at Ds.3..	35,957	5				
		Export Duty......Ds. 2,871 6						
		Weighing and Shipping 1,273 0						
			4,144	6				
			40,102	3				
		Commission, 3 per Cent.	1,203	0				
		Cost......	41,305	3...	at 50d.	8,605	5	9
May 12	9	To Sandoval & Co. Buenos Ayres.						
		Their ⅓ Proceeds of Sales.............33,770		3...	at 50d.	7,035	9	11
		£				21,106	9	2

SANDOVAL & CO. MANAGERS $\frac{1}{3}$; OURSELVES $\frac{1}{3}$; D. WALKER $\frac{1}{3}$.   *Cr.*   (2)

1817.							£.	s.	d.
May 1	9	By Sandoval & Co. Buenos Ayres.							

Their Account Sales 15th January.

	Dls.	Rs.	Exch.
100 Pieces Baize........at Ds.85....	8,500	0	
120 Pieces Ditto........at 90....	10,800	0	
80 Pieces Ditto........at 95....	7,600	0	
300 Pieces Blue Cloths...at 55....	16,500	0	
200 Pieces...Ditto......at 57....	11,400	0	
100 Pieces Scarlet Ditto..at 75....	7,500	0	

900 Pieces Woollens 62,300   0

CHARGES.

	Ds.	Rs.
Duties and Custom-House Charges..	11,873	4
Postages and Petty Charges, $\frac{1}{2}$ p^r C^t..	311	4
Warehouse Rent 1 per Cent.......	623	0
Commission and Guarantee, 6 per C^t	3,738	0

                                                16,546   0

Net Proceeds .... 45,754 0...at 50*d*.   9,532   1   8

May 12	9	By Sandoval & Co. Buenos Ayres.

Their Account Sales 10th February.

	No.	Ds.	Dls.	Rs.
400 Pieces Printed Calicos ..1 & 2..at 14....			5,600	0
400 Pieces ....Ditto ......3 & 4..at 17....			6,800	0
200 Pieces ....Ditto ...... 5 ..at 20....			4,000	0
400 Pieces White Linens ...1 & 2..at 22....			8,800	0
400 Pieces ....Ditto......3 & 4..at 27....			10,800	0
200 Pieces ....Ditto ...... 5 ..at 32....			6,400	0
400 Pieces Printed Linens ..1 & 2..at 27....			10,800	0
400 Pieces ....Ditto .....3 & 4..at 32....			12,800	0
200 Pieces ....Ditto ..... 5 ..at 37			7,400	0

3,000 Pieces Cottons and Linens.............. 73,400

CHARGES.

	Dls.	Rs.
Duties and Custom-House Charges ..	12,338	0
Postages and Petty Charges. $\frac{1}{4}$ p^r C^t ..	367	0
Warehouse Rent, 1 per Cent.	734	0
Commission and Guarantee, 6 p^r C^t..	4,404	0

                                                17,843   0

Net Proceeds ....55,557 0...at 50*d*.   11,574   7   6

                                                21,106   9   2

(3)   *Dr.*   JOINT RETURNS PER DIANA FROM BUENOS AYRES;

1817.				£.	s.	d.	£.	s.	d.
May 1	14	To Roberts & Smith, London.							
		Insurance of £14,000 on Hides, with Private Underwriters, at 4 Guineas per Cent.		588	0	0			
		Policy Duty ¼ per Cent.		35	0	0	623	0	0
1	A 8	To Insurance, £3,500 by Ourselves on Dollars, at 2½ Guineas per Cent.		91	17	6			
		Policy Duty ¼ per Cent.		8	15	0	100	12	6
14	1	To Cash, Charges on 15,000 Dollars :							
		Freight 1 per Cent. on Sale £3,350. 9. 1.		33	10	1			
		Landing, Porterage, Weighing, &c. ⅛ per Cent. . .		4	3	9			
		Brokerage ⅛ per Cent.		4	3	9	41	17	7
15	1	To Cash, Duty on 15,523 Hides . . . . at 9½ d. .		614	9	0			
		Entry, Landing, Sorting, and Weighing		90	14	3			
		Tons. cwt. qr. lb. Freight on 186 14 2 17 at £6. 10. per Ton		1213	15	3			
		Primage 5 per Cent. . . . . on. . . . Ditto		60	13	9	1,979	12	3
19	3	To Promiscuous Charges, Postages, and Sundry Expenses :							
		½ per Cent. on Sale of Hides, £13,977. 5. 8. . . .		69	17	9			
		On Dollars		2	10	0	72	7	9
19	1	To Cash, Brokerage on Hides ½ per Cent.					69	17	9
19	2	To Commission, 1 per Ct on Sale of Dollars, £3,350. 9. 1.		33	10	1			
		3 per Ct on Sale of Hides, £13,977. 5. 8.		419	6	4			
		¼ per Ct on Insurance, . . £17,500. 0. 0.		43	15	0	496	11	5
19	3	To Interest, on Bill No. 665, £2,000 due 14 June, 26 days		7	2	6			
		4 months on Sale of Hides, £13,977. 5. 8. . . .		232	19	1	240	1	7
19	2	To Guarantee, 2 per Cent. on Sale of Hides, £13,977. 5. 8.		279	10	11			
		½ per Cent. on Underwriters, £17,500. 0. 0.		87	10	0	367	0	11
19	13	To David Walker, London, His Half Net Proceeds.	7,668	6	6				
19	5	To Adventure per Diana, . . Our . . Ditto . . . . Ditto.	7,668	6	6		15,336	13	0
						£	19,327	14	9

OURSELVES MANAGERS ½; DAVID WALKER ½.   *Cr.*   (3)

1817.				£.	s.	d.
May 12	1	By Bills Receivable, No. 665 on Belfield & Brown, due 14 June		2,000	0	0
14	1	By Cash, sold 15,000 Dollars ex Diana, Oz. dwts. Weight 12,969 10 at 5s. 2d. per oz.....................		3,350	9	1
17	12	By Peter Walsingham, London. (1 & 3 ms.) lbs. £. s. d. 1,700 Hides A weighing Net 44,560... at 9d... 1,671 0 0 1,237 Ditto B ditto........ 32,562... at 8d... 1,085 8 0 1,892 Ditto C ditto........ 51,216... at 7d... 1,493 16 0		4,250	4	0
17	13	By Hammond & Morley, London. (1 & 3 ms.) lbs. 899 Hides A weighing Net 25,948... at 9d... 973 1 0 3,000 Ditto B ditto........ 80,901... at 8d... 2,696 14 0 800 Ditto C ditto........ 21,247... at 7d... 619 14 1		4,289	9	1
19	13	By James Donald & Sons, London. (1 & 3 ms.) lbs. 2,000 Hides A weighing Net 55,022... at 9d... 2,063 6 6 2,495 Ditto B ditto........ 65,901... at 8d... 2,196 14 0 1,500 Ditto C ditto........ 40,375... at 7d... 1,177 12 1 15,523 Hides.		5,437	12	7
		£		19,327	14	9

(4)   *Dr.*   JOINT COTTON PER BRITANNIA, FROM RIO DE

Ourselves ½

1817.				£.	s.	d.
May 8	8	To Monteiro & Costa, Rio Janeiro, for our half Invoice:				

	No.	Bags.		Arrobas.	lbs.		Mil-Reas.
H	1 to 100..	100....	Net	397	16	at 8.000....	3,180.000
	101 to 200.	.100....	Ditto ...	384	24	at 8.500....	3,270.375
	201 to 300..	100. ...	Ditto ...	402	8	at 9.000....	3,620.250

300 Bags .....1,184 16   Rs. 10,070.625

CHARGES.

Arrobas. lb.

Duty on 1,184 16 at 600 Rs. per Arroba. ... Rs. 710.700

Brokerage on Ditto at   40.... per Ditto........ 47.380

New Duty on 300 Bags at 100 Rs. per Bag 30.000

Marking.....Ditto....at 30 Rs. Ditto......   9.000

Repairing Bags 14.400

811.480

Rs. 10,882.105

Commission 3 per Cent. 326.463

Rs. 11,208.568

Our ½ Proportion .... Rs. 5,604.284

| At the Exchange of 60*d.* per Milrea......................... | 1,401 | 1 | 5 |

| £ | 1,401 | 1 | 5 |

JANEIRO, JAMES HORNER AND SON, MANAGERS. Cr. (4)
James Horner & Son, London, ½.

			£.	s.	d.
1817.					
May 28	13	By James Horner & Son, London, for our ½ Proceeds, as per Account Sales.			

150 Bags to Whitaker & Co. at 3 months.

	£.	s.	d.
Net Weight, 18,963 lbs...at 1s. 9d...1,659		5	3

150 Ditto to Christopher Bland, at 3 months.

Net Weight, 19,018 lbs...at 1s. 10d...1,743 6 4

300 Bags. £ 3,402 11 7

CHARGES.

	£.	s.	d.
Insurance on £ 4,000 at 3 Guineas per Cent. .	126	0	0
Policy Duty ¼ per Cent....................	10	0	0
Guarantee, ½ per Cent....................	20	0	0
Duty on 37,981 lbs. at 8s. 7d. per 100 lb......	163	0	0
Freight on 1,184 ½ Arrobas at 4s. 6d.	266	10	3
Primage 5 per Cent.......................	13	6	6
Landing, Dock Dues, Cartage, &c.	16	12	8
Mending, Sampling, and Weighing..........	19	10	0
Postages and Sundry Expenses ½ per Cent.....	17	0	3
Brokerage on Sale, ½ per Cent..............	17	0	3
Commission 3 per Cent. on Sale	102	1	7
Guarantee, 1 ½ per Cent. on Ditto	51	0	9
Interest, ...3 months on Ditto	42	10	8

864 12 11

£ 2,537 18 8

	£.	s.	d.
......................Our ½ Proportion	1,268	19	4
May 28 1 By Loss, our Half Share	132	2	1
	1,401	1	5

(5)   *Dr.*   JOINT OIL PER SENEGAGLIA, FROM

1817.				£.	s.	d.
May 7	7	To Malatesta & Co. Leghorn, Our ½ Amount of Invoice.				
		M No. 1 to 42 .. 42 Casks Gallipoli, Cost .... Pezze 6,573 S. 18 D. 3				
		Casks and Shipping Charges....... 477 17 4				
		7,051 15 7				
		Commission 3 per Cent. 211 11 1				
		P. 7,263 6 8				
		Our Half, P. 3,631. 13. 4. at 48*d.* per Pezza....		726	6	8
May 7	14	To Roberts & Smith, Insurance of £1,800 at 2 Gs. with Policy ¼ per Ct.		42	6	0
7	A 8	To Insurance, ... £ 200 by Ourselves at 2 Gs. and Ditto		4	14	0
21	1	To Cash, paid for Import Duty and Custom-House Charges . 307 3 9				
		Freight and Primage 55 1 4				
		Landing, Cartage, and Sundry 19 17 11				
				382	3	0
May 30	1	To Cash, paid Brokerage on Sale ½ per Cent.		10	5	10
30	3	To Promiscuous Charges, ½ per Cent. for Postages, &c.		10	5	10
30	2	To Commission. ... 3 per Cent. on Sales 61 15 0				
		¼ per Cent. on Insurance £ 2,000..... 5 0 0				
				66	15	0
30	2	To Guarantee ..... 2 per Cent. on Sales 41 3 4				
		½ per Cent. on Underwriters £2,000 .. 10 0 0				
				51	3	4
30	3	To Interest........ 4 months on Sales		34	6	2
30	7	To Malatesta & Co..... Their Half Net Proceeds ...... £ 728 4 5		601	19	2
30		To Transfer to Account below, Our Half Ditto.......... 728 4 5				
				1,456	8	10
				2,058	8	0
May 30		To Transfer from Account above, Our Half Invoice		726	6	8
30	1	To Profit		1	17	9
				728	4	5

MALATESTA AND CO. LEGHORN—EACH ONE HALF. *Cr.* (5)

1817.				£.	s.	d.
May 30		By Transfer to Account below		726	6	8
May 28	12	By Thomas Jackson & Son, London. (4 ms. Cash.)				
		11 Casks containing 1,314 Gallons at £98 per Tun		542	12	5
May 29	11	By Philip Wanstead, London. (4 ms. Cash.)				
		18 Casks containing 2,111 Gallons at £99 per Tun		885	10	11
May 30	12	By David Hunter & Co. London. (4 ms. Cash.)				
		13 Casks containing 1,526 Gallons at £97 per Tun		627	4	3
				2,058	8	0
May 30		By Transfer from Account above, Our Half N. P.		728	4	5

(6)　　　*Dr.*　　　JOINT COFFEE PER REGENT, FROM MONTEIRO AND COSTA,

Ourselves $\frac{2}{5}$, Monteiro & Costa $\frac{2}{5}$

1817.			3,000 Bags.	£.	s.	d.
May 30	14		To Roberts & Smith, London, Insurance of £14,000 with Private Underwriters, at 3 Guineas per Cent. 441 0 0			
			Policy Duty $\frac{1}{4}$ per Cent. 35 0 0			
				476	0	0
30	A 8		To Insurance, £1,000 by Ourselves at 3 Guineas per Cent. . . 31 10 0			
			Policy Duty $\frac{1}{4}$ per Cent. 2 10 0			
				34	0	0
				510	0	0

RIO DE JANEIRO—OURSELVES MANAGERS. *Cr.* (6)

Nicholson & Co. London, $\frac{1}{5}$.

(7)		*Dr.*	EXCHANGE	£.	s.	d.
1817.				£.	s.	d.
May 5	1	To Bills Receivable, (No. 658) 5,000 Pezze on Leghorn, at 48*d.* per Pezza		1,000	0	0
		Remitted to Rimaverde & Co. Lisbon, where 5,000 Pezze at				
		840 Reas per Pezza give .... Rs. 4,200. 000		....	....	....
15	1	To Bills Receivable, (No. 667) 5,000 Pezze on Leghorn at 48*d.* per Pezza		1,000	0	0
		Remitted to Lorenzo Davila, Cadiz, to purchase a Bill on Lisbon,				
		and remit the same to Rimaverde & Co. Lisbon.				
		5,000 Pezze at 156 Piastres per 100 Pezze, give 7,800 Piastres.				
		7,800 Piastres at 550 Reas per Piastre......... Rs. 4,290. 000		....	....	....
26	1	To Bills Receivable, (No. 674) 5,000 Pezze on Leghorn, at 48*d.* per Pezza		1,000	0	0
		Remitted to Lorenzo Davila, Cadiz, to purchase a Bill on Paris,				
		and remit the same to Rimaverde & Co. Lisbon.				
		5,000 Pezze at 156 Piastres per 100, give ...... 7,800 Piastres.				
		7,800 Piastres at 113 Sous per Piastre........ 44,070 Francs.				
		44,070 Francs at 100 Reas per Franc........... Rs. 4,407. 000		....	....	....
31	1	To Profit		170	10	3
				3,170	10	3

ARBITRATIONS.   *Cr.*   (7)

1817.				£.	s.	d.
May 3	1	By Bills Receivable, No. 656, our Draft on Rimaverde & Co. Lisbon.				
. . . .	. . . .	. . . . Rs. 4,200.000 Exchange at 59*d.* per Milrea		1,032	10	0
14	1	By Bills Receivable, No. 666, Our Draft on Rimaverde & Co. Lisbon.				
. . . .	. . . .	. . . . Rs. 4,290.000 at the Exchange of 59*d.* per Milrea		1,054	12	6
24	1	By Bills Receivable, No. 673, our Draft on Rimaverde & Co. Lisbon.				
. . . .	. . . .	. . . . Rs. 4,407.000 at the Exchange of 59*d.* per Milrea		1,083	7	9
				3,170	10	3

(8)   *Dr.*   INSURANCE.

1817.			£.	s.	d.
May 10	14	To Roberts & Smith, Total Loss of our Subscription per James to Revel	250	0	0
16	A 9	To Partial Average on our Subscription £ 300 per Nancy to Buenos Ayres, at 15 per Cent.	76	0	6
24	14	To Roberts & Smith, Return Premium on £ 200 per Columbus, at 1 per Cent.	2	0	0
31	1	To Profit	195	8	1
31		To Balance, Premiums on Risks pending.	1,135	4	2
			1,658	12	9

PER CONTRA. *Cr.* (8)

1817.			*£.*	*s.*	*d.*
April 30		By Balance, Premiums on Risks pending	1,346	11	3
May 1	A 3	By Joint Returns per Diana, from Buenos Ayres, £3,500 on Silver at 2½ Guineas per Cent.....................................	100	12	6
2	14	By Roberts & Smith, London, our Subscription per Ellen to Smyrna, £400 at 4 per Cent.....................................	16	0	0
3	C 3	By Tallow per Neptune from Buenos Ayres, £500 at 4 Guineas......	22	5	0
5	C 2	By Woollens per Wellington to Rio de Janeiro, £500 at 3 Guineas....	17	0	0
7	14	By Roberts & Smith, London, our Subscription per George to Lima, £250 at 8 per Cent.....................................	20	0	0
7	A 5	By Gallipoli Oil per Senegaglia from Leghorn, £200 at 2 Guineas	4	14	0
12	14	By Roberts and Smith, London, our Subscription per Sarah from Lisbon, £400 at 2 per Cent.....................................	8	0	0
19	14	By Roberts & Smith, London, our Subscription per Alexander to Riga, £500 at 3 per Cent.....................................	15	0	0
19	A 1	By Joint Mission per Trafalgar to Buenos Ayres, £1,000 at 3 Guineas .	34	0	0
24	14	By Roberts & Smith, London, our Subscription per Brahmin from Calcutta, £300 at 10 per Cent...............................	30	0	0
29	14	By Roberts & Smith, London, our Subscription per Anne to Bahia, £350 at 3 per Cent.....................................	10	10	0
30	A 6	By Coffee per Regent from Rio de Janeiro, £1,000 at 3 Guineas per Cent...	34	0	0
			1,658	12	9
May 31		By Balance, Premiums on Risks pending	1,135	4	2

(9)   *Dr.*   PARTIAL

1817.				£.	s.	d.
May 16	14	To Roberts & Smith, London.				

Partial Loss per Nancy to Buenos Ayres, 10 Bales Woollens **M** No. 1 to 10, Insured at £2,500.

Which, in a sound state, would have sold (as per Certificate) for..........................	Ds. 14,540	
But, in consequence of Damage by Salt Water, sold (as per Account Sales) for	11,286	
Depreciation...	Ds. 3,254	

Therefore, If 14,540 Ds. lose 3,254 Ds. £2,500 will lose £ 559 9 10

CHARGES.

Survey and Consular Documents ..... Ds. 127	4
Expenses of Auction Sale 236	4
Ds. 364	0

At the Exchange of 48d. per Dollar....	72	16	0
Postages of Documents.....................	1	5	8
Loss on £2,500 at £25. 6s. 10d. per Cent...... £633	11	6	

£25. 6. 10. per Cent. on our Subscription of £300 is .... | 76 | 0 | 6

				£.	s.	d.
21	2	To Commission 2 per Cᵗ on Loss per Catharine £ 595. 19. . 11 18 4				
21	6	To Kaminski & Co. Net Recovery on Ditto 581 1 1				
				592	19	5
				668	19	11

AVERAGE. *Cr.* (9)

1817.				£.	s.	d.
May 16	A 8	By Insurance, Partial Loss per Nancy, as opposite		76	0	6
21	14	By Roberts & Smith, London.				

Partial Loss per Catharine to Riga on 20 Hhds. Sugar insured by them at £1,500; which, if sound, would have sold (as per Certificate) for   Roubles. 16,500

But, in consequence of Average, sold (as per Account Sales) for   10,650

Depreciation ... Rs. 5,850

Therefore, If 16,500 Roubles lose 5,850; £1,500 will lose £531 16 4

CHARGES.

Survey and Consular Documents .... Rs. 187

Expenses of Auction Sale 315

Roubles...... 502

At the Exchange of 2s. 6d. per Rouble .	62	15	0
Postages of Documents.....................	1	7	8
Loss.................................	595	19	0
Less Brokerage on Recovery ½ per Cent.	2	19	7

	£.	s.	d.
	592	19	5
	668	19	11

Dr.   CASH.   (1)

1817.			RECEIPTS, &c.	£.	s.	d.
April 30			To Balance	6,637	5	9
May 1	1		To Bills Receivable, due No. 518 and 519	1,726	10	0
2	1		To Bills Receivable, sold No. 653, our Draft on Malatesta & Co.	621	6	6
3	3		To Interest, Discount from Stansfield & Nephew, 1¼ per Cent. on £ 1,251. 5. 0.	15	12	10
3	1		To Bills Receivable, sold No. 656, our Draft on Rimaverde & Co.	1,032	10	0
5	1		To..... Ditto..... due No. 536, 524, and 522	2,701	17	2
10	1		To..... Ditto..... due No. 528, 531, and 525	1,563	13	8
10	3		To Interest, Disc^t from Peterson & Grenville, 2 per Cent. on £1,392. 8. 6.	27	17	0
10	3		To Ditto... Ditto on Bills Payable, No. 219, due 12 July 63 days £1,377. 14. 5.	11	17	9
14	A 3		To Joint Returns per Diana, Proceeds of Silver	3,350	9	1
14	1		To Bills Receivable, sold No. 666, our Draft on Rimaverde & Co.	1,054	12	6
15	12		To Rogers & Wilson..	1,366	8	6
16	1		To Bills Receivable, due No. 537 to 540	2,192	17	8
21	4		To Debentures, Drawback per Mary	388	19	2
23	11		To William Fleetwood's Assignees, Dividend of 6s. 8d. per £ final	195	18	9
23	1		To Bills Receivable, due No. 520 and 521	1,635	10	0
23	1		To..... Ditto. .... sold No. 672, our Draft on Muller & Schmidt	505	10	6
24	1		To..... Ditto..... sold No. 673, our Draft on Rimaverde & Co.	1,083	7	9
26	1		To..... Ditto..... due No. 523	1,500	0	0
28	C 3		To Tallow per Neptune, 50 Serrons sold for	234	1	8
29	13		To James Horner & Son, our ½ Cotton ex Britannia	1,268	19	4
29	1		To Bills Receivable, due No. 529	1,000	0	0
				30,115	5	7
May 31			To Balance	5,872	5	2

		PAYMENTS, &c.	£.	s.	d.
1817.					
May 1	15	By John Hamilton, Private Account	500	0	0
2	1	By Bills Payable, due No. 154 to 156	1,861	5	6
3	11	By Stansfield & Nephew	1,251	5	0
5	C 1	By Sugar per Roderic, Dock Charges	67	3	6
5	C 2	By Woollens per Wellington, Shipping Charges	90	5	1
5	1	By Bills Receivable, bought No. 658 on Leghorn	1,000	0	0
5	15	By Charles Simpson, Check to George Smith	176	17	6
5	1	By Bills Receivable, bought No. 657 on Rio de Janeiro	526	3	10
5	C 1	By Sugar per Roderic, Brokerage on Sale	15	11	9
7	1	By Bills Payable, due No. 138, 179, and 147	978	17	0
10	10	By Peterson & Grenville	1,392	8	6
10	1	By Bills Payable, discounted No. 219	1,377	14	5
12	15	By John Hamilton, Check to Randolph & Co.	238	10	0
12	1	By Bills Payable, due No. 144	1,000	0	0
14	A 3	By Joint Returns per Diana, Charges on Dollars	41	17	7
15	3	By Interest, Discount to Rogers & Wilson, 1¼ per Cent. on £1,366. 8. 6.	17	1	7
15	1	By Bills Receivable, bought No. 667 on Leghorn	1,000	0	0
15	A 3	By Joint Returns per Diana, Duty and Charges on Hides	1,979	12	3
17	1	By Bills Payable, due No. 148 to 150	1,350	0	0
19	A 1	By Joint Mission per Trafalgar, Duty and Shipping Charges	775	10	6
19	C 3	By Tallow per Neptune, Duty and Landing Charges	208	17	2
19	A 3	By Joint Returns per Diana, Brokerage on Sale	69	17	9
20	13	By David Walker, Balance	1,955	12	4
21	C 3	By Tallow per Neptune, Freight and Primage	284	18	5
21	A 5	By Joint Oil per Senegaglia, Duty and Charges	382	3	0
22	15	By John Hamilton, Private Account	300	0	0
22	1	By Bills Payable, due No. 162, 158, and 145	1,924	0	7
26	1	By Bills Receivable, bought No. 674 on Leghorn	1,000	0	0.
26	15	By Charles Simpson, Private Account	150	0	0
26	1	By Bills Payable, due No. 166 and 167	937	9	6
28	C 3	By Tallow per Neptune, Brokerage on Sale	13	11	10
30	A 5	By Joint Oil per Senegaglia Ditto Ditto	10	5	10
30	1	By Bills Payable, due No. 146	500	0	0
31	1	By Bills Receivable, bought No. 678 on Leghorn	728	4	5
31	3	By Promiscuous Charges, for Postages, Stamps, Salaries, Wages, &c. this month, as per Book of Sundry Expenses	137	15	7
31		By Balance	5,872	5	2
			30,115	5	7

Dr.   BILLS RECEIVABLE.   (1)

When and how obtained.			No.	Drawn By.		Date.	Term.	Order of.	Drawn on.
1817.						1817.			
Apr.30	. .	To Balance	. . .	. . . .		. . .	. . .	. . . .	. . . .
May 2	7	To Malatesta & Co. .	√ 653	Ourselves	London	May 2	30 d. s.	Bradford & Co.	Malatesta & Co. Leghorn.
3	12	To Rogers & Wilson	654	Milner & Son . .	Leeds .	Apr.30	3 m.	Rogers & Wilson	Belfield & Brown London.
			655	Woodfall & Co. .	Bristol	25	. . .	Ditto	Watson & Son Ditto.
3	A7	To Exch. Arbitrations	√ 656	Ourselves	London	May 3	60 d. s.	Grandison & Co.	Rimaverde & Co. Lisbon.
5	1	To Cash	√ 657	Charles Horsfall	Ditto	. . .	. . .	Ourselves	Paramo & Co. Rio Jan.
5	1	To Cash	√ 658	Mellin & Green .	London	4	30 d. s.	Ditto	Nicolini & Son Leghorn.
7	12	To Peter Walsingham	√ 659	Ourselves	Ditto	7	3 m.	Order	Pet. Walsingham London.
8	7	To Casanova & Co. .	660	Nondimeno & Co.	Naples	Apr. 5	2 m.	Casanova & Co.	Weldon & Co. Ditto.
			661	Pietro Rosa . . .	Ditto	7	30 d. s.	Ditto	Marblay & Son Ditto.
10	12	To Dd. Hunter & Co.	662	Chas. Evergreen	London	May 3	2 m.	Slater & Son . .	Borland & White Ditto.
			663	Fox & Glover .	Manchr.	Apr. 7	3 m.	Order	Nelson & Smith Ditto.
			664	Alex. Campbell .	Glasgow	20	. . .	Ditto	Caulfield & Co. Ditto.
12	A3	{ Joint Returns per } { Diana . . . . . }	665	Montenegro & Co.	Buen.Ay.	Feb. 5	30 d. s.	Sandoval & Co.	Belfield & Brown Ditto.
14	A7	To Exch. Arbitrations	√ 666	Ourselves	London	May 12	60 d. s.	Grandison & Co.	Rimaverde & Co. Lisbon.
15	1	To Cash	√ 667	Watkinson & Co.	Ditto	10	30 d. s.	Ourselves	Buonocore & Co. Leghorn.
17	6	To Muller & Schmidt	668	Handel & Co. . .	Hambh.	Apr.30	2 m.	Muller & Schmidt	Weston & Grey London.
19	11	To Philip Wanstead	669	C. Gregson . . .	Hull	May 10	3 m.	Philip Wanstead	Charles Lumb Ditto.
			670	John Gregory . .	Liverpl.	Apr.25	4 m.	John Henderson	Parbet & Co. . . Ditto.
21	12	To T. Jackson & Son	671	Newman & Co. .	Dublin	15	3 m.	Evergreen & Son	S. Tomlinson . . Ditto.
23	6	To Muller & Schmidt	√ 672	Ourselves	London	May 23	30 d. s.	James Herman	Muller & Schmidt Hambro'.
24	A7	To Exch. Arbitrations	√ 673	Ditto	Ditto	24	60 d. a.	Randolph & Son	Rimaverde & Co. Lisbon.
26	1	To Cash	√ 674	Frazer & Smith .	Ditto	20	30 d. s.	Ourselves	Bentivoglio & Co. Leghorn.
28	6	To Vanderloo & Co.	675	Schmidt & Co.	Amsterd.	10	2 m.	Vanderloo & Sons	Mitchell & Co. . London.
28	11	To Philip Wanstead .	√ 676	Ourselves	London	28	3 m.	Campbell & Co.	P. Simpson . . . Ditto.
29	12	To Dd. Hunter & Co.	677	Brander & Son .	Nottingh.	Apr.15	. . .	D. Hunter & Co.	Crompton & Son Ditto.
31	1	To Cash	√ 678	John King . . .	London	May 28	30 d. s.	Ourselves	Colomella & Co. Leghorn.
May 31		To Balance	. . .	, ...		. . .	. . .	. . . .	. . . .

(1)   PER CONTRA.   *Cr.*

Due.		£.	s.	d.			When and how disposed of.	No.		£.	s.	d.
1817.					1817.							
....	....	29,178	7	6	May 1	1	By Cash, due	518	1,000 0 0			
....	Sterling Bill ... 48d.	621	6	6				519	726 10 0	1,726	10	0
July 23	£756 10 0				2	1	By Cash, ... sold	653	Sterling Bill .. 48d.	621	6	6
28	381 12 8	1,138	2	8	3	1	By Ditto, ... ditto	656	Rs. 4,200.000 at 59d.	1,032	10	0
....	Rs. 4,200.000 at 59d.	1,032	10	0	5	8	By Monteiro & Costa, remitted	657	Rs. 2,104.767 at 60d.	526	3	10
....	Rs. 2,104.767 at 60d.	526	3	10	5	A7	By Exchange Arbitrations ...	658	P. 5,000 ... at 48d.	1,000	0	0
....	P. 5,000 ... at 48d.	1,000	0	0	5	1	By Cash, ... due	536	876 5 10			
Aug. 10	....	973	6	8				524	1,325 11 4			
June 8	1,000 0 0							522	500 0 0	2,701	17	2
10	648 2 10	1,648	2	10	10	1	By Cash, ... due	528	374 18 8			
July 6	738 15 0							531	750 0 0			
10	281 12 6							525	438 15 0	1,563	13	8
23	500 0 0	1,520	7	6								
June 14	Sterling Bill .. 50d.	2,000	0	0	14	1	By Cash, ... sold	666	Rs. 4,290.000 at 59d.	1,054	12	6
....	Rs. 4,290.000 at 59d.	1,054	12	6	15	A7	By Exchange Arbitrations ..	667	P. 5,000 ... at 48d.	1,000	0	0
....	P. 5000 ... at 48d.	1,000	0	0	16	1	By Cash, ... due	537	639 3 7			
July 3	....	1,000	0	0				538	450 0 0			
Aug. 13	375 10 0							539	718 12 9			
28	500 0 0	875	10	0				540	385 1 4	2,192	17	8
July 18	....	461	6	9	22	11	By Macnamara & Sons, remitted	659	....	973	6	8
....	Sterling Bill at 32s. 6d.	505	10	6	22	6	By Muller & Schmidt, protested	547	....	500	0	0
....	Rs. 4,407.000 at 59d.	1,083	7	9	23	1	By Cash, ... due	520	1,000 0 0			
....	P. 5,000 ... at 48d.	1,000	0	0				521	635 10 0	1,635	10	0
July 13	....	1,278	13	6	23	1	By Cash, ... sold	672	Sterling Bill, at 32s. 6d.	505	10	6
Aug. 31	....	926	1	0	24	1	By Ditto ... ditto	673	Rs. 4,407.000 at 59d.	1,083	7	9
July 18	....	837	17	4	26	A7	By Exchange Arbitrations ...	674	P. 5,000 ... at 48d.	1,000	0	0
....	Sterling Bill . at 48d.	728	4	5	26	1	By Cash, ... due	523	....	1,500	0	0
					28	10	By Campbell & Douglas, remitted	676	....	926	14	0
					29	1	By Cash, ... due	529	....	1,000	0	0
					31	7	By Malatesta & Co. remitted .	678	Sterling Bill .. 48d.	728	4	5
					31		By Balance		....	27,117	19	7
		50,390	4	3						50,390	4	3
....	....	27,117	19	7								

2 L

Dr.   BILLS PAYABLE.   (1)

1817.			No.	£.	s.	d.	£.	s.	d.
May 2	1	To Cash . . . . due	154	500	0	0			
			155	432	15	6			
			156	928	10	0	1,861	5	6
7	1	To Cash . . . . due	138	265	11	8			
			179	483	5	4			
			147	230	0	0	978	17	0
10	1	To Cash, Discounted Monteiro & Costa's Draft	219	. . .	. .	. .	1,377	14	5
12	1	To Cash . . . . due	144	. . .	. .	. .	1,000	0	0
17	1	To Cash . . . . due	148	400	0	0			
			149	350	0	0			
			150	600	0	0	1,350	0	0
22	1	To Cash . . . . due	162	786	4	10			
			158	500	0	0			
			145	637	15	9	1,924	0	7
26	1	To Cash . . . . due	166	350	0	0			
			167	587	9	6	937	9	6
30	1	To Cash . . . . due	146	. . .	. .	. .	500	0	0
31		To Balance	. . .	. . .	. .	. .	19,860	19	7
							29,790	6	7

(1)   PER CONTRA.   *Cr.*

When accepted.	Folio.	Drawn by.	No.	Order of.	Date and Term.			When due.		£.	s.	d.
1817. April 30		By Balance	...	....	...	...	...	...	....	21,826	11	4
May 2	10	By Hargreaves & Sons	215	James Smith	London	May 1	3 m.	Aug. 4	....	516	8	0
3	6	By Kaminski & Co.	216	Wilson & Co.	Riga	Mar.25	30 d. s.	June 5	....	752	15	6
5	10	By Williams & Heywood	217	Order	London	May 5	3 m.	Aug. 8	500 0 0			
			218	Ditto	Ditto	....	....	....	238 12 6	738	12	6
10	8	By Monteiro & Costa	√219	Contanova&Co.	Rio Jan.	Feb. 27	60 d. s.	July 12	5,604. 284 at 59d.	1,377	14	5
2	11	By Macnamara & Sons	220	Henry Lamb,	London	May 10	3 m.	Aug.13	654 15 6			
			221	Ditto	Ditto	....	....	....	491 7 10	1,146	3	4
15	7	By Malatesta & Co.	222	Jordan & Sons,	Leghorn	Apr. 15	2 m.	June18	P.3,631.13.4 at48d.	726	6	8
19	10	By Hargreaves & Sons	223	Order	London	May 18	3 m.	Aug.21	....	267	7	4
21	6	By Le Maitre & Sons	224	Pierre Maret,	Bourdx.	May 5	2 m.	July 8	....	500	0	0
26	10	By Williams & Heywood	225	George Hase	London	24	3 m.	Aug.27	661 17 6			
			226	Ditto	Ditto	....	....	....	450 0 0	1,111	17	6
30	6	By Kaminski & Co.	227	Hall & Best ..	Riga	Apr. 20	30 d. s.	July 2	....	826	10	0
										29,790	6	7
May 31		By Balance	...	....	...	...	...	...	....	19,860	19	7

INDEX TO THE

LEDGER.

N	Folio	**T**	Folio
		Three per Cent. Funds 4	

O		**U**	

P		**V**	
Profit 1		Vanderloo & Co. . . . . ✓ 6	
Promiscuous Charges 3			
Peterson & Grenville 10			

Q		**W**	
		Williams & Heywood 10	
		Wanstead, Philip 11	
		Walsingham, Peter 12	
		Walker, David. 13	

R		**X**	
Rogers & Wilson 12			
Roberts & Smith (Insurance Account) 14			
Roberts & Smith (Subscription Account) . . . 14			

S		**Y & Z**	
Stock 1			
Sandoval & Co. (Sterling Account) 9			
Sandoval & Co. (Spanish Account) 9			
Stansfield & Nephew 11			
Simpson, Charles (Private Account) 15			

(1)   *Dr.*   STOCK.

1817.				£.	.	d.
May 31	15	To John Hamilton, Transfer		1,041	10	11
31	15	To Charles Simpson, Ditto		327	12	2
31		To Balance		57,497	6	7
				58,866	9	8

Dr.   PROFIT.

1817.						
May 31	1	To Loss, Transfer		412	3	1
31	1	To Stock		3,220	6	8
				3,632	9	9

Dr.   LOSS.

1817.						
May 28	A 4	To Joint Cotton per Britannia		132	2	1
31	2	To Guarantee		201	6	7
31	3	To Interest		78	14	5
				412	3	1

PER CONTRA. *Cr.* (1)

1817.				£.	s.	d.
April 30		By Balance..		55,415	5	1
May 31	3	By Interest		230	17	11
31	1	By Profit		3,220	6	8
				58,866	9	8
May 31		By Balance.......................................		57,497	6	7

PER CONTRA. *Cr.*

1817.						
May 10	8	By Monteiro & Costa		23	7	0
19	5	By Adventure per Diana..........................		1,955	12	4
30	A 5	By Joint Oil per Senegaglia		1	17	9
31	A 7	By Exchange Arbitrations		170	10	3
31	A 8	By Insurance....................................		195	8	1
31	2	By Commission		1,207	19	0
31	3	By Promiscuous Charges		77	15	4
				3,632	9	9

PER CONTRA. *Cr.*

1817.						
May 31	1	By Profit, Transfer		412	3	1
				412	3	1

(2)   *Dr.*   COMMISSION.

1817.				£	s.	d.
May 31	1	To Profit		1,207	19	0
				1,207	19	0

Dr.   GUARANTEE.

1817.						
May 23	11	To William Fleetwood's Assignees, Loss...................		391	17	6
31		To Balance on Debts and Risks Outstanding................		875	11	8
				1,267	9	2

PER CONTRA. *Cr.* (2)

1817.				£.	s.	d.
May 5	C 1	By Sugar per Roderic		101	0	4
5	C 2	By Woollens per Wellington		53	13	6
19	A 1	By Joint Mission per Trafalgar		390	4	3
19	A 3	By Joint Returns per Diana		496	11	5
21	A 9	By Partial Average per Catharine		11	18	4
28	C 3	By Tallow per Neptune		87	16	2
30	A 5	By Joint Oil per Senegaglia		66	15	0
				1,207	19	0

PER CONTRA. *Cr.*

1817.						
April 30		By Balance on Debts and Risks Outstanding		405	17	8
May 5	C 1	By Sugar per Roderic		77	6	10
5	C 2	By Woollens per Wellington		12	10	0
19	A 1	By Joint Mission per Trafalgar		90	0	0
19	A 3	By Joint Returns per Diana		367	0	11
28	C 3	By Tallow per Neptune		62	3	10
30	A 5	By Joint Oil per Senegaglia		51	3	4
31	1	By Loss		201	6	7
				1,267	9	2
May 31		By Balance on Debts and Risks Outstanding		875	11	8

2 M

(3)   *Dr.*   INTEREST.

1817.				£.	s.	d.
May 5	C 2	To Woollens per Wellington		27	9	0
15	1	To Cash, Rogers & Wilson		17	1	7
19	A 1	To Joint Mission per Trafalgar		234	0	7
31	1	To Stock, 1 month's Interest		230	17	11
				509	9	1

Dr.   PROMISCUOUS

1817.						
May 31	1	To Cash...		137	15	7
31	1	To Profit		77	15	4
				215	10	11

PER CONTRA. *Cr.* (3)

1817.				£.	s.	d
May 3		1	By Cash, Stansfield & Nephew	15	12	10
5	C 1		By Sugar per Roderic	51	19	1
10		1	By Cash, Peterson & Grenville	27	17	0
10		1	By Ditto, Bills Payable No 219	11	17	9
19	A 1		By Joint Mission per Trafalgar	3	16	6
19	A 3		By Joint Returns per Diana	240	1	7
28	C 3		By Tallow per Neptune	41	8	2
30	A 5		By Joint Oil per Senegaglia	34	6	2
31		15	By John Hamilton	3	0	11
31		15	By Charles Simpson	0	14	8
31		1	By Loss	78	14	5
				509	9	1

CHARGES. *Cr.*

1817.				£.	s.	d
May 5	C 1		By Sugar per Roderic	15	11	9
5	C 2		By Woollens per Wellington	11	17	2
19	A 1		By Joint Mission per Trafalgar	86	6	1
19	A 3		By Joint Returns per Diana	72	7	9
22		6	By Muller & Schmidt	5	10	6
28	C 3		By Tallow per Neptune	13	11	10
30	A 5		By Joint Oil per Senegaglia	10	5	10
				215	10	11

(4)   *Dr.*   DEBENTURES.

1817.				£.	s.	d.
April 30		To Balance		829	14	5
May 19	A 1	To Joint Mission per Trafalgar		458	16	9
				1,288	11	2
May 31		To Balance		899	12	0

Dr.   THREE PER CENT.

1817.			£.	s.	d.
April 30		To Balance............. £10,000 at 60	6,000	0	0

Dr.   ADVENTURE PER ROLLA

1817.			£.	s.	d.
April 30		To Balance	10,593	10	0

PER CONTRA. *Cr.* (4)

1817.				£.	s.	d.
May 21	1	By Cash, Drawback per Mary		388	19	2
31		By Balance		899	12	0
				1,288	11	2

FUNDS. *Cr.*

TO LIMA. *Cr.*

(5)   *Dr.*   ADVENTURE PER BRAHMIN

1817.				£.	s.	d.
April 30		To Balance..		17,127	17	3

Dr.   ADVENTURE PER DIANA

1817.						
April 30		To Balance, ... our ⅓ Proportion...............		5,712	14	2
May 19	1	To Profit.......................................		1,955	12	4
				7,668	6	6

Dr.   ADVENTURE PER TRAFALGAR

1817.						
May 19	A 1	To Joint Mission, ... our ⅓ Proportion...............		5,712	14	2

TO CALCUTTA.   *Cr.*   (5)

TO BUENOS AYRES.   *Cr.*

1817.				£.	s.	d.
May 19	A 3	By Joint Returns, ... Our ½ Proportion..............		7,668	6	6
				7,668	6	6

TO BUENOS AYRES.   *Cr.*

Drs.   LE MAITRE AND SONS,   (6)

1817.				£.	s.	d.
May 21	1	To Bills Payable		500	0	0
31		To Balance		1,215	18	8
				1,715	18	8

Drs.   VANDERLOO AND CO.

1817.			£	s	d
April 30	To Balance		3,632	6	8
May 31	To Balance		2,353	13	2

Drs.   MULLER AND SCHMIDT,

1817.				£	s	d
April 30		To Balance		2,150	14	6
May 22	1	To Bills Receivable, No. 547 protested		500	0	0
22	3	To Promiscuous Charges, Protest, &c.		5	10	6
				2,656	5	0
May 31		To Balance		1,150	14	6

Drs.   KAMINSKI AND CO.

1817.				£	s	d
May 3	1	To Bills Payable		752	15	6
30	1	To Ditto		826	10	0
31		To Balance		1,239	0	4
				2,818	5	10

(6)   BOURDEAUX.   *Crs.*

1817.			£	s.	d.
April 30	By Balance		1,715	18	8
May 31	By Balance		1,215	18	8

AMSTERDAM.   *Crs.*

1817.					
May 28	1	By Bills Receivable	1,278	13	6
31		By Balance	2,353	13	2
			3,632	6	8

HAMBURGH.   *Crs.*

1817.					
May 17	1	By Bills Receivable	1,000	0	0
23	1	By Ditto, our Re-draft	505	10	6
31		By Balance..	1,150	14	6
			2,656	5	0

RIGA.   *Crs.*

1817.					
April 30		By Balance	2,237	4	9
May 21	A 9	By Partial Average per Catharine	581	1	1
			2,818	5	10
May 31		By Balance..	1,239	0	4

Drs.		CASANOVA AND CO.		(7)

1817.			£.	s.	d.
April 30		To Balance	1,648	2	10

Drs.		MALATESTA AND CO. LEGHORN,

1817.			£.	s.	d.
April 30		To Balance	2,476	7	8
May 31	1	To Bills Receivable	728	4	5
			3,204	12	1

Drs.		MALATESTA AND CO. LEGHORN,

1817.			Pezze.	S.	D.	Exch.			
May 2	7	To Sterling Account, Transfer	9,275	5	10	48d.	1,855	1	2
15	1	To Bills Payable..........................	3,631	13	4	48d.	726	6	8
		P.	12,906	19	2	.....	2,581	7	10

(7)   **NAPLES.**   *Crs.*

1817.				£.	s.	d.
May 8	1	By Bills Receivable		1,648	2	10

STERLING ACCOUNT.   *Crs.*

1817.				£.	s.	d.
April 30	7	By Italian Account, Transfer............................		1,855	1	2
May 2	1	By Bills Receivable		621	6	6
30	A 5	By Joint Oil per Senegaglia, their ½ Proceeds...............		728	4	5
				3,204	12	1

ITALIAN ACCOUNT.   *Crs.*

1817.			Pezze.	S.	D.	Exch.			
April 30		By Balance ......·...................	9,275	5	10	48d.	1,855	1	2
May 7	A 5	By Joint Oil pr Senegaglia, our ½ Invoice ..	3,631	13	4	48d.	726	6	8
		P.	12,906	19	2	.....	2,581	7	10

Drs.   MONTEIRO AND COSTA, RIO JANEIRO,   (8)

1817.			£.	s.	d.
April 30		To Balance	482	6	6
May 5	C 2	To Woollens per Wellington	2,421	17	3
			2,904	3	9

Drs.   MONTEIRO AND COSTA, RIO JANEIRO,

1817.			Mil-	Reas.	Exch.			
May 5	8	To Sterling Account, Transfer	2,622	033	60	655	10	2
5	1	To Bills Receivable, our Remittance......	2,104	767	60	526	3	10
10	1	To Bills Payable, .. their Draft	5,604	284	59	1,377	14	5
10	1	To Profit .... on Exchange	....	....	....	23	7	0
		Rs.	10,331	084	....	2,582	15	5

(8) STERLING ACCOUNT. *Crs.*

			£.	s.	d.
1817.					
May 5	C 1	By Sugar per Roderic......................................	2,248	13	7
5	8	By Brazilian Account, Transfer...........................	655	10	2
			2,904	3	9

BRAZILIAN ACCOUNT. *Crs.*

			Mil-	Reas.	Exch.	£.	s.	d.
1817.								
April 30		By Balance.........................	4,726	800	60	1,181	14	0
May 8	A 4	By Joint Cotton per Britannia, our ½ Invoice	5,604	284	60	1,401	1	5
		Rs.	10,331	084	....	2,582	15	5

Drs.   SANDOVAL AND CO. BUENOS AYRES,   (9)

1817.				£.	s.	d.
May 19	A 1	To Joint Mission per Trafalgar, their ⅓ share		5,712	14	2
				5,712	14	2
May 31		To Balance		1,663	2	0

Drs.   SANDOVAL AND CO. BUENOS AYRES,

1817.			Dollars.	Rs.	Exch.			
May 1	A 2	To Joint Proceeds ex Diana	45,754	0	50d.	9,532	1	8
12	A 2	To ....Ditto.....Ditto	55,557	0	50d.	11,574	7	6
		Ds.	101,311	0	....	21,106	9	2

(9)   STERLING ACCOUNT.   *Crs.*

1817.			£.	s.	d.
April 30		By Balance	2,154	13	2
May 28	C 3	By Tallow per Neptune	1,894	19	0
31		By Balance	1,663	2	0
			5,712	14	2

SPANISH ACCOUNT.   *Crs.*

1817.			Dollars.	Rs.	Exch.			
May 1	A 2	By Joint Proceeds ex Diana ... Bill......	9,696	0	50d.	2,020	0	0
1	A 2	By ....Ditto......Ditto....Dollars....	16,539	2	50d.	3,445	13	6
12	A 2	By ....Ditto......Ditto....Hides.....	41,305	3	50d.	8,605	5	9
12	A 2	By ....Ditto......Ditto....their ⅓ share	33,770	3	50d.	7,035	9	11
		Ds.	101,311	0	....	21,106	9	2

Drs.   PETERSON AND GRENVILLE,   (10)

1817.				£.	s.	d.
May 10	1	To Cash		1,392	8	6

Drs.   CAMPBELL AND DOUGLAS,

1817.						
May 28	1	To Bills Receivable		926	14	0
31		To Balance		1,847	10	0
				2,774	4	0

Drs.   HARGREAVES AND SONS,

1817.						
May 2	1	To Bills Payable		516	8	0
19	1	To Ditto		267	7	4
31		To Balance		45?	5	6
				1,238	0	10

Drs.   WILLIAMS AND HEYWOOD,

1817.						
May 5	1	To Bills Payable		738	1?	6
26	1	To Ditto		1,111	17	6
31		To Balance		3,670	10	0
				5,521	0	0

(10)   LONDON.   *Crs.*

1817.			£.	s.	d.
April 30		By Balance	1,392	8	6

LONDON.   *Crs.*

1817.					
April 30		By Balance	926	14	0
May 14	A 1	By Joint Mission per Trafalgar	1,847	10	0
			2,774	4	0
May 31		By Balance	1,847	10	0

LONDON   *Crs.*

1817.					
April 30		By Balance	783	15	4
May 3	C 2	By Woollens per Wellington	454	5	6
			1,238	0	10
May 31		By Balance	454	5	6

LONDON.   *Crs.*

1817.					
April 30		By Balance	1,850	10	0
May 2	C 2	By Woollens per Wellington	490	10	0
7	A 1	By Joint Mission per Trafalgar	3,180	0	0
			5,521	0	0
May 31		By Balance	3,670	10	0

(11)   *Drs.*   MACNAMARA AND SONS,

1817.				£.	s.	d.
May 12	1	To Bills Payable		1,146	3	4
22	1	To Bills Receivable....................................		973	6	8
31		To Balance		8,622	7	8
				10,741	17	8

Drs.   STANSFIELD AND NEPHEW,

1817.						
May 3	1	To Cash		1,251	5	0
31		To Balance		4,145	12	6
				5,396	17	6

Drs.   WILLIAM FLEETWOOD'S ASSIGNEES,

1817.						
April 30		To Balance		587	16	3
				587	16	3

Dr.   PHILIP WANSTEAD,

1817.						
April 30		To Balance		2,826	9	10
May 1	C 1	To Sugar per Roderic..................................		1,480	4	7
29	A 5	To Joint Oil per Senegaglia		885	10	11
				5,192	5	4
May 31		To Balance		3,390	1	4

LONDON. *Crs.* (11)

1817.				£.	s.	d.
April 30		By Balance		2,516	17	8
May 17	A 1	By Joint Mission per Trafalgar		6,700	0	0
24	C 4	By Linens for Sandoval & Co.		1,525	0	0
				10,741	17	8
May 31		By Balance		8,622	7	8

LONDON. *Crs.*

1817.						
May 3	C 2	By Woollens per Wellington		1,251	5	0
10	A 1	By Joint Mission per Trafalgar		4,145	12	6
				5,396	17	6
May 31		By Balance		4,145	12	6

LONDON. *Crs.*

1817.						
May 23	1	By Cash, final Dividend of 6s. 8d. per £		195	18	9
23	2	By Guarantee, Loss		391	17	6
				587	16	3

LONDON. *Cr.*

1817.						
May 19	1	By Bills Receivable		875	10	0
28	1	By Ditto		926	14	0
31		By Balance		3,390	1	4
				5,192	5	4

(12)   *Drs.*   THOMAS JACKSON AND SON,

1817.				£.	s.	d.
April 30			To Balance	1,581	5	0
May 3	C 1		To Sugar per Roderic...............................	737	13	7
28	A 5		To Joint Oil per Senegaglia	545	12	10
				2,864	11	5
May 31			To Balance	2,403	4	8

Dr.   PETER WALSINGHAM,

1817.						
April 30			To Balance	973	6	8
May 17	A 3		To Joint Returns per Diana	4,250	4	0
24	C 3		To Tallow per Neptune	784	9	7
				6,008	0	3
May 31			To Balance	5,034	13	7

Drs.   ROGERS AND WILSON,

1817.						
April 30			To Balance	2,504	11	2

Drs.   DAVID HUNTER AND CO.

1817.						
April 30			To Balance	3,065	12	7
May 5	C 1		To Sugar per Roderic...	899	5	0
30	A 5		To Joint Oil per Senegaglia	627	4	3
				4,592	1	10
May 31			To Balance	2,233	17	0

LONDON.   *Crs.*   (12)

1817.				£.	s.	d.
May 21	1	By Bills Receivable		461	6	9
31		By Balance		2,403	4	8
				2,864	11	5

LONDON.   *Cr.*

1817.						
May 7	1	By Bills Receivable		973	6	8
31		By Balance		5,034	13	7
				6,008	0	3

LONDON.   *Crs.*

1817.						
May 3	1	By Bills Receivable......................................		1,138	2	8
15	1	By Cash		1,366	8	6
				2,504	11	2

LONDON.   *Crs.*

1817.						
May 10	1	By Bills Receivable......................................		1,520	7	6
29	1	By Ditto		837	17	4
31		By Balance		2,233	17	0
				4,592	1	10

(13)   *Drs.*   HAMMOND AND MORLEY,

1817.				£.	s.	d.
May 17	A.3	To Joint Returns per Diana		4,289	9	1
22	C 3	To Tallow per Neptune		1,153	6	2
				5,442	15	3
May 31		To Balance		5,442	15	3

Drs.   JAMES DONALD AND SONS,

1817.						
May 19	A 3	To Joint Returns per Diana		5,437	12	7
26	C 3	To Tallow per Neptune		546	14	0
				5,984	6	7
May 31		To Balance		5,984	6	7

Dr.   DAVID WALKER,

1817.						
May 19	A 1	To Joint Mission per Trafalgar, his $\frac{1}{3}$ share		5,712	14	2
20	1	To Cash		1,955	12	4
				7,668	6	6

Drs.   JAMES HORNER AND SON,

1817.						
May 28	A 4	To Joint Cotton per Britannia, our $\frac{1}{2}$ share		1,268	19	4

LONDON. *Crs.* (13)

1817.			£.	s.	d.
May 31	By Balance		5,442	15	3

LONDON. *Crs.*

1817.					
May 31	By Balance		5,984	6	7

LONDON. *Cr.*

1817.					
May 19	A 3	By Joint Returns per Diana, his ½ share	7,668	6	6

LONDON. *Crs.*

1817.					
May 29	1	By Cash	1,268	19	4

(14)   *Drs.*   ROBERTS AND SMITH, BROKERS, LONDON.

1817.				£.	s.	d.
May 21	A 9	To Partial Average per Catharine to Riga		592	19	5
31		To Balance		4,810	1	7
				5,403	1	0

Drs.   ROBERTS AND SMITH, BROKERS, LONDON.

1817.			£.	s.	d.
April 30		To Balance	587	12	6
May 2	A 8	To Insurance per Ellen to Smyrna, .. £400 at 4 per Cent. ...	16	0	0
7	A 8	To Ditto.... per George to Lima, ... 250 at 8 Ditto......	20	0	0
12	A 8	To Ditto.... per Sarah from Lisbon . 400 at 2 Ditto......	8	0	0
19	A 8	To Ditto.... per Alexander to Riga .. 500 at 3 Ditto......	15	0	0
24	A 8	To Ditto.... per Brahmin from Calcutta 300 at 10 Ditto......	30	0	0
29	A 8	To Ditto.... per Anne to Bahia ..... 350 at 3 Ditto......	10	10	0
			687	2	6
May 31		To Balance	359	2	0

ACCOUNT OF THEIR INSURANCES.   *Crs.*   (14)

1817.			£.	s	d.
April 30		By Balance	3,526	15	0
May 1	Λ 3	By Joint Returns per Diana from Buenos Ayres, £ 14,000 at 4 Gᶜ	623	0	0
3	C 3	By Tallow per Neptune . . . from Ditto. . . . . . 2,000 at 4	89	0	0
5	C 2	By Woollens per Wellington to Rio de Janeiro 2,000 at 3	68	0	0
7	A 5	By Joint Oil per Senegaglia . . . . 1,800 at 2	42	6	0
19	A 1	By Joint Mission per Trafalgar to Buenos Ayres 17,000 at 3	578	0	0
30	A 6	By Joint Coffee per Regent . . . . 14,000 at 3	476	0	0
			5,403	1	0
May 31		By Balance	4,810	1	7

ACCOUNT OF OUR SUBSCRIPTIONS.   *Crs.*

1817.					
May 10	A 8	By Insurance, Total Loss per James	250	0	0
16	A 9	By Partial Average per Nancy to Buenos Ayres.	76	0	6
24	A 8	By Insurance, Return Premium per Columbus	2	0	0
31		By Balance	359	2	0
			687	2	6

(15)   *Dr.*   JOHN HAMILTON,

1817.				£.	s.	d.
May 1	1	To Cash		500	0	0
12	1	To Ditto, Randolph & Co.		238	10	0
22	1	To Ditto		300	0	0
31	3	To Interest		3	0	11
				1,041	10	11

Dr.   CHARLES SIMPSON,

1817.						
May 5	1	To Cash, George Smith		176	17	6
26	1	To Ditto		150	0	0
31	3	To Interest		0	14	8
				327	12	2

PRIVATE ACCOUNT.   *Cr.*   (15)

				£.	s.	d.
1817. May 31	1	By Stock		1,041	10	11
				1,041	10	11

PRIVATE ACCOUNT.   *Cr.*

1817. May 31	1	By Stock		327	12	2
				327	12	2

(1)   *Dr.*   THE JOINT ESTATE OF JOHN HAMILTON

		30th April 1817.	£.	s.	d.
B P	1	To Bills Payable, Amount Outstanding	21,826	11	4
		£. s. d.			
A	8	To Insurance, ... Premiums on Risks Pending 1,346 11 3			
L	2	To Guarantee, ... Del Credere on Debts Ditto 405 17 8	1,752	8	11
L	6	To Le Maitre & Sons, Bourdeaux, due to them 1,715 18 8			
L	6	To Kaminski & Co. Riga, ... ditto ditto.......... 2,237 4 9			
L	7	To Malatesta & Co. Leghorn, Italian Account.......... 1,855 1 2			
L	8	To Monteiro & Costa, Rio Janeiro, Brazilian Account ... 1,181 14 0			
L	9	To Sandoval & Co. Buenos Ayres, Sterling Ditto....... 2,154 13 2			
L	10	To Peterson & Grenville, London, due to them........ 1,392 8 6			
L	10	To Campbell & Douglas, Ditto..... ditto........... 926 14 0			
L	10	To Hargreaves & Sons, ... Ditto..... ditto........... 783 15 4			
L	10	To Williams & Heywood, Ditto..... ditto............ 1,850 10 0			
L	11	To Macnamara & Sons,... Ditto..... ditto........... 2,516 17 8			
L	14	To Roberts & Smith, Account Insurances, London 3,526 15 0	20,141	12	3
			43,720	12	6
L	1	To Stock, our Net Capital	55,415	5	1
		£	99,135	17	7

AND CHARLES SIMPSON, LONDON. *Cr.* (1)

		30th April 1817.	£.	s.	d.
			£.	*s.*	*d.*			
C	1	By Cash,............Balance in hand............. 6,637 5 9			
B R	1	By Bills Receivable..... Ditto... ditto.............. ... 29,178 7 6			
L	4	By Debentures .... Ditto... ditto............... 829 14 5			
L	4	By Three per Cent. Funds 6,000 0 0	42,645	7	8
C	1	By Sugar per Roderic, Charges................ 539 16 4			
L	4	By Adventure per Rolla to Lima 10,593 10 0			
L	5	By Ditto..... per Brahmin to Calcutta 17,127 17 3			
L	5	By Ditto..... per Diana to Buenos Ayres 5,712 14 2	33,973	17	9
L	6	By Vanderloo & Co. Amsterdam, due from them 3,632 6 8			
L	6	By Muller & Schmidt, Hambro'.. ditto.............. 2,150 14 6			
L	7	By Casanova & Co. Naples ..... ditto.............. 1,648 2 10			
L	7	By Malatesta & Co. Leghorn, ... Sterling Account...... 2,476 7 8			
L	8	By Monteiro & Costa, Rio de Janeiro, Ditto.......... 482 6 6			
L	11	By William Fleetwood's Assignees, London 587 16 3			
L	11	By Philip Wanstead, ... London, due from him 2,826 9 10			
L	12	By Thomas Jackson & Son, Ditto.... ditto.......... 1,581 5 0			
L	12	By Peter Walsingham, ... Ditto.... ditto......... 973 6 8			
L	12	By Rogers & Wilson,...... Ditto.... ditto......... 2,504 11 2			
L	12	By David Hunter & Co. .... Ditto.... ditto.......... 3,065 12 7			
L	14	By Roberts & Smith, Account Subscriptions 587 12 6	22,516	12	2
		£	99,135	17	7

(2)   *Dr.*   THE JOINT ESTATE OF JOHN HAMILTON

		31st May 1817.	£.	s.	d.
B P	1	To Bills Payable,........ Amount outstanding	19,860	19	7
			£. s. d.		
A	8	To Insurance, ... Premiums on Risks Pending 1,135 4 2			
L	2	To Guarantee,..... Del Credere on Debts Ditto 875 11 8	2,010	15	10
L	6	To Le Maitre & Sons, ... Bourdeaux.. due to them 1,215 18 8			
L	6	To Kaminski & Co. .... Riga......... ditto.... 1,239 0 4			
L	10	To Campbell & Douglas, ... London. ditto.... 1,847 10 0			
L	10	To Hargreaves & Sons, ... Ditto... ditto.... 454 5 6			
L	10	To Williams & Heywood, ... Ditto... ditto.... 3,670 10 0			
L	11	To Macnamara & Sons, ... Ditto...ditto.... 8,622 7 8			
L	11	To Stansfield & Nephew, ... Ditto...Ditto.... 4,145 12 6			
L	14	To Roberts & Smith (Acct Insurances) Ditto...ditto.... 4,810 1 7	26,005	6	3
			47,877	1	8
L	1	To Stock, our Net Capital.................................	57,497	6	7
		£	105,374	8	3

AND CHARLES SIMPSON, LONDON.   *Cr.*   (2)

		31st May 1817.	£.	s.	d.

			£.	s.	d.	£.	s.	d.
C	1	By Cash,............Balance in hand.............	5,872	5	2			
B R	1	By Bills Receivable, ...Ditto...ditto..............	27,117	19	7			
L	4	By Debentures,........Ditto...ditto..............	899	12	0			
L	4	By Three per Cent. Funds	6,000	0	0	39,889	16	9
C	4	By Linens for Sandoval & Co. Buenos Ayres...........	1,525	0	0			
A	6	By Joint Coffee per Regent, Premiums	510	0	0			
L	4	By Adventure per Rolla to Lima	10,593	10	0			
L	5	By Ditto.....per Brahmin to Calcutta	17,127	17	3			
L	5	By Ditto. ....per Trafalgar to Buenos Ayres...........	5,712	14	2	35,469	1	5
L	6	By Vanderloo & Co. Amsterdam, ...due from them...	2,353	13	2			
L	6	By Muller & Schmidt, Hambro',.......ditto........	1,150	14	6			
L	9	By Sandoval & Co. Buenos Ayres,.......ditto........	1,663	2	0			
L	11	By Philip Wanstead, ... London,....ditto........	3,390	1	4			
L	12	By Thomas Jackson & Son,..Ditto......ditto........	2,403	4	8			
L	12	By Peter Walsingham, ...Ditto......ditto........	5,034	13	7			
L	12	By David Hunter & Co. ....Ditto......ditto........	2,233	17	0			
L	13	By Hammond & Morley, ...Ditto......ditto........	5,442	15	3			
L	13	By James Donald & Sons,...Ditto. .....ditto........	5,984	6	7			
L	14	By Roberts & Smith (Account Subscriptions).........	359	2	0	30,015	10	1
					£	105,374	8	3

INDEX TO THE PARTNERSHIP LEDGER.

Dr.   JOINT CAPITAL.   (1)

1817.				£.	s.	d.
April 30		To Balance		55,415	5	1
May 31	1	To Interest		230	17	11
31	1	To Profit		3,220	6	8
				58,866	9	8
May 31		To Balance		57,497	6	7

Dr.   PROFIT.

1817.						
May 31	2	To John Hamilton, his Moiety		1,610	3	4
31	2	To Charles Simpson, Ditto		1,610	3	4
				3,220	6	8

Dr.   INTEREST.

1817						
May 31	2	To John Hamilton		127	5	7
31	2	To Charles Simpson		103	12	4
				230	17	11

(1)   PER CONTRA.   *Cr.*

1817.				£.	s.	d.
May 31	2	By John Hamilton, withdrawn		1,041	10	11
31	2	By Charles Simpson, ditto		327	12	2
31		By Balance		57,497	6	7
				58,866	9	8

PER CONTRA.   *Cr.*

1817.						
May 31	1	By Joint Capital		3,220	6	8
				3,220	6	8

PER CONTRA.   *Cr.*

1817.						
May 31	1	By Joint Capital		230	17	11
				230	17	11

Dr.   JOHN HAMILTON.   (2)

1817.				£.	s.	d.
May 31	1	To Joint Capital, withdrawn		1,041	10	11
31		To Balance		31,243	9	7
				32,285	0	6

Dr.   CHARLES SIMPSON.

1817.						
May 31	1	To Joint Capital, withdrawn		327	12	2
31		To Balance		26,253	17	0
				26,581	9	2

(2) PER CONTRA. *Cr.*

1817.			£.	s.	d.
April 30		By Balance	30,547	11	7
May 31	1	By Interest	127	5	7
31	1	By Profit	1,610	3	4
			32,285	0	6
May 31		By Balance	31,243	9	7

PER CONTRA. *Cr.*

1817.					
April 30		By Balance	24,867	13	6
May 31	1	By Interest	103	12	4
31	1	By Profit	1,610	3	4
			26,581	9	2
May 31		By Balance	26,253	17	0

SET V.

BANKERS' BOOKS.

CONCERN . . . . A PARTNERSHIP.

CAPITAL . . . . INVARIABLE.

BUSINESS . . . . CONTINUED.

RESULT . . . . PROFITABLE.

OBSERVATIONS.

BANKING is the most simple of all businesses in regard to its Books; for, having no Merchandise Account, nor any account analogous to it, its Day Books consist of the Money Accounts alone, namely, the Cash, the Bills Receivable, and the Bills Payable, or London Bankers' Acceptances. In the Deposite Accounts, money is borrowed by the Bank at 4 per cent Interest. In the Loan Accounts, money is lent by the Bank on Securities at 5 per cent Interest. In the Exchange Accounts, Interest is reckoned on both sides at 5 per cent, with a charge by the Bank for Commission and Stamps.

Besides these Accounts, there are the promiscuous transactions for which no personal accounts are opened, and which may be classed under the general title of Discounts; for, either the Banker discounts the customer's Bill, or the customer discounts the Banker's. In these transactions, it is not supposed necessary to state the several parts of the profit accruing from Interest, from Stamps, and from Commission: the general result alone is shewn in the Account of Promiscuous Discounts. But if the particulars be desirable, they may easily be obtained by a Memorandum-Book kept for the purpose. In the other Accounts, these branches of the profits are distinctly stated and collected.

Interest, however, is the great source of the Provincial Banker's emolument. The circulation of Notes on Demand creates a capital which, invested in beneficial securities, rains a golden shower on the Bank, without endangering the public Creditor.. And as Interest is here the great channel of profit, so it engrosses a principal share of the Accounts. In the Personal Accounts, Interest columns are ruled on the left of the principal column; and at every entry the Interest is calculated to the next half yearly period of settlement, and immediately recorded. The two general periods for the Balance of Interest, are the 30th of June and the 31st of December. This simultaneous entry of the Interest with the Principal, prevents the enormous accumulated labour of a general set of Interest Accounts Current for the entire six months. At the periods mentioned, the Balance of Interest is struck through all the Accounts, and carried to the principal column, as well as the charges for Stamps and Commission.

In the Customers' Books (which are merely open Accounts Current) the Interest is entered only in its half-yearly Balance, along with the other charges.

The business being given for the month of June, the periodical close of the Interest Accounts, and the result of the whole half-year, are exhibited, by stating against the Balances on the 31st of May the Interests accrued during the preceding five months.

The mark [✓] against the Numbers of the Bills Receivable denotes the Bills paid away. By this means the specific Bills which compose the Balance, may be seen without reference to the Portfolio, the unmarked Bills being those that remain on hand.

The Book of Notes on Demand requires no exemplification, being a mere Memorandum-Book, with columns for the Numbers, Dates, Values, Signatures, and Countersigns of the Notes issued. When the Notes are finally withdrawn, the respective Numbers are marked as paid and annulled.

In consequence of the numerous entries to Promiscuous Discounts and the London Bankers' Accounts, it may promote convenience to separate them from the Ledger, and record each of them in a distinct Book.

The Proprietors of this Bank are, Peter Smith, John Brown, Charles Langdon, and George Williams, of whom the first has a third share, the last a sixth, and the two others each a fourth. The conditions of the Partnership are, to maintain an invariable capital of £30,000, and to distribute the result of the business in the ratio of the shares.

It has already been explained in the Ninth Chapter, that an invariable Stock requires a particular process in the equilibration of the Accounts. When Stock is variable, the results of the Profit, Loss, and Private Accounts, are transferred to it;

but, as an invariable Stock excludes all fluctuation, so it admits no entries in its Account after the first record of the capital.

The result of the Profit Account is, therefore, first carried down as its own Balance, and then transferred in shares to the respective Private Accounts of the Partners. Their Accounts of shares in the capital remain, like the Joint Stock, invariable in the Partnership Ledger; whilst their Private Accounts with the Bank resemble the other Personal Accounts, being equally subject to Interest, and either Debtors or Creditors, according as they are borrowers or depositors.

When the capital of a Bank is variable, the mode of keeping the Stock Account, and appropriating the shares of Profit, may be seen in the preceding Set of Books.

In the present case of invariable property, it may be objected to the Partnership Ledger, that, as it receives no entries after the first record of the Joint Capital and the shares, it may be dispensed with altogether, and its purpose be equally accomplished by a Memorandum in the first blank page of the Ledger. To this objection there are two answers:

Firstly, A subject so important as the Shares of Capital ought to be recorded in regular, systematic Accounts, and not be committed to the care of a mere Memorandum.

Secondly, Accounts ought to be adapted, not merely to present purposes, but also to future contingencies. So long as there is no alteration either in the Capital, in the Shares, or in the Proprietors, a Memorandum may serve the purpose of recording the Shares: but it must be observed, that the permanency of the Capital, &c. relates to the present system of the business, and not to absolute exclusion of change; the Capital may hereafter be extended or reduced, present Partners may withdraw, new ones may accede, and correspondent alterations take place in the Shares. To record transactions of this description, the Partnership Ledger will be found indispensable.

ACCOUNT WITH THE LONDON BANKER.

When the Provincial Banker keeps with his London Banker only one Account, debited with remittances, &c. and credited with drafts, &c. this Account will shew the general Balance between them, and answer the internal purposes of system; but it is totally inadequate to the important external object of checking the London Banker's Accounts Current. For these Accounts Current consisting solely of Cash receipts and disburses, they present no basis of comparison with an Account composed chiefly of Bills Receivable and Payable falling due in endless diversity of combinations and dates. Nor will a mere Calendar of due Bills and Acceptances remedy this inadequacy : the actual encashments will ever vary from the calculations, as well from errors of date in the register, as from postponements in the payment of due Remittances, and the presentation of due Acceptances. In the latter especially, the irregularities and variations are of frequent occurrence; and it must be observed, that the Calendar is not merely inefficient from its inability to check the individual entries, but also from its having no jurisdiction on the opening Balance of the Account Current, nor on the difference existing in that Balance, as produced by the combination of differences in the preceding Account.

Hence the Provincial Banker who keeps only one general Account with the London Banker, may continue from year to year his imperfect examinations of Accounts Current, without ever ascertaining the conformity of their Books; and when at length the connexion is closed, there may become apparent an important difference which may have existed or accumulated undiscovered during a long series of years. The disadvantage will in this case fall to the Country Banker; for the London Banker is defended by his regular Accounts Current, the Balances of which have never been disavowed, because they could never be examined. The following arrangement would remove this inconvenience.

Instead of one general Account, let the Provincial Banker keep with his London Banker three specific Accounts, which may be briefly distinguished by the letters A, B, C; and to each of which, in extensive concerns, a separate Book may be allotted.

> A, is the Account of the London Banker's Acceptances;
> B, the Account of the Bills remitted to him;
> C, the Cash Account.

The Acceptance Account is credited for the drafts, and debited to the Cash Account for the due amounts registered in the Calendar. The Bill Account is debited for the remittances, and credited by the Cash Account for the due amounts similarly registered. The Cash Account is, therefore, chiefly composed of transfers from the other Accounts, but it also receives all immediate cash transactions.

Let each of these Accounts be ruled with double columns for money, and in the internal columns transcribe the London Banker's Account Current. These columns being regularly equilibrated, and their Balances carried forwards, whatever differences occur between the London and Provincial Balances in the specific Accounts, the combination of those Balances will always shew conformity in the general state of the Account. For though the London Banker transmits only the Cash Account, his Acceptance and Bill Accounts may be regularly and correctly formed. The Debit entries of the Cash supply the Credit entries of the Bills; and the Debit entries of the latter agree with the Provincial, being vouched by the London acknowledgments of Remittances.

In like manner, the Credit entries of the Cash supply the Debit entries of the Acceptances, the Credit entries of which will agree with the Provincial.

In the following Ledger is exemplified this combined record of the London and Provincial Accounts; and in the Inventory the disagreeing Balances of Acceptances, Bills, and Cash, are shewn to be reconciled by the conformity of the General Balances.

It must, however, be observed, that this general correspondence is necessarily produced by the construction of the Accounts in a series of transfers: and, therefore, it does not prove the correctness of the London Banker's Account Current. It is merely an arrangement preparatory to the proof itself, which is obtained by the following examinations:

Firstly, The Acceptances paid must be checked by the original Drafts returned as vouchers of the payments. This process will ascertain the correctness of the London Balance of Acceptances.

Secondly, The London Balance of Bills must be checked by the list of Bills in hand, which the London Banker ought always to transmit with his Account Current.

Thirdly, The correctness of the London Balances of Acceptances and Bills clearly proves the correctness of the London Balance of Cash. For the general result of the three London Balances is always accurate, by its correspondence with the result of the three Provincial Balances; so that we have a correct general Balance, composed of three particular Balances, A, B, C; whereof the first, A, and second, B, being proved correct, the third, C, must also be correct; for, if it were otherwise, it would necessarily destroy that accuracy of the general Balance, which has in the first instance been established.

We may hence deduce the utility of constructing the London Banker's Acceptance and Bill Accounts; for, though it is the Cash Account alone that he transmits, yet its Balance cannot be immediately checked; and its correctness can be ascertained solely by inference from the examination of the Balances of Acceptances and Bills.

This plan of the London Banker's Account was suggested by an ingenious friend, whose unassuming merit would not permit a more explicit acknowledgment.

SET V.

THE BOOKS

OF

PETER SMITH, JOHN BROWN, CHARLES LANGDON,

AND GEORGE WILLIAMS,

BANKERS, LEEDS.

---

1. CASH.
2. BILLS RECEIVABLE.
3. BILLS PAYABLE.
4. LEDGER.
5. INVENTORY.
6. PARTNERSHIP LEDGER.

Dr. CASH. (1)

1817.		RECEIPTS.	£.	s.	d.
May 31		To Balance	12,050	7	11
June 2	4	To Promiscuous Discounts	256	3	3
3	4	To Ditto...... Ditto	173	15	8
3	10	To Grandison, Neville, & Co. Bank of England Notes	5,000	0	0
4	4	To Promiscuous Discounts	121	15	8
5	17	To Henry Bath	500	0	0
5	4	To Promiscuous Discounts	270	12	5
6	4	To Ditto...... Ditto	186	12	0
7	4	To Ditto...... Ditto	91	7	10
9	4	To Ditto...... Ditto	75	12	8
10	4	To Ditto...... Ditto	83	2	10
11	18	To Ellen Wilton	25	0	0
11	4	To Promiscuous Discounts	90	15	4
12	4	To Ditto...... Ditto	65	0	0
13	4	To Ditto...... Ditto	87	12	8
14	4	To Ditto...... Ditto	99	11	6
16	4	To Ditto...... Ditto	137	11	7
17	6	To Notes on Demand, Re-issued, 4,000 of £1 .... £4,000 300 of 2 .... 600 80 of 5 400	5,000	0	0
18	5	To Promiscuous Discounts	234	15	8
		Carried forward .... £	24,549	17	0

(1)   PER CONTRA.   *Cr.*

		PAYMENTS.	£.	s.	d.
1817.					
June 2	16	By Samuel Winsford & Co. Notes	200	0	0
2	4	By Promiscuous Discounts	73	1	6
2	21	By Charles Langdon	50	0	0
3	13	By Billington & Co. Notes	300	0	0
3	4	By Promiscuous Discounts	134	8	3
4	17	By Sir Charles Slade, his Check to J. Wilton	74	18	0
4	14	By John Evergreen, Check to Charles Smith	32	10	0
5	11	By Simpson & White, Notes	250	0	0
5	4	By Promiscuous Discounts	140	19	8
5	21	By George Williams	40	0	0
6	4	By Promiscuous Discounts	49	10	0
6	12	By Johnson & Sons, Notes	200	0	0

7	6	By Notes on Demand, withdrawn 4,000 of £1 . . . . £4,000
		                   300 of 2 600
		                    80 of 5 400
			5,000	0	0

7	4	By Promiscuous Discounts	345	17	6
7	20	By Peter Smith	100	0	0
7	16	By Samuel Winsford & Co. Check to John Holt	26	14	3
9	15	By Hunt & Milner, Notes	150	0	0
9	4	By Promiscuous Discounts	70	1	4
9	12	By Johnson & Sons, Check to T. Wallis	35	15	0
10	14	By John Evergreen, Notes	200	0	0
10	4	By Promiscuous Discounts	100	0	0
11	20	By John Brown	50	0	0
11	4	By Promiscuous Discounts	179	16	10
11	14	By John Evergreen, Check to Hartley & Co.	41	3	8
12	4	By Promiscuous Discounts	155	8	8
12	11	By Simpson & White, Notes	250	0	0
13	4	By Promiscuous Discounts	197	12	6
13	12	By Johnson & Sons, Check to B. Saunders	38	10	0
14	4	By Promiscuous Discounts	77	0	4
14	13	By Billington & Co. Notes	200	0	0
14	15	By Hunt & Milner, Check to Robert Bland	19	16	6
16	15	By Hunt & Milner, Notes	150	0	0
16	4	By Promiscuous Discounts	267	18	6
16	21	By George Williams	20	0	0
17	18	By Mrs. Risingham	25	0	0
17	5	By Promiscuous Discounts	160	4	10
18	17	By Sir Charles Slade, Check to R. Townsend	54	13	6
18	16	By Samuel Winsford & Co. Check to T. Grant	21	11	0
		Carried forward . . . . £	9,482	11	10

Dr.   CASH.   (2)

1817.			RECEIPTS.	Brought forward	£.	s.	d.
					24,549	17	0
June 19	5		To Promiscuous Discounts		63	10	10
20	5		To Ditto....... Ditto		81	12	6
21	5		To Ditto....... Ditto		58	13	9
23	5		To Ditto....... Ditto		228	10	5
24	5		To Ditto....... Ditto		77	11	7
25	5		To Ditto....... Ditto		139	12	6
26	6		To Notes on Demand, Issued .. 3,000 of 1 £............£3,000				
			200 of 2 400				
			20 of 5 100				
					3,500	0	0
27	5		To Promiscuous Discounts		58	7	6
28	5		To Ditto....... Ditto		180	13	5
29	17		To James Arnold's Assignees, a final Dividend of 6s. 8d. on £631. 17. 6		210	12	6
					29,149	2	0
June 30			To Balance		11,070	16	2

(2)   PER CONTRA.   *Cr.*

		PAYMENTS. Brought forward	£. 9,482	s. 11	d. 10
1817.					
June 19	11	By Simpson & White, Notes	250	0	0
19	5	By Promiscuous Discounts	244	17	6
20	21	By Charles Langdon	30	0	0
20	12	By Johnson & Sons, Notes	200	0	0
21	5	By Promiscuous Discounts	99	4	0
21	14	By John Evergreen, Check to S. Milne	47	10	0
23	16	By Samuel Winsford & Co. Notes	300	0	0
23	5	By Promiscuous Discounts	168	11	5
24	5	By Ditto...... Ditto	108	17	10
24	14	By John Evergreen, Notes	200	0	0
25	18	By Mrs. Risingham	20	0	0
25	10	By Grandison, Neville, & Co. Bank of England Notes	5,000	0	0
25	5	By Promiscuous Discounts	238	10	0
26	11	By Simpson & White, Notes	150	0	0
26	5	By Promiscuous Discounts	98	1	6
26	17	By Sir Charles Slade, Check to Harris & Son	127	15	0
27	13	By Billington & Co. Notes	200	0	0
27	17	By Henry Bath, Check to Tomlinson & Co.	83	2	9
27	5	By Promiscuous Discounts	234	12	6
28	18	By William Trueman	50	0	0
28	5	By Promiscuous Discounts	147	3	10
29	5	By Ditto...... Ditto	322	14	4
30	3	By Stamps this month	107	12	6
30	3	By Bank Expenses, Postages this month	14	10	4
30	22	By Charles Wilfred, .. Balance of Salary	20	0	0
30	22	By John Simpson,.... Ditto .... Ditto	15	0	0
30	22	By George Riley, ... Ditto .... Ditto	10	0	0
30	22	By John Wilkes, ... Ditto .... Ditto	5	0	0
30	22	By James Thompson, Ditto .... Ditto	5	0	0
30	3	By Bank Expenses, Half Year's Rent of Bank	52	10	0
30	3	By .... Ditto..... Worthington & Co. Engravers	25	13	6
30	3	By .... Ditto..... John Nolan, Stationer	19	7	0
30		By Balance	11,070	16	2
			29,149	2	0

Dr.   BILLS RECEIVABLE.   (1)

When received.	Folio.	From whom received.	No.	By whom Drawn.	Date.		Term.	To whose Order.	On whom Drawn.
1817.						1817.			
May 31		To Balance	...	....	......	......	.....	....	....
June 2	11	To Simpson & White	✓ 537	Simpson & White	Leeds	June 2	2 m.	Ourselves	James White & Co. London.
			✓ 538	Ditto	Ditto	2	2 m.	Ditto	Ditto .... Ditto.
			✓ 539	Ditto.	Ditto	2	2 m.	Ditto	Ditto .... Ditto.
2	16	To S. Winsford & Co.	✓ 540	S. Winsford & Co.	Ditto	2	2 m.	Ditto	Rogers & Pearson, Ditto.
2	4	To Promiscuous Discts.	✓ 541	Glengary & Co. .	Manchr.	May 25	2 m.	Ancouts & Son	Richardson & Co. Ditto.
3	12	To Johnson & Sons	✓ 542	McGregor & Co.	Glasgow	16	3 m.	McFarlane & Co.	Macnamara & Sons Ditto.
			✓ 543	James Camelford	Edinbro'	April 29	3 m.	Order	Archibald Lumb, Ditto.
3	13	To Billington & Co. ...	✓ 544	Billington & Co.	Leeds	June 3	2 m.	Ourselves	Samuel Westwood, Ditto.
3	4	To Promiscuous Discts.	✓ 545	Maundrell & Co.	Leeds	May 25	2 m.	John Smith . . .	Robert Griffith ... Ditto.
			✓ 546	John Bentley ...	Wakefd.	27	2 m.	James Ball	Mountain & Sons, Ditto.
			✓ 547	Samuel Newton	York	June 2	2 m.	John Ouse	Fairfax & Co..... Ditto.
			✓ 548	Peter Jones	Leeds	3	2 m.	Simon Laurel ..	Snowden & Sons, Ditto.
4	13	To Billington & Co. ...	✓ 549	Billington & Co.	Ditto	4	2 m.	Ourselves	Samuel Westwood, Ditto.
			✓ 550	Ditto	Ditto	4	2 m.	Ditto	Ditto .... Ditto.
4	4	To Promiscuous Discts.	✓ 551	Durham Bank ..	......	May 10	3 m.	James Conder .	Grandison & Co. Ditto.
5	14	To John Evergreen ...	✓ 552	John Evergreen	Leeds	June 5	30 d. s.	Ourselves	{ Ramon Miranda & Co. ..... } Cadiz.
5	4	To Promiscuous Discts.	✓ 553	T. Northmore ..	Preston	May 30	2 m.	Wm. Kenworthy	Davison & Grant, London.
			✓ 554	Hungerford & Co.	Leeds	June 2	2 m.	Philip West ...	Strawman & Co. Ditto.
			✓ 555	John Brown ...	Halifax	3	3 m.	Himself	Charles White ... Ditto.
5	11	To Simpson & White	✓ 556	Simpson & White	Leeds	5	2 m.	Ourselves	James White & Co. Ditto.
6	15	To Hunt & Milner ..	✓ 557	Hunt & Milner..	Ditto	5	2 m.	Order	Milner & Hunt ... Ditto.
6	12	To Johnson & Sons ..	✓ 558	Johnson & Sons	Ditto	6	2 m.	Ourselves	Anandale & Sons, Ditto.
6	4	To Promiscuous Discts.	✓ 559	Bolland & Co. ...	Manchr.	May 23	2 m.	William Smith .	Nathaniel Brown, Ditto.
			✓ 560	Maundrel & Co.	Leeds	June 4	2 m.	Joshua Bland ..	Kippax & Co...... Ditto.
		Carried forward ...	....	....	......	....	.....	....	....

(1)   PER CONTRA.   *Cr.*

Debit side (1)

When due.	£	s.	d.	£	s.	d.
1817.						
. . . . .	. . .	. .	. .	6,758	15	0
Aug. 5	500	0	0			
5	200	0	0			
5	300	0	0	1,000	0	0
5	. . .	. .	. .	200	0	0
July 28	. . .	. .	. .	73	15	0
Aug. 19	863	17	.6			
1	648	9	0	1,512	6	6
6	. . .	. .	. .	300	0	0
July 28	15	10	0			
30	27	5	6			
Aug. 5	43	11	0			
6	50	0	0	136	6	6
7	400	0	0			
7	350	0	0	750	0	0
13	. . .	. .	. .	500	0	0
{ Negotd. June 10 } at36¼d.	. . .	. .	. .	1,374	18	10
Aug. 2	19	15	8			
5	30	0	0			
Sept. 6	92	7	6	142	3	2
Aug. 8	. . .	. .	. .	250	0	0
8	. . .	. .	. .	1,200	0	0
9	. . .	. .	. .	200	0	0
July 26	234	18	0			
Aug. 7	50	0	0	284	18	0
. . . . .	. . .	. .	. .	14,683	3	0

Credit side (PER CONTRA. Cr.)

Folio.	How disposed of.	No.	When due.	£	s.	d.	£	s.	d.
1817.			**1817.**						
June 2 / 11	By Simpson & White ...	516	July 20	627	15	0			
		522	Aug. 13	330	0	0	957	15	0
2 / 9	By Grandison Neville & Co.	540	Aug. 5	200	0	0			
		510	July 23	1,000	0	0			
		518	24	500	0	0			
		527	25	837	16	8	2,537	16	8
3 / 9	By Grandison Neville & Co.	535	26	1,200	0	0			
		529	27	413	18	4			
		521	28	350	0	0			
		544	Aug. 6	300	0	0			
		504	July 29	472	15	0			
		507	30	826	10	0	3,563	3	4
4 / 13	By Billington & Co.	537	Aug. 5	500	0	0			
		538	5	200	0	0			
		548	6	50	0	0	750	0	0
4 / 4	By Promiscuous Discounts	541	July 28	73	15	0			
		545	28	15	10	0			
		546	30	27	5	6			
		547	Aug. 5	43	11	0			
		530	July 31	100	0	0			
		520	Aug. 1	50	0	0			
		515	2	50	0	0	360	1	6
5 / 14	By John Evergreen	539	5	300	0	0			
		549	7	400	0	0			
		550	7	350	0	0			
		551	13	500	0	0	1,550	0	0
5 / 9	By Grandison Neville & Co	542	19	863	17	6			
		556	8	250	0	0			
		543	1	648	9	0			
		552	June 10	1,374	18	10	3,137	5	4
	Carried forward	....	.....	....			12,856	1	10

Dr.   BILLS RECEIVABLE.   (2)

When received.	Folio.	From whom received.	No.	By whom drawn.		Date.		Term.	To whose Order.	On whom Drawn.
1817.						1817.				
		Brought forward ...	....	....	......	...	....	....	....
June 7	16	To S. Winsford & Co.	√ 561	Stuart & Kirk,	Edinbro'	June 2	3 m.	S. Winsford & Co.	Jacob Hall ...... London.
			√ 562	Tandem & Co.	Dublin	May 28	2 m.	Ditto	Sir S. Black & Co. Ditto.
			√ 563	Winsford & Co.	Leeds	June 7	2 m.	Ourselves	Philander & Mills Ditto.
9	4	To Proms. Discounts	√ 564	Sandford&Merton,	York	2	3 m.	Verdon & Co. ..	Worthington & Sons, Ditto.
			√ 565	Philip Westerman	Leeds	3	2 m.	James Horn ...	Philip Maude & Co. Ditto.
9	12	To Johnson & Sons	√ 566	Ossiphoff & Co.	Riga	Apr. 20	3 m.	Dombrowski & Co.	Bartleman & Co. Ditto.
9	4	To Proms. Discounts	√ 567	Anderton & Smith	Hull	May 15	2 m.	John White ...,	Broadman & Sons Ditto.
			√ 568	Luke Green	Wakefd.	20	2 m.	Philip Brown ..	Barringdale & Co. Ditto.
			√ 569	Robert Smith ..	Leeds	June 8	2 m.	John Penny	Grandison & Co. Ditto.
9	15	To Hunt & Milner	√ 570	Hunt & Milner	Ditto	9	2 m.	Ourselves	Milner & Hunt, . . Ditto.
10	11	To Simpson & White	√ 571	Simpson & White	Ditto	10	2 m.	Ditto	James White & Co. Ditto.
			√ 572	Ditto	Ditto	10	2 m.	Ditto	Ditto .... Ditto.
10	4	To Proms. Discounts	√ 573	James Strange	Manchr.	Feb. 15	6 m.	Himself	Woodfall & Ward, Ditto.
10	14	To John Evergreen	√ 574	Roger Bland ...	Bristol	Apr. 26	3 m.	Order	Macnamara & Co. Ditto.
11	14	To John Evergreen	√ 575	Ordonez & Co.	Madrid	May 1	2 m.	John Evergreen	Madrigues & Co. Ditto.
			√ 576	Rambouillet & Co.	Paris	15	2 m.	Perrault & Co.	Legrand & Co. .... Ditto.
11	4	To Proms. Discounts	√ 577	John Ryder	Rochdale	June 3	2 m.	James Lord ...	Whitaker & Co. .. Ditto.
			√ 578	Samuel Gore ...	Macclesf.	Apr. 1	3 m.	T. Johnson	Benjamin Briar, .. Ditto.
			√ 579	John Price	Paisley	May 2	3 m.	Robert Taylor ..	Macnamara & Co. Ditto.
			√ 580	James Naylor ..	Dundee	10	2 m.	Philip Green ...	Rowlandson & Co. Ditto.
12	11	To Simpson & White	√ 581	Simpson & White	Leeds	June 12	2 m.	Ourselves	James White & Co. Ditto.
12	13	To Billington & Co.	√ 582	Billington & Co.	Ditto	12	2 m.	Ditto	Samuel Westwood, Ditto.
			√ 583	Ditto	Ditto	12	2 m.	Ditto	Ditto .... Ditto.
12	4	To Proms. Discounts	√ 584	David Spink ...	Otley	June 5	2 m.	William North .	Brownson & Co. . Ditto.
			√ 585	John West	Wetherby	May 15	3 m.	Robert White ..	Carter & Sons, ... Ditto.
			√ 586	Robert Black ..	Tadcaster	10	2 m.	John Smith ...	Strawman & Co. Ditto.
13	16	To S. Winsford & Co.	√ 587	Rimaverde & Co.	Lisbon	20	30 d. s.	Braga & Co.	Guimarraens & Co. Ditto.
13	4	To Proms. Discounts	√ 588	Morley & Co. ..	Bradford	June 6	2 m.	Order	Archibald Ward, Ditto.
14	15	To Hunt & Milner	√ 589	Hunt & Milner	Leeds	13	2 m.	Ourselves	Milner & Hunt, .. Ditto.
			√ 590	Ditto	Ditto	13	2 m.	Order	Ditto .... Ditto.
14	13	To Billington & Co.	√ 591	Billington & Co.	Ditto	14	2 m.	Ourselves	Samuel Westwood, Ditto.
14	4	To Promis. Discounts	√ 592	Morgan & Leek	St. Asaph	May 23	2 m.	Themselves	Glendower & Co. Ditto.
			√ 593	Milton & Miles	Leicester	Apr. 15	3 m.	John Smith	Castleford & Sons, Ditto.
			√ 594	William Ford	Leeds	June 10	2 m.	James Hope ...	Westman & White, Ditto.
		Carried forward ...	....	....	......	....	....	....	....

(2)   PER CONTRA.   *Cr.*

When due.	£.	s.	d.	£.	s.	d.
1817.						
....	....	.	.	14,683	3	0
Sept. 5.	743	10	0			
July 31	382	15	0			
Aug. 10	500	0	0	1,626	5	0
Sept. 5	200	0	0			
Aug. 6	150	0	0	350	0	0
July 23	....	.	.	958	13	6
18	17	10	0			
23	20	0	0			
Aug. 11	33	12	8	71	2	8
12	....	.	.	150	0	0
13	400	0	0			
13	600	0	0	1,000	0	0
18	....	.	.	329	17	6
July 29	....	.	.	187	10	0
4	743	15	0			
18	600	0	0	1.343	15	0
Aug. 6	27	10	0			
July 4	40	0	0			
Aug. 5	50	0	0			
July 13	64	12	6	182	2	6
Aug. 15	....	.	.	250	0	0
15	500	0	0			
15	500	0	0	1,000	0	0
8	100	0	0			
18	100	0	0			
July 13	175	18	6	375	18	6
18	....	.	.	1,427	7	9
Aug. 9	....	.	.	200	0	0
16	250	0	0			
16	450	0	0	700	0	0
17	....	.	.	200	0	0
July 26	19	5	4			
18	25	0	0			
Aug. 13	33	11	6	77	16	10
....	...	.	.	25,113	12	3

Folio	How disposed of	No.	When due.	£.	s.	d.	£.	s.	d.
1817.			1817.						
	Brought forward	....	......	....	.	.	12,856	1	10
June 7	15	By Hunt & Milner	563	Aug. 10	500	0	0			
		561	Sept. 5	743	10	0	1,243	10	0
7	4	By Promiscuous Discounts	553	Aug. 2	19	15	8			
		555	Sept. 6	92	7	6			
		554	Aug. 5	30	0	0			
		560	7	50	0	0	192	3	2
9	12	By Johnson & Sons	558	9	200	0	0			
		564	Sept. 5	200	0	0			
		565	Aug. 6	150	0	0			
		562	July 31	382	15	0	932	15	0
10	11	By Simpson & White ...	566	23	....	.	.	958	13	6
10	4	By Promiscuous Discounts	567	July 18	17	10	0			
		568	23	20	0	0			
		569	Aug. 11	33	12	8	71	2	8
11	9	By Grandison Neville & Co.	570	12	150	0	0			
		574	July 29	187	10	0			
		559	26	234	18	0			
		576	18	600	0	0			
		373	Aug. 18	329	17	6			
		575	July 4	743	15	0	2,246	0	6
12	13	By Billington & Co.	571	Aug. 13	400	0	0			
		572	13	600	0	0	1,000	0	0
12	4	By Promiscuous Discounts	577	6	27	10	0			
		578	July 4	40	0	0			
		579	Aug. 5	50	0	0	117	10	0
13	9	By Grandison Neville & Co.	581	15	250	0	0			
		587	July 18	1,427	7	9			
		580	13	64	12	6			
		586	13	175	18	6			
		584	Aug. 8	100	0	0			
		585	18	100	0	0	2,117	18	9
14	15	By Hunt & Milner	583	15	500	0	0			
		588	9	200	0	0	700	0	0
	Carried forward	....	....	....	.	.	22,435	15	5

Dr.   BILLS RECEIVABLE.   (3)

When received.	Folio.	From whom rece ved.	No.	By whom Drawn.		Date.	Term.	To whose Order.	On whom Drawn.	
1817.						1817.				
		Brought forward ...	...	....	......	....	....	....	....	
June 16	11	To Simpson & White	√595	Simpson & White	Leeds	June16	2 m.	Order	James White & Co.	London.
16	15	To Hunt & Milner ..	√596	Hunt & Milner	Ditto	16	2 m.	Ourselves	Milner & Hunt,	.. Ditto.
16	4	To Proms. Discounts	√597	Duncan Campbell	Inverness	Apr.28	3 m.	James Forbes ...	Archibald Stuart,	Ditto.
			√598	Somerset & Co.	Bristol	May16	2 m.	Wrighton & Co.	Simon Swift	Ditto.
17	5	To Proms. Discounts	√599	John Lumley ..	Leeds	June 5	2 m.	Josiah Green ..	Charles Ashton ...	Ditto.
			√600	Roger Maude ..	Ditto	9	2 m.	James West ...	Jamieson & Co. ..	Ditto.
			√601	John Hey	Ditto	15	2 m.	James Hudson	George Corney ...	Ditto.
18	12	To Johnson & Sons	√602	Pendragon &Lister	Baltimore	Apr.30	30 d. s.	Johnson & Sons	Strawman & Co. ..	Ditto.
18	13	To Billington & Co.	√603	Billington & Co.	Leeds	June16	2 m.	Ourselves	Samuel Westwood,	Ditto.
			√604	Ditto	Ditto	16	2 m.	Ditto	Ditto	Ditto.
			√605	Ditto	Ditto	16	2 m.	Ditto	Ditto	Ditts.
19	11	To Simpson & White	√606	Simpson & White	Ditto	19	2 m.	Ourselves	James White & Co.	Ditto.
19	14	To John Evergreen	√607	John Evergreen	Ditto	19	3 m.	Order	Philipson & Hart,	Ditto.
19	5	To Proms. Diccounts	√608	T. Nelson	Hull	May10	3 m.	James Grant ...	Wellwood & Sons,	Ditto.
			√609	James Smith ...	Malton	27	3 m.	Peter Pole	Robert North	Ditto.
			√610	Musgrave & Co. .	Leeds	June15	2 m.	Mary Scott	Forrester & Co. . .	Ditto.
20	15	To Hunt & Milner ..	√611	Hunt & Milner	Ditto	20	2 m.	Order	Milner & Hunt, ..	Ditto.
			√612	Ditto	Ditto	20	2 m.	Ourselves	Ditto	Ditto.
20	12	To Johnson & Sons	√613	Macartney & Co.	Edinbro'	May 1	3 m.	Gregson & Co.	Alexander & Sons,	Ditto.
20	5	To Proms. Discounts	√614	Philip Wells ...	Newcastle	Apr.15	3 m.	John Boler	Blanchard & Smith,	Ditto.
21	16	To S. Winsford & Co.	√615	Vanderloo & Co.	Amsterd.	June 5	2 m.	Jac. Mussullbach	Turvin & Wilde,	Ditto.
23	12	To Johnson & Sons .	√616	Johnson & Sons	Leeds	20	3 m.	Themselves	Wolverton & Co.	Ditto.
			√617	Ditto	Ditto	23	2 m.	Ourselves	McFarlane & Co.	Glasgow.
23	16	To S. Winsford & Co.	√618	Anderson & Co.	Glasgow	May10	3 m.	R. Griffith	Hodson & Best . .	London.
23	5	To Proms. Discounts	√619	Charles Scott ..	Dundee	June 4	2 m.	John Douglas ..	Archibald Muir ...	Ditto.
			√620	Reginald & Sons	Lancaster	May 1	3 m.	Thomas Duncan	Highfield & Flower,	Ditto.
			√621	Dodson & Co. ..	Manchr.	June10	2 m.	Order	Williamson & Co.	Ditto.
24	5	To Proms. Discounts	√622	Lamprey & Sons	Liverpool	Apr.30	3 m.	T. Drinkwater	Glenarvon & Sons,	Ditto.
24	11	To Simpson & White	623	Simpson & White	Leeds	June24	2 m.	Ourselves	James White & Co.	Ditto.
			√624	Ditto	Ditto	24	2 m.	Ditto	Ditto	Ditto.
24	14	To John Evergreen	√625	Rimaverde & Co.	Lisbon	May31	30 d. s.	Marrocos & Co.	Peter Swift	Ditto.
			626	John Evergreen	Leeds	June24	2 m.	Ourselves	Herman & Co. ...	Ditto.
		Carried forward ...	....	....	......	....	....	....	....	..

(3)

PER CONTRA.   *Cr.*

When due.	£.	s.	d.	£.	s.	d.	Folio.	How disposed of.	No.	When due.	£.	s.	d.	£.	s.	d.
1817.								1817.		1817.						
....	....	.	.	25,113	12	3		Brought forward	....	......	....	.	.	22,435	15	5
Aug. 19	....	.	.	1,200	0	0	June16 11	By Simpson & White ...	557	Aug. 8	....	.	.	1,200	0	0
19	....	.	.	150	0	0	16 4	By Promiscuous Discounts	597	July 31	150	0	0			
July 31	150	0	0						593	18	25	0	0			
19	500	0	0											175	0	0
				650	0	0	18 12	By Johnson & Sons	582	Aug. 15	....	.	.	500	0	0
Aug. 8	63	15	0				18 13	By Billington & Co.	601	18	50	0	0			
12	48	10	6						590	16	450	0	0			
18	50	0	0						598	July 19	500	0	0			
				162	5	6								1,000	0	0
July 23	....	.	.	2,000	0	0	18 9	By Grandison Neville & Co.	591	Aug. 17	200	0	0			
Aug. 19	200	0	0						602	July 23	2,000	0	0			
19	300	0	0						592	26	19	5	4			
19	500	0	0						594	Aug. 13	33	11	6			
				1,000	0	0			589	16	250	0	0			
22	....	.	.	250	0	0			599	8	63	15	0			
Sept. 22	....	.	.	1,291	4	6			600	12	48	10	6			
Aug. 13	150	0	0						596	19	150	0	0			
30	200	0	0											2,765	2	4
18	76	18	6				19 9	By Grandison Neville & Co.	606	22	250	0	0			
				•426	18	6			607	Sept. 22	1,291	4	6			
23	375	15	0						609	Aug. 30	200	0	0			
23	624	5	0						608	13	150	0	0			
				1,000	0	0								1,891	4	6
4	....	.	.	200	0	0	19 5	By Promiscuous Discounts	610	18	....	.	.	76	18	6
July 18	....	.	.	100	0	0	20 15	By Hunt & Milner	604	19	300	0	0			
Aug. 8	....	.	.	1.736	19	0			605	19	500	0	0			
Sept. 23	713	18	8						603	19	200	0	0			
Aug. 26	850	0	0											1,000	0	0
				1,563	18	8	23 12	By Johnson & Sons.....	595	19	1,200	0	0			
13	....	.	.	325	15	0			611	23	375	15	0			
7	37	15	0											1,575	15	0
4	48	3	10				23 9	By Grandison Neville & Co.	613	4	200	0	0			
13	84	6	8						618	13	325	15	0			
				170	5	6			615	8	1,736	19	0			
2	....	.	.	400	0	0			621	13	84	6	8			
27	500	0	0						620	4	48	3	10			
27	500	0	0											2,395	4	6
				1,000	0	0	24 11	By Simpson & White ...	622	2	400	0	0			
July 29	938	18	6						612	23	624	5	0			
Aug. 27	200	0	0											1,024	5	0
				1,138	18	6	24 5	By Promiscuous Discounts	619	7	37	15	0			
									614	July 18	100	0	0			
														137	15	0
......	.	.	.	39,879	17	5		Carried forward	....	......	....	.	.	36,177	0	3

Dr.   BILLS RECEIVABLE.   (4)

When received.	Folio.	From whom received.	No.	By whom Drawn.		Date.	Term.	To whose Order.	On whom Drawn.
1817.						1817.			
		Brought forward ..	....	....	......	......	....	....	....
June 25	13	To Billington & Co.	√ 627	Billington & Co.	Leeds	June25	2 m.	Ourselves	Samuel Westwood London.
			√ 628	Ditto	Ditto	25	2 m.	Ditto	Ditto .... Ditto.
			√ 629	Ditto	Ditto	25	2 m.	Ditto	Ditto .... Ditto.
25	5	To Proms. Discounts	√ 630	Simon Fraser ..	Glasgow	May 11	3 m.	James Campbell	Levant & Noble .. Ditto.
			√ 631	Ringwell & Co.	Leeds	June12	2 m.	Order	Bustard & Bell ... Ditto.
26	5	To Proms. Discounts	√ 632	Woodhouse & Son	Ditto	May 5	3 m.	Charles Fielding	Merlin & Drew ... Ditto.
26	11	To Simpson & White	633	Simpson & White	Ditto	June26	2 m.	Ourselves	James White & Co. Ditto.
27	5	To Proms. Discounts	634	John Nelson ...	Bradford	20	2 m.	George Pearce ..	Pattison & Pratt .. Ditto.
			√ 635	Wormwood & Co.	Huddersf.	15	2 m.	T. Pilchard	Risingham & Co. . Ditto.
			√ 636	Wimbleton & Co.	Leeds	2	3 m.	Charles Bland ..	Bertrand & More, Ditto.
27	13	To Billington & Co.	637	Billington & Co.	Ditto	27	2 m.	Ourselves	Samuel Westwood, Ditto.
28	16	To S. Winsford & Co.	638	S. Winsford & Co.	Ditto	28	30 d. s.	Order	J. Guimmarraens, Oporto.
28	5	To Proms. Discounts	√ 639	John King	Halifax	20	3 m.	T. Whitehead ..	S. Marsden & Sons, London.
29	5	To Ditto	√ 640	Westerman & Co.	Huddersf.	May23	3 m.	James Nettleton	Rosendale & Co. Ditto.
			641	Rowlandson & Co.	Wakefd.	June25	2 m.	Order	Brightman & Rich, Ditto.
			642	John Cromack	Pontefr.	26	2 m.	Peter Clark	Solomon Law ... Ditto.
			643	Adamson & Sons	Leeds	27	2 m.	Conder & Smith	Archibald Kendal, Ditto.
29	15	To Hunt & Milner	644	Hunt & Milner .	Ditto	28	2 m.	Order	Milner & Hunt .. Ditto.
			645	Ditto	Ditto	28	2 m.	Ditto	Ditto .... Ditto.
			646	Ditto	Ditto	28	2 m.	Ditto	Ditto .... Ditto.
June 30		To Balance	....	....	......	....	....	....	....

(4)

When due.	£.	s.	d.	£.	s.	d.
1817.						
....	....	.	.	39,879	17	5
Aug. 28	200	0	0			
28	300	0	0			
28	300	0	0	800	0	0
14	90	11	6			
15	150	0	0	240	11	6
8	....	.	.	200	0	0
29	....	.	.	150	0	0
23	87	8	4			
18	50	0	0			
Sept. 5	100	0	0	237	8	4
Aug. 30	....	.	.	200	0	0
....	....	.	.	1,000	0	0
Sept. 23	....	.	.	150	0	0
Aug. 26	75	10	0			
28	100	0	0			
29	64	18	6			
30	238	5	9	478	14	3
Aug. 31	750	0	0			
31	318	12	6			
31	381	7	6	1,450	0	0
				44,786	11	6
....	....	.	.	3,990	12	7

PER CONTRA. *Cr.*

	Fo.	How disposed of.	No.	When due.	£.	s.	d.	£.	s.	d.
1817.		Brought forward	....	1817.	....	.	.	36,177	0	3
June25	13	By Billington & Co.	616	Sept. 23	713	18	8			
			630	Aug. 14	90	11	6	804	10	2
26	9	By Grandison & Co......	631	15	150	0	0			
			632	8	200	0	0			
			625	July 29	938	18	6	1,288	18	6
26	5	By Promiscuous Discounts	636	Sept. 5	....	.	.	100	0	0
28	16	By S. Winsford & Co.	629	Aug. 28	300	0	0			
			635	18	50	0	0			
			627	28	200	0	0			
			639	Sept. 23	150	0	0			
			628	Aug. 28	300	0	0	1,000	0	0
29	15	By Hunt & Milner	617	26	850	0	0			
			624	27	500	0	0			
			640	26	75	10	0	1,425	10	0
30		By Balance	623	Aug. 27	500	0	0			
			626	27	200	0	0			
			633	29	150	0	0			
			634	23	87	8	4			
			637	30	200	0	0			
			638	......	1,000	0	0			
			641	28	100	0	0			
			642	29	64	18	6			
			643	30	238	5	9			
			644	31	750	0	0			
			645	31	318	12	6			
			646	31	381	7	6	3,990	12	7
								44,786	11	6

Dr.   BILLS PAYABLE.   (1)

	Fo.	Drawn On and Accepted By.	Nos.	Due.	£.	s.	d.	£.	s.	d.
1817.				1817.						
June 2	8	To Grandison Neville & Co.	403 to 405	Aug. 5	. . .	. .	. .	257	5	0
3	8	. . . . . . Ditto	406 to 407	6	174	10	0			
			408 to 410	6	1,514	7	6			
								1,688	17	6
4	8	. . . . . . Ditto	411 to 413	7	. . .	. .	. .	258	16	6
5	8	. . . . . . Ditto	414 to 415	8	. . .	. .	. .	271	19	0
6	8	. . . . . . to Ditto	416 to 418	9	. . .	. .	. .	226	18	6
7	8	. . . . . . Ditto	419 to 420	10	612	0	8			
			422	10	91	15	0			
								703	15	8
7	8	. . . . . . Ditto	421	Sept. 10	. . .	. .	. .	1,000	0	0
9	8	. . . . . . Ditto	423	Aug. 12	. . .	. .	. .	75	17	6
10	8	. . . . . . Ditto	424 to 425	13	. . .	. .	. .	233	8	6
11	8	. . . . . . Ditto	426 to 428	14	1,350	0	0			
			429	14	91	3	0			
								1,441	3	0
12	8	. . . . . . Ditto	430 to 432	15	. .	. .	. .	. 165	4	0
13	8	. . . . . . Ditto	433	16	87	19	0			
			434 to 436	16	1,453	7	6			
								1,541	6	6
14	8	. . . . . . Ditto	437	17	. . .	. .	. .	100	0	0
16	8	. . . . . . Ditto	438 to 440	19	. . .	. .	. .	237	13	0
18	8	. . . . . . Ditto	441 to 442	21	. . .	. .	. .	235	17	6
		Carried forward	. . . . . .	. . . . .	. . .	. .	. .	8,438	2	2

(1)   PER CONTRA.   *Cr.*

1817.	Folio.	Drawn on Account of.	Drawn By.	Order of.	No.	Date.	Term.	When due.	£.	s.	d.	£.	s.	d.
						1817.		1817.						
June 2	4	By Proms. Discounts	Ourselves	James Temple	403	June 2	2 m.	Aug. 5	100	0	0			
		Ditto	Charles Beaton	404	2	2 m.	5	30	0	0			
		Ditto	John Willis	405	2	2 m.	5	127	5	0			
												257	5	0
3	4	By Proms. Discounts	Ourselves	Jonathan Peterson ..	406	3	2 m.	6	74	10	0			
		Ditto	Edward Johnson ...	407	3	2 m.	6	100	0	0			
												174	10	0
3	12	By Johnson & Sons	Johnson & Sons	William Smith	408	3	2 m.	6	378	15	0			
		Ditto	Hartley & King	409	3	2 m.	6	735	12	6			
		Ditto	Samuel Wilson	410	3	2 m.	6	400	0	0			
												1,514	7	6
4	4	By Proms. Discounts	Ourselves ......,	George Gill & Son .	411	4	2 m.	7	45	0	0			
		Ditto	James Tremain	412	4	2 m.	7	77	3	6			
		Ditto	Mansfield & Co. ...	413	4	2 m.	7	136	13	0			
												258	16	6
5	4	By Proms. Discounts	Ourselves	Warburton & Son ..	414	5	2 m.	8	200	0	0			
		Ditto	Philip Crosse	415	5	2 m.	8	71	19	0			
												271	19	0
6	4	By Proms. Discounts	Ourselves	Charles West......	416	6	2 m.	9	87	8	6			
		Ditto	Peter McFarlane ...	417	6	2 m.	9	100	0	0			
		Ditto	John Crow	418	6	2 m.	9	39	10	0			
												226	18	6
7	16	By S. Winsford & Co.	S. Winsford & Co.	John Hopkins	419	7	2 m.	10	239	14	0			
		Ditto	George King & Son .	420	7	2 m.	10	372	6	8			
												612	0	8
7	16	By S. Winsford & Co.	Ditto	Maclean & Co.	421	7	3 m.	Sept.10	1,000	0	0	1,000	0	0
7	4	By Proms. Discounts	Ourselves......	Order	422	7	2 m.	Aug.10	....	.	.	91	15	0
9	4	By Ditto	Ditto	Congreve & Sons ...	423	9	2 m.	12	....	.	.	75	17	6
10	4	By Ditto.	Ourselves	Order	424	10	2 m.	13	83	8	6			
		Ditto	Ditto	425	10	2 m.	13	150	0	0			
												233	8	6
11	14	By John Evergreen	Ourselves	John Evergreen	426	11	2 m.	14	500	0	0			
		Ditto	Ditto	427	11	2 m.	14	500	0	0			
		Ditto	Ditto	428	11	2 m.	14	350	0	0			
												1,350	0	0
11	4	By Proms. Discounts	Ourselves	Order	429	11	2 m.	14				91	3	0
12	4	By Ditto.	Ditto	Samuel Lucas	430	12	2 m.	15	50	0	0			
		Ditto	Peter Harrison	431	12	2 m.	15	65	4	0			
		Ditto	Order	432	12	2 m.	15	50	0	0			
												165	4	0
13	4	By Proms. Discounts	Ourselves......	James Pearson	433	13	2 m.	16	....	.	.	87	19	0
13	16	By S. Winsford & Co.	S. Winsford & Co.	Miles Smeaton	434	13	2 m.	16	463	17	6			
		Ditto	Chas. Hardman & Co.	435	13	2 m.	16	289	10	0			
		Ditto	Philips, Johnson & Co.	436	13	2 m.	16	700	0	0			
												1,453	7	6
14	4	By Proms. Discounts	Ourselves	Order	437	14	2 m.	17	....	.	.	100	0	0
16	4	By Ditto	Ditto	Ditto	438	16	2 m.	19	37	13	0			
		Ditto	Samuel Ford	439	16	2 m.	19	150	0	0			
		Ditto	Anthony Thwaite ...	440	16	2 m.	19	50	0	0			
												237	13	0
18	5	By Proms. Discounts	Ourselves......	Order	441	18	2 m.	21	200	0	0			
		Ditto	James Windsor	442	18	2 m.	21	35	17	6			
												235	17	6
		Carried forward ...	....	....	....	....	....	....	....	.	.	8,438	2	2

2 T 2

Dr.   BILLS PAYABLE.   (2)

1817.	Fo.	Drawn On and Accepted By.	Nos.	Due.	£.	s.	d.	£.	s.	d.
				1817.						
		Brought forward	. . . .	. . . .	. . . . .	. .	. .	8,438	2	2
June 18		To Grandison Neville & Co.	443 to 445	Sept. 21	. . . . .	. .	. .	1,535	11	3
19	8	. . . . Ditto	446	Aug. 22	63	15	0			
			447 to 449	22	1,327	15	0			
								1,391	10	0
20	8	. . . . Ditto	450 to 451	23	. . . . .	. .	. .	181	18	0
21	8	. . . . . . Ditto	452	24	. . . . .	. .	. .	58	17	6
21	8	. . . . . . Ditto	453 to 456	Sept. 24	. . . . .	. .	. .	1,727	4	8
23	8	. . . . . . Ditto	457 to 458	Aug. 26	. . . . .	. .	. .	229	10	0
24	8	. . . . Ditto	459 to 461	27	227	17	0			
			462 to 464	27	952	10	2			
								1,180	7	2
25	8	. . . . Ditto	465 to 466	28	. . . . .	. .	. .	140	5	0
27	8	. . . . . . Ditto	467	29	. . . . .	. .	. .	58	11	0
28	8	. . . . . . Ditto	468 to 470	31	. . . . .	. .	. .	181	10	0
29	8	. . . . . . Ditto	471 to 472	Sept. 1	. . . . .	. .	. .	150	0	0
								15,273	6	9

(2)   PER CONTRA.   *Cr.*

	Folio.	Drawn on Account of.	Drawn By.	Order of.	No.	Date.	Term.	Due.	£.	s.	d.	£.	s.	d.
1817.						1817.		1817.						
		Brought forward ..	. . . .	. . . .	. . .	. . .	. . . .	. . . .	. . .	.	.	8,438	2	2
June 18	12	By Johnson & Sons .	Johnson & Sons .	Whiteson & Co. . . .	443	June18	3 m.	Sep. 21	387	12	9			
		Ditto	John Wood	444	18	3 m.	21	815	10	0				
		Ditto	Charles Pierce	445	18	3 m.	21	332	8	6				
												1,5 35	11	3
19	5	By Proms. Discounts	Ourselves	Order	446	19	2 m.	Aug.22	. . .	.	.	63	15	0
19	14	By John Evergreen	Ditto	Samuel Robinson . .	447	19	2 m.	22	450	0	0			
			Ditto	Order	448	19	2 m.	22	627	15	0			
			Ditto	Jackson & Smith . .	449	19	2 m.	22	250	0	0			
												1,327	15	0
20	5	By Proms. Discounts	Ourselves	Order	450	20	2 m.	23	81	18	0			
			Ditto	Ditto	451	20	2 m.	23	100	0	0			
												181	18	0
21	5	By Proms. Discounts	Ourselves	Order	452	21	2 m.	24	. . .	.	.	58	17	6
21	16	By S. Winsford & Co.	S. Winsford & Co.	Mallinson & Co. . . .	453	21	3 m.	Sep. 24	426	13	6			
			Ditto	Order	454	21	3 m.	24	500	0	0			
			Ditto	Peter Lord	455	21	3 m.	24	372	16	8			
			Ditto	Charles Ringwell . .	456	21	3 m.	24	427	14	6			
												1,727	4	8
23	5	By Proms. Discounts	Ourselves	Nelson & Lord . . .	457	23	2 m.	Aug.26	79	10	0			
			Ditto	Order	458	23	2 m.	26	150	0	0			
												229	10	0
24	5	By Proms. Discounts	Ourselves	Graham & Sons . . .	459	24	2 m.	27	77	17	0			
			Ditto	Order	460	24	2 m.	27	50	0	0			
			Ditto	Wilson & Baker . . .	461	24	2 m.	27	100	0	0			
												227	17	0
24	14	By John Evergreen	Ourselves	John Evergreen . . .	462	24	2 m.	27	263	18	6			
			Ditto	Peter Walstrom . . .	463	24	2 m.	27	350	0	0			
			Ditto	John Evergreen . . .	464	24	2 m.	27	338	11	8			
												952	10	2
25	5	By Proms. Discounts	Ourselves	Order	465	25	2 m.	28	90	5	0			
			Ditto	Samuel Ball	466	25	2 m.	28	50	0	0			
												140	5	0
27	5	By Proms. Discounts	Ditto	Philip North	467	26	2 m.	29	. . .	.	.	58	11	0
28	5	By Proms. Discounts	Ourselves	Order	468	28	2 m.	31	50	0	0			
			Ditto	Ditto	469	28	2 m.	31	81	10	0			
			Ditto	Ditto	470	28	2 m.	31	50	0	0			
												181	10	0
29	5	By Proms. Discounts	Ourselves	John Waterford . . .	471	29	2 m.	Sep. 1	100	0	0			
			Ditto	Order	472	29	2 m.	1	50	0	0			
												150	0	0
												15,273	6	9

A

	Folio
Arnold's Assignees, James	17

B

Bank Expenses	3
Billington & Co.	13
Bath, Henry......................	17
Brandon, Mary	18
Barnard, Samuel	19
Brown, John (Private Account).	20

C

Commission	2

D

Davison, John	19

E

Evergreen, John	14

F

Five per Cent. Funds	7

G

	Folio
Grandison, Neville, & Co. Acc^t A	8
......Ditto ....Ditto B	9
......Ditto ....Ditto C	10

H

Hunt & Milner	15

I

Joint Stock	1
Interest	2
India Stock	7
Johnson & Sons	12

K

L

Loss	1
Langdon, Charles (Private Account)	21

M

LEDGER.

N	Folio	U	Folio
Notes on Demand 6			

O	V

P		W	
Profit 1		Winsford & Co. Samuel 16	
Promiscuous Discounts. 4, 5		Wilton, Ellen 18	
		Watson, Sir Henry 19	
		Williams, George (Private Account) 21	
		Wilfred, Charles 22	
		Wilkes, John 22	

R		X	
Risingham, Mrs. 18			
Riley, George 22			

S		Y	
Stamps 3			
Stock Dividends 6			
Simpson & White 11			
Slade, Sir Charles 17			
Smith, Peter (Private Account) 20			
Simpson, John 22			

T		Z	
Three per Cent. Funds 7			
Trueman, William 18			
Thompson, James 22			

Dr.   JOINT STOCK.   (1)

			£.	s.	d.

Dr.   PROFIT.

1817.				£.	s.	d.
June 30	1	To Loss, Transfer		963	17	0
30		To Balance		3,303	16	8
				4,267	13	8
June 30	20	To Peter Smith, ... his ⅓ share....................		1,101	5	7
30	20	To John Brown,..... his ¼ ditto.....................		825	19	2
30	21	To Charles Langdon, . his ¼ ditto.....................		825	19	2
30	21	To George Williams, . his ⅙ ditto....................		550	12	9
				3,303	16	8

Dr.   LOSS.

1817.				£.	s.	d.
June 30	3	To Stamps		256	12	6
30	3	To Bank Expenses		496	12	0
30	17	To James Arnold's Assignees		210	12	6
				963	17	0

(1) PER CONTRA. *Cr.*

			£.	s.	d.
1817.					
May 31		By Balance, Permanent Capital	30,000	0	0

PER CONTRA. *Cr.*

1817.			£	s	d
June 30	2	By Interest	3,396	11	10
30	2	By Commission	123	15	0
30	5	By Promiscuous Discounts	747	6	10
			4,267	13	8
June 30		By Balance, Net Gain this Half Year	3,303	16	8
			3,303	16	8

PER CONTRA. *Cr.*

1817.					
June 30	1	By Profit, Transfer...................................	963	17	0
			963	17	0

Dr.   INTEREST.   (2)

1817.				£	s.	d.
June 30	14	To John Evergreen		37	5	5
30	17	To Sir Charles Slade		64	6	4
30	17	To Henry Bath		43	18	5
30	18	To Mrs. Risingham		33	3	10
30	18	To William Trueman		14	19	10
30	18	To Mary Brandon		10	0	0
30	18	To Ellen Wilton		4	1	1
30	20	To Peter Smith		14	12	1
30	1	To Profit..		3,396	11	10
				3,618	18	10

Dr.   COMMISSION.

1817.						
June 30	10	To Grandison, Neville, & Co.		271	17	6
30	1	To Profit..		123	15	0
				395	12	6

(2)   PER CONTRA.   *Cr.*

1817.				£.	s.	d.
June 30	6	By Stock Dividends, 3 per Cent. Funds		1,200	0	0
30	6	By..... Ditto...... 5 per Cent. Funds		1,000	0	0
30	6	By.... Ditto..... India Stock		400	0	0
30	10	By Grandison, Neville, & Co.		169	15	2
30	11	By Simpson & White		199	4	3
30	12	By Johnson & Sons		45	1	2
30	13	By Billington & Co.		113	16	3
30	15	By Hunt & Milner		77	5	9
30	16	By Samuel Winsford & Co.		8	3	3
30	19	By Sir Henry Watson		187	10	0
30	19	By John Davison		85	0	0
30	19	By Samuel Barnard		125	0	0
30	20	By John Brown		2	15	3
30	21	By Charles Langdon		3	5	6
30	21	By George Williams		2	2	3
				3,618	18	10

PER CONTRA.   *Cr.*

1817.						
June 30	11	By Simpson & White		56	5	0
30	12	By Johnson & Sons		86	0	0
30	13	By Billington & Co.		·49	10	0
30	14	By John Evergreen		71	12	6
30	15	By Hunt & Milner		50	10	0
30	16	By Samuel Winsford & Co.		81	15	0
				395	12	6

Dr.   STAMPS.   (3)

1817.				£.	s.	d.
May 31		To Balance		217	13	6
June 30	2	To Cash		107	12	6
				325	6	0

Dr.   BANK EXPENSES.

1817.				£	s	d
May 31		To Balance		59	11	2
June 30	2	To Cash, Postages this Month		14	10	4
30	2	To Ditto, Half Year's Rent of Bank		52	10	0
30	2	To Ditto, Worthington & Co. Engravers		25	13	6
30	2	To Ditto, John Nolan, Stationer		19	7	0
30	22	To Charles Wilfred, Half Year's Salary		150	0	0
30	22	To John Simpson, ... Ditto.... Ditto		75	0	0
30	22	To George Riley, ... Ditto.... Ditto		50	0	0
30	22	To John Wilkes, ... Ditto.... Ditto		25	0	0
30	22	To James Thompson, Ditto.... Ditto		25	0	0
				496	12	0

(3)   PER CONTRA.   *Cr.*

1817.				£.	s.	d.
June 30	11	By Simpson & White		9	15	0
30	12	By Johnson & Sons		8	2	6
30	13	By Billington & Co.		8	17	6
30	14	By John Evergreen		22	10	0
30	15	By Hunt & Milner		11	16	0
30	16	By Samuel Winsford & Co.		7	12	6
30	1	By Loss		256	12	6
				325	6	0

PER CONTRA.   *Cr.*

1817.						
June 30	1	By Loss		496	12	0
				496	12	0

Dr.   PROMISCUOUS   (4)

1817.				£.	s.	d.
June 2	1	To Cash		73	1	6
2	1	To Bills Payable		257	5	0
3	1	To Cash		134	8	3
3	1	To Bills Payable		174	10	0
4	1	To Bills Receivable		360	1	6
4	1	To Bills Payable		258	16	6
5	1	To Cash		140	19	8
5	1	To Bills Payable		271	19	0
6	1	To Cash		49	10	0
6	1	To Bills Payable		226	18	6
7	2	To Bills Receivable		192	3	2
7	1	To Cash		345	17	6
7	1	To Bills Payable		91	15	0
9	1	To Cash		70	1	4
9	1	To Bills Payable		75	17	6
10	2	To Bills Receivable		71	2	8
10	1	To Cash		100	0	0
10	1	To Bills Payable		233	8	6
11	1	To Cash		179	16	10
11	1	To Bills Payable		91	3	0
12	1	To Cash		155	8	8
12	2	To Bills Receivable		117	10	0
12	1	To Bills Payable		165	4	0
13	1	To Cash		197	12	6
13	1	To Bills Payable		87	19	0
14	1	To Cash		77	0	4
14	1	To Bills Payable		100	0	0
16	3	To Bills Receivable		175	0	0
16	1	To Cash		267	18	6
16	1	To Bills Payable		237	13	0
		Carried forward............£		4,980	1	5

(4)		DISCOUNTS.		*Cr.*	

1817.			£.	s.	d.
May 31		By Balance	589	14	8
June 2	1	By Cash	256	3	3
2	1	By Bills Receivable	73	15	0
3	1	By Cash	173	15	8
3	1	By Bills Receivable	136	6	6
4	1	By Cash	121	15	8
4	1	By Bills Receivable	500	0	0
5	1	By Cash	270	12	5
5	1	By Bills Receivable	142	3	2
6	1	By Cash	186	12	0
6	1	By Bills Receivable	284	18	0
7	1	By Cash	91	7	10
9	2	By Bills Receivable	350	0	0
9	1	By Cash	75	12	8
9	2	By Bills Receivable	71	2	8
10	1	By Cash	83	2	10
10	2	By Bills Receivable	329	17	6
11	1	By Cash	90	15	4
11	2	By Bills Receivable	182	2	6
12	1	By Cash	65	0	0
12	2	By Bills Receivable	375	18	6
13	1	By Cash	87	12	8
13	2	By Bills Receivable	200	0	0
14	1	By Cash	99	11	6
14	2	By Bills Receivable	77	16	10
16	1	By Cash	137	11	7
16	3	By Bills Receivable	650	0	0
		Carried forward £	5,703	8	9

Dr.   PROMISCUOUS   (5)

1817.				£.	s.	d.
			Brought forward	4,930	1	5
June 17	1		To Cash	160	4	10
18	1		To Bills Payable	235	17	6
19	3		To Bills Receivable	76	18	6
19	2		To Bills Payable	63	15	0
19	2		To Cash	244	17	6
20	2		To Bills Payable	181	18	0
21	2		To Cash	99	4	0
21	2		To Bills Payable	58	17	6
23	2		To Cash	168	11	5
23	2		To Bills Payable	229	10	0
24	3		To Bills Receivable	137	15	0
24	2		To Cash	108	17	10
24	2		To Bills Payable	227	17	0
25	2		To Cash	238	10	0
25	2		To Bills Payable	140	5	0
26	4		To Bills Receivable	100	0	0
26	2		To Cash	98	1	6
27	2		To Bills Payable	58	11	0
27	2		To Cash	234	12	6
28	2		To Bills Payable	181	10	0
28	2		To Cash	147	3	10
29	2		To Bills Payable	150	0	0
29	2		To Cash	322	14	4
30	1		To Profit......................................	747	6	10
				9,393	0	6

(5)		DISCOUNTS.			Cr.		
				£.	s.	d.
1817.		Brought forward		5,703	8	9
June 17	2	By Bills Receivable		162	5	6
18	1	By Cash..............................		234	15	8
19	3	By Bills Receivable..............................		426	18	6
19	2	By Cash		63	10	10
20	3	By Bills Receivable..............................		100	0	0
20	2	By Cash		81	12	6
21	2	By Ditto		58	13	9
23	3	By Bills Receivable		170	5	6
23	2	By Cash		228	10	5
24	3	By Bills Receivable		400	0	0
24	2	By Cash		77	11	7
25	4	By Bills Receivable		240	11	6
25	2	By Cash		139	12	6
26	4	By Bills Receivable		200	0	0
27	2	By Cash		58	7	6
27	4	By Bills Receivable		237	8	4
28	2	By Cash		180	13	5
28	4	By Bills Receivable		150	0	0
29	4	By Ditto		478	14	3
				9,393	0	6

Dr. NOTES ON DEMAND. (6)

1817.				Amount of Notes.			£.	s.	d.
				£1	£2	£5			
June 7	1	To Cash, withdrawn		4,000	600	400	5,000	0	0
30		To Balance		70,000	20,000	10,000	100,000	0	0
				74,000	20,600	10,400	105,000	0	0

Dr. STOCK DIVIDENDS.

1817.			£.	s.	d.
June 30	2	To Interest, ½ Year on £80,000 Three per Cents. due 5 July	1,200	0	0
30	2	To Ditto... Ditto.... on 40,000 Five per Cents..... Ditto...	1,000	0	0
30	2	To Ditto... Ditto.... on 10,000 India Stock ......Ditto...	400	0	0
			2,600	0	0
June 30		To Balance	2,600	0	0

(6) PER CONTRA. *Cr.*

1817.				Amount of Notes.			£.	s.	d.
				£ 1.	£ 2.	£ 5.			
May 31		By Balance		67,000	19,600	9,900	96,500	0	0
June 17	1	By Cash, Re-issued................		4,000	600	400	5,000	0	0
26	2	By Ditto, Issued		3,000	400	100	3,500	0	0
				74,000	20,600	10,400	105,000	0	0
June 30		By Balance		70,000	20,000	10,000	100,000	0	0

PER CONTRA. *Cr.*

1817.			£.	s.	d.
June 30		By Balance	2,600	0	0
			2,600	0	0

Dr.   THREE PER CENT FUNDS.   (7)

1817.			£.	s.	d.
May 31	To Balance.................................. 80,000 at 55..		44,000	0	0

Dr.   FIVE PER CENT FUNDS.

1817.					
May 31	To Balance ....40,000 at 90..		36,000	0	0

Dr.   INDIA STOCK.

1817.					
May 31	To Balance......................,...........10,000 at 150..		15,000	0	0

(7) PER CONTRA. *Cr.*

PER CONTRA. *Cr.*

PER CONTRA. *Cr.*

Drs.   GRANDISON, NEVILLE, AND CO. BANKERS, LONDON.   (8)

1817.				Their Account.			Our Account.		
				£.	s.	d.	£.	s.	d.
June 2	10	To Cash Account....... due		892	5	4	715	12	6
3	10	To.... Ditto .... ditto		2,408	10	0	2,308	10	0
5	10	To.... Ditto .... ditto..........		1,000	0	0	1,000	0	0
6	10	To. .. Ditto .... ditto..........		710	17	11	572	11	8
9	10	To.... Ditto .... ditto.		1,083	18	2	933	18	2
10	10	To.... Ditto .... ditto..........		412	5	0	412	5	0
12	10	To.... Ditto .... ditto..........		1,837	12	11	1,764	19	6
14	10	To. .. Ditto .... ditto..........		1,000	0	0	1,000	0	0
16	10	To.... Ditto .... ditto..........		200	0	0	237	17	10
17	10	To.... Ditto .... ditto..........		596	7	5	658	9	7
18	10	To.... Ditto .... ditto..........		2,280	10	0	2,721	11	6
20	10	To.... Ditto .... ditto..........		263	14	0	163	14	0
21	10	To.... Ditto .... ditto..........		1,367	8	0	926	6	6
23	10	To.... Ditto .... ditto..........		1,000	0	0	1,000	0	0
25	10	To.... Ditto .... ditto..........		1,128	13	4	1,278	13	4
26	10	To.... Ditto .... ditto..........		638	15	9	806	5	9
28	10	To.... Ditto .... ditto..........		1,500	0	0	1,500	0	0
30	10	To.... Ditto .... ditto..........		643	17	6	693	17	6
30		To Balance		43,224	18	0	42,857	8	0
				62,189	13	4	61,552	0	10

(8)   ACCEPTANCE ACCOUNT.   *Crs.*

			Their Account.			Our Account.		
1817.			£.	s.	d.	£.	s.	d.
May 31		By Balance	46,916	6	7	46,278	14	1
June 2	1	By Bills Payable	257	5	0	257	5	0
3	1	By...Ditto	1,688	17	6	1,688	17	6
4	1	By...Ditto	258	16	6	258	16	6
5	1	By...Ditto	271	19	0	271	19	0
6	1	By...Ditto	226	18	6	226	18	6
7	1	By...Ditto	703	15	.8	703	15	8
7	1	By...Ditto	1,000	0	0	1,000	0	0
9	1	By...Ditto	75	17	6	75	17	6
10	1	By...Ditto	233	8	6	233	8	6
11	1	By...Ditto	1,441	3	0	1,441	3	0
12	1	By...Ditto	165	4	0	165	4	0
13	1	By...Ditto	1,541	6	6	1,541	6	6
14	1	By...Ditto	100	0	0	100	0	0
16	1	By...Ditto	237	13	0	237	13	0
18	1	By...Ditto	235	17	6	235	17	6
18	2	By...Ditto	1,535	11	3	1,535	11	3
19	2	By...Ditto	1,391	10	0	1,391	10	0
20	2	By...Ditto	181	18	0	181	18	0
21	2	By...Ditto	58	17	6	58	17	6
21	2	By...Ditto	1,727	4	8	1,727	4	8
23	2	By...Ditto	229	10	0	229	10	0
24	2	By...Ditto	1,180	7	2	1,180	7	2
25	2	By...Ditto	140	5	0	140	5	0
27	2	By...Ditto	58	11	0	58	11	0
28	2	By...Ditto	181	10	0	181	10	0
29	2	By...Ditto	150	0	0	150	0	0
			62,189	13	4	61,552	0	10
June 30		By Balance	43,224	18	0	42,857	8	0

Dr.   GRANDISON, NEVILLE, AND CO. BANKERS, LONDON.   (9)

1817.				Their Account.			Our Account.		
				£.	s.	d.	£.	s.	d.
May 31			To Balance	38,796	18	10	38,596	18	10
June 2	1		To Bills Receivable	2,537	16	8	2,537	16	8
3	1		To Ditto	3,563	3	4	3,563	3	4
5	1		To Ditto	3,137	5	4	3,137	5	4
11	2		To Ditto	2,246	0	6	2,246	0	6
13	2		To Ditto	2,117	18	9	2,117	18	9
18	3		To Ditto	2,765	2	4	2,765	2	4
19	3		To Ditto	1,891	4	6	1,891	4	6
23	3		To Ditto	2,395	4	6	2,395	4	6
26	4		To Ditto	1,288	18	6	1,288	18	6
				60,739	13	3	60,539	13	3
June 30			To Balance	40,801	8	5	40,501	8	5

(9)   BILL ACCOUNT.   *Crs.*

1817.				Their Account.			Our Account		
				£.	s.	d.	£.	s.	d.
June 2	10	By Cash Account..............due....		1,235	10	0	1,035	10	0
4	10	By ...Ditto.................ditto....		687	16	6	837	16	6
5	10	By ...Ditto.................ditto....		789	12	4	789	12	4
7	10	By ...Ditto.................ditto....		2,494	3	8	2,344	3	8
9	10	By ...Ditto.................ditto....		1,500	0	0	1,500	0	0
11	10	By ...Ditto.................ditto....		975	17	3	975	17	3
13	10	By ...Ditto.................ditto....		1,408	4	7	1,108	4	7
14	10	By ...Ditto.................ditto....		1,439	11	6	1,739	11	6
17	10	By ...Ditto.................ditto....		500	0	0	500	0	0
19	10	By ...Ditto.................ditto....		691	16	6	691	16	6
21	10	By ...Ditto.................ditto....		1,506	9	8	2,006	9	8
23	10	By ...Ditto.................ditto....		926	18	0	426	18	0
24	10	By ...Ditto.................ditto....		1,678	7	6	1,678	7	6
26	10	By ...Ditto.................ditto....		888	9	10	888	9	10
27	10	By ...Ditto.................ditto....		2,054	15	0	2,054	15	0
30	10	By ...Ditto.................ditto....		1,160	12	6	1,460	12	6
30		By Balance		40,801	8	5	40,501	8	5
				60,739	13	3	60,539	13	3

Drs.   GRANDISON NEVILLE AND CO. BANKERS, LONDON.   (10)

1817.			Their Account.			Dr. Interest 5 per Cent.			Our Account.		
			£.	s.	d.	£.	s.	d.	£.	s.	d.
May 31		To Balance..................	6,358	19	3	178	2	9	5,921	6	9
June 2	9	To Bill Account, ...due	1,235	10	0	3	19	5	1,035	10	0
4	9	To ... Ditto..... ...ditto....	687	16	6	2	19	8	837	16	6
5	9	To ... Ditto.........ditto....	789	12	4	2	14	I	789	12	4
7	9	To ...Ditto......... ditto....	2,494	3	8	7	7	8	2,344	3	8
9	9	To ...Ditto......... ditto....	1,500	0	0	4	6	3	1,500	0	0
11	9	To ...Ditto......... ditto....	975	17	3	2	10	9	975	17	3
13	9	To ...Ditto......... ditto....	1,408	4	7	2	11	7	1,108	4	7
14	9	To ...Ditto......... ditto....	1,439	11	6	3	16	3	1,739	11	6
17	9	To ...Ditto......... ditto....	500	0	0	0	17	10	500	0	0
19	9	To ... Ditto......... ditto....	691	16	6	1	0	10	691	·16	6
21	9	To ... Ditto......... ditto....	1,506	9	8	2	9	6	2,006	9	8
23	9	To ...Ditto......... ditto....	926	18	0	0	8	2	426	18	0
24	9	To ...Ditto......... ditto....	1,678	7	6	1	7	7	1,678	7	6
25	2	To Cash, Bank of England Notes	5,000	0	0	3	8	6	5,000	0	0
26	9	To Bill Account, ...due	888	9	10	0	9	9	888	9	10
27	9	To ...Ditto......... ditto....	2,054	15	0	0	16	10	2,054	15	0
30	9	To ...Ditto......... ditto....	1,160	12	6	....	..	..	1,460	12	6
30		To Difference of Int. in their Acct.	......	..	..	5	19	7			
30	2	To Interest..................	169	15	2	....	..	..	169	15	2
			31,466	19	3	225	7	0	31,129	6	9
June 30		To Balance	7,230	6	5	....	..	..	7,162	16	5

(10)   CASH ACCOUNT.   *Crs.*

1817.				Their Account.			Cr. Interest 5 per Cent.			Our Account.		
				£.	s.	d.	£.	s.	d.	£.	s.	d.
June 2	8		By Acceptance Account, due ...	892	5	4	2	14	11	715	12	6
3	8		By ..... Ditto .... ditto...	2,408	10	0	8	10	9	2,308	10	0
3	1		By Cash, Bank of England Notes	5,000	0	0	18	9	10	5,000	0	0
5	8		By Acceptance Account, due ...	1,000	0	0	3	8	6	1,000	0	0
6	8		By ...... Ditto ...... ditto...	710	17	11	1	17	8	572	11	8
9	8		By ...... Ditto ..... ditto...	1,083	18	2	2	13	9	933	18	2
10	8		By ...... Ditto ..... ditto...	412	5	0	1	2	7	412	5	0
12	8		By ...... Ditto ..... ditto...	1,837	12	11	4	7	0	1,764	19	6
14	8		By ...... Ditto ..... ditto...	1,000	0	0	2	3	10	1,000	0	0
16	8		By ...... Ditto ..... ditto...	200	0	0	0	9	1	237	17	10
17	8		By ...... Ditto ..... ditto...	596	7	5	1	3	5	658	9	7
18	8		By ...... Ditto ...... ditto...	2,280	10	0	4	9	6	2,721	11	6
20	8		By ...... Ditto ..... ditto...	263	14	0	0	4	6	163	14	0
21	8		By ...... Ditto ..... ditto...	1,367	8	0	1	2	10	926	6	6
23	8		By ...... Ditto ..... ditto...	1,000	0	0	0	19	2	1,000	0	0
25	8		By ...... Ditto ..... ditto...	1,128	13	4	0	17	6	1,278	13	4
26	8		By ...... Ditto ..... ditto...	638	15	9	0	8	10	806	5	9
28	8		By ...... Ditto ..... ditto...	1,500	0	0	0	8	2	1,500	0	0
30	8		By ...... Ditto ..... ditto...	643	17	6	....	..	..	693	17	6
30			By Balance of Interest	......	..	..	169	15	2			
30	2		By Commiss^n ¼ p^r C^t on £108,750	271	17	6	....	..	..	271	17	6
30			By Balance.................	7,230	6	5	....	..	..	7,162	16	5
				31,466	19	3	225	7	0	31,129	6	9

Drs.   SIMPSON AND WHITE,   (11)

1817.				5 per Cent.	Dr. Interest.			Cr. Interest.					
					£.	s.	d.	£.	s.	d.	£.	s.	d.
May 31		To Balance		183	15	4	....	..	..	4,173	15	8	
June 2	1	To Bills Receivable		....	..	..	3	14	3	957	15	0	
5	1	To Cash		0	17	1	....	..	..	250	0	0	
10	2	To Bills Receivable		....	..	..	3	0	4	958	13	6	
12	1	To Cash		0	12	4	....	..	..	250	0	0	
16	3	To Bills Receivable		....	..	..	6	8	2	1,200	0	0	
19	2	To Cash		0	7	6	....	..	..	250	0	0	
24	3	To Bills Receivable		....	..	..	6	8	6	1,024	5	0	
2	2	To Cash		0	1	8	....	..	..	150	0	0	
30		To Transfer opposite		33	1	7	19	11	3				
30	2	To Interest		....	..	..	....	..	..	199	4	3	
30	3	To Stamps		....	..	..	....	..	..	9	15	0	
30	2	To Commission, ¼ p^r C^t on £22,500		....	..	..	....	..	..	56	5	0	
				218	15	6				9,479	13	5	
June 30		To Balance		....	..	..	....	..	..	4,379	13	5	

(11)   LEEDS.   *Crs.*

1817.		5 per Cent.	Dr. Interest.			Cr. Interest.					
			£.	s.	d.	£.	s.	d.	£.	s.	d.
June 2	1	By Bills Receivable	4	18	7	....	..	..	1,000	0	0
5	1	By .... Ditto	1	6	9	....	..	..	250	0	0
10	2	By .... Ditto	6	0	7	....	..	..	1,000	0	0
12	2	By .... Ditto	1	11	6	....	..	..	250	0	0
16	3	By .... Ditto	8	4	4	....	..	..	1,200	0	0
19	2	By .... Ditto	1	16	4	....	..	..	250	0	0
24	3	By .... Ditto	7	18	10	....	..	..	1,000	0	0
26	4	By .... Ditto	1	4	8	....	..	..	150	0	0
30		By Transfer opposite	33	1	7	19	11	3			
30		By Balance of Interest	....	..	..	199	4	3			
30		By Balance	....	..	..	....	..	..	4,379	13	5
						218	15	6	9,479	13	5

Drs.   JOHNSON AND SONS,   (12)

1817.				5 per Cent.	Dr. Interest.			Cr. Interest.					
					£.	s.	d.	£.	s.	d.	£.	s.	d.
June 3	1	To Bills Payable		....	..	..	7	14	0	1,514	7	6
6	1	To Cash		0	13	2	....	..	..	200	0	0
9	2	To Bills Receivable		....	..	..	5	6	4	932	15	0
9	1	To Cash		0	2	1	....	..	..	35	15	0
13	1	To Ditto ....,........		0	1	9	....	..	..	38	10	0
18	3	To Bills Receivable		....	..	..	3	3	0	500	0	0
18	2	To Bills Payable		....	..	..	17	9	7	1,535	11	3
20	2	To Cash		0	5	6	....	..	..	200	0	0
23	3	To Bills Receivable		....	..	..	10	19	11	1,575	15	0
30		To Transfer opposite		88	11	6	44	12	10			
30	2	To Interest		....	..	..	....	..	..	45	1	2
30	3	To Stamps...............		....	..	..	....	..	..	8	2	6
30	2	To Commission $\frac{1}{4}$ pr Ct on £34,400		....	..	..	....	..	..	86	0	0
				89	14	0				6,671	17	5
June 30		To Balance		....	..	..	....	..	..	104	11	3

| (12) | | LEEDS. | | | Crs. |

1817.			5 per Cent.	Dr. Interest.			Cr. Interest.					
				£.	s.	d.	£.	s.	d.	£.	s.	d.
May 31		By Balance		53	10	0	....	..	..	132	7	6
June 3	1	By Bills Receivable		8	15	1	....	..	..	1,512	6	6
6	1	By ....Ditto		1	1	11	....	..	..	200	0	0
9	2	By ....Ditto		3	0	4	....	..	..	958	13	6
18	3	By ....Ditto		6	6	0	....	..	..	2,000	0	0
20	3	By ....Ditto		0	19	2	....	..	..	200	0	0
23	3	By ....Ditto		14	19	0	....	..	..	1,563	18	8
30		By Transfer opposite		88	11	6	44	12	10			
30		By Balance of Interest		....	..	..	45	1	2			
30		By Balance		....	..	..	....	..	..	104	11	3
				89	14	0				6,671	17	5

Drs.   BILLINGTON AND CO.   (13)

1817			5 per Cent.	Dr. Interest.			Cr. Interest.					
				£.	s.	d.	£.	s.	d.	£.	s.	d
May 31		To Balance		107	5	10	....	..	..	1,285	4	10
June 3	1	To Cash		1	2	2	....	..	..	300	0	0
4	1	To Bills Receivable		....	..	..	3	14	1	750	0	0
12	2	To Ditto		....	..	..	6	0	7	1,000	0	0
14	1	To Cash		0	8	9	....	..	..	200	0	0
18	3	To Bills Receivable		....	..	..	4	10	8	1,000	0	0
25	4	To Ditto		....	..	..	8	17	4	804	10	2
27	2	To Cash		0	1	8	....	..	..	200	0	0
30		To Transfer opposite		28	0	6	23	2	8			
30	2	To Interest		....	..	..	....	..	..	113	16	3
30	3	To Stamps		....	..	..	....	..	..	8	17	6
30	2	To Commission ¼ pr Ct on £19,800		....	..	..	....	..	..	49	10	0
				136	18	11				5,711	18	9
June 30		To Balance		....	..	..	....	..	..	1,461	18	9

(13)   LEEDS.   *Crs.*

1817.			5 per Cent.	Dr. Interest.			Cr. Interest.					
				£.	s.	d.	£.	s.	d.	£.	s.	d.
June 3	1	By Bills Receivable		1	10	5	....	..	..	300	0	0
4	1	By ... Ditto....................		3	18	0	....	..	..	750	0	0
12	2	By ... Ditto....................		6	6	0	....	..	..	1,000	0	0
14	2	By ... Ditto....................		1	6	4	....	..	..	200	0	0
18	3	By ... Ditto....................		6	17	0	....	..	..	1,000	0	0
25	4	By ... Ditto....................		6	9	4	....	..	..	800	0	0
27	4	By ... Ditto....................		1	13	5	....	..	..	200	0	0
30		By Transfer opposite		28	0	6	23	2	8			
30		By Balance of Interest		....	..	..	113	16	3			
30		By Balance		....	..	..	....	..	..	1,461	18	9
							136	18	11	5,711	18	9

2 Z

Dr.   JOHN EVERGREEN,   (14)

1817.			5 per Cent.	Dr. Interest.			Cr. Interest.					
				£.	s.	d.	£.	s.	d.	£.	s.	d.
June 4	1	To Cash		0	2	4	....	..	..	32	10	0
5	1	To Bills Receivable		....	..	..	8	7	10	1,550	0	0
10	1	To Cash		0	11	0	....	..	..	200	0	0
11	1	To Bills Payable		....	..	..	8	6	6	1,350	0	0
11	1	To Cash		0	2	2	....	..	..	41	3	8
19	2	To Bills Payable		....	..	..	9	12	10	1,327	15	0
21	2	To Cash		0	1	2	....	..	..	47	10	0
24	2	To Bills Payable		....	..	..	7	11	4	952	10	2
24	2	To Cash		0	3	3	....	..	..	200	0	0
30		To Transfer opposite		22	16	0	33	18	6			
30		To Balance of Interest		37	5	5						
30	3	To Stamps		....	..	..	....	..	..	22	10	0
30	2	To Commission, ¼ pr Cᵗ on £28,650		....	..	..	....	..	..	71	12	6
				61	1	4				5,795	11	4
June 30		To Balance		....	..	..	....	..	..	154	7	1

			5 per Cent.	Dr. Interest.			Cr. Interest.					
1817.				£.	s.	d.	£.	s.	d.	£.	s.	d.
May 31		By Balance	....	....	..	..	23	7	6	267	12	0
June 5	1	By Bills Receivable	....	....	..	..	3	15	4	1,374	18	10
10	2	By ... Ditto...........	....	0	14	10	....	..	..	187	10	0
11	2	By ... Ditto...........	....	1	17	9	....	..	..	1,343	15	0
19	3	By ... Ditto...........	....	14	17	1	....	..	..	1,291	4	6
24	3	By ... Ditto...........	....	5	6	4	....	..	..	1,138	18	6
30		By Transfer opposite	22	16	0	33	18	6				
30	2	By Interest	....	....	..	..	....	..	..	37	5	5
30		By Balance	....	....	..	..	....	..	..	154	7	1
							61	1	4	5,795	11	4

(14) LEEDS. *Cr.*

Drs.   HUNT AND MILNER,   (15)

1817.			5 per Cent. £	s.	d.	Dr. Interest. £	s.	d.	Cr. Interest. £	s.	d.	£	s.	d.
May 31		To Balance	75	18	3							216	12	6
June 7	2	To Bills Receivable							9	12	7	1,243	10	0
9	1	To Cash	0	8	8							150	0	0
14	2	To Bills Receivable							4	4	11	700	0	0
14	1	To Cash	0	0	11							19	16	6
16	1	To Ditto	0	5	9							150	0	0
20	3	To Bills Receivable							6	17	0	1,000	0	0
29	4	To Ditto							11	4	0	1,425	10	0
30		To Transfer opposite	32	10	8	31	18	6						
30	3	To Stamps										11	16	0
30	2	To Interest										77	5	9
30	2	To Commission ¼ per Cᵗ on £20,200										50	10	0
			109	4	3							5,045	0	9
June 30		To Balance										395	0	9

(15)   LEEDS.   *Crs.*

			5 per Cent.			Dr. Interest.			Cr. Interest.					
1817.						£.	s.	d.	£.	s.	d.	£.	s.	d.
June 6	1	By Bills Receivable				6	8	2	.....	....	....	1,200	0	0
9	2	By.... Ditto				0	17	8	.....	....	....	150	0	0
14	2	By.... Ditto				4	10	1	.....	....	....	700	0	0
16	3	By.... Ditto				1	0	7	.....	....	....	150	0	0
20	3	By.... Ditto				7	7	11	.....	....	....	1,000	0	0
29	4	By.... Ditto				12	6	3	.....	....	....	1,450	0	0
30		By Transfer opposite				32	10	8	31	18	6			
30		By Balance of Interest				.....	....	....	77	5	9			
30		By Balance				.....	....	....	.....	....	....	395	0	9
									109	4	3	5,045	0	9

Drs.   SAMUEL WINSFORD AND CO.   (16)

1817.			5 per Cent. / Dr. Interest.			Cr. Interest.					
			£.	s.	d.	£.	s.	d.	£.	s.	d.
June 2	1	To Cash	0	15	4	....	....	....	200	0	0
7	1	To Bills Payable	....	....	....	3	8	8	612	0	8
7	1	To Ditto	....	....	....	9	17	3	1,000	0	0
7	1	To Cash	0	1	8	....	....	....	26	14	3
13	1	To Bills Payable	....	....	....	9	7	2	1,453	7	6
18	1	To Cash	0	0	8	....	....	....	21	11	0
21	2	To Bills Payable	....	....	....	20	6	11	1,727	4	8
23	2	To Cash	0	5	9	....	....	....	300	0	0
28	4	To Bills Receivable	....	....	....	8	11	0	1,000	0	0
30		To Transfer opposite	58	10	10	51	11	0			
30	2	To Interest	....	....	....	....	....	....			
30	3	To Stamps	....	....	....	....	....	....	8	3	3
30	2	To Commission, ¼ per Cᵗ on £32,700	....	....	....	....	....	....	7	12	6
									81	15	0
			59	14	3				6,438	8	10
June 30		To Balance	....	....	....	....	....	....	40	18	4

			5 per Cent.	Dr. Interest.			Cr. Interest.					
(16)						LEEDS.				*Crs.*		
1817.				£.	s.	d.	£.	s.	d.	£.	s.	d.
May 31		By Balance		31	10	10	.....	....	....	81	3	9
June 2	1	By Bills Receivable		0	19	8	.....	....	....	200	0	0
7	2	By Ditto		11	5	1	.....	....	....	1,626	5	0
13	2	By Ditto		3	10	4	.....	....	....	1,427	7	9
21	3	By Ditto		9	5	7	.....	....	....	1,736	19	0
23	3	By Ditto		1	19	4	.....	....	....	325	15	0
28	4	By Ditto		.....	....	....	.....	....	....	1,000	0	0
30		By Transfer opposite		58	10	10	51	11	0			
30		By Balance of Interest		.....	....	....	8	3	3			
30		By Balance		.....	....	....	.....	....	....	40	18	4
							59	14	3	6,438	8	10

Drs.   JAMES ARNOLD'S   (17)

1817.			£.	s.	d.
May 31	To Balance		421	5	0
			421	5	0

Dr.   SIR CHARLES SLADE,

1817.			4 per Cent. Interest.					
			£.	s.	d.			
June 4	1	To Cash	0	4	3	74	18	0
18	1	To Ditto	0	1	6	54	13	6
26	2	To Ditto	0	1	2	127	15	0
30		To Balance of Interest	64	6	4			
30		To Balance	.....	....	....	2,806	19	10
			64	13	3	3,064	6	4

Dr.   HENRY BATH,

1817.			4 per Cent. Interest.					
June 27	2	To Cash.............................	0	0	6	83	2	9
30		To Balance of Interest..................	43	18	5			
30		To Balance............................	.....	....	....	1,460	15	8
			43	18	11	1,543	18	5

(17) ASSIGNEES, LEEDS. *Crs.*

1817.				£.	s.	d.
June 29	2	By Cash, Dividend of 6s. 8d. on £631. 17. 6.		210	12	6
30	1	By Loss..		210	12	6
				421	5	0

LEEDS. *Cr.*

			4 per Cent. Interest.					
1817.			£.	s.	d.	£.	s.	d.
May 31		By Balance	64	13	3	3,000	0	0
June 30	2	By Interest	......	....	....	64	6	4
			64	13	3	3,064	6	4
June 30		By Balance	......	....	....	2,806	19	10

LEEDS. *Cr.*

			4 per Cent. Interest.					
1817.								
May 31		By Balance	42	11	6	1,000	0	0
June 5	1	By Cash	1	7	5	500	0	0
30	2	By Interest	......	....	....	43	18	5
			43	18	11	1,543	18	5
June 30		By Balance	......	....	....	1,460	15	8

Dr.   MRS. RISINGHAM,   (18)

1817.				4 per Cent. Interest.					
				£.	s.	d.	£.	s.	d.
June 17	1	To Cash		0	0	8	25	0	0
25	2	To Ditto		0	0	2	20	0	0
30		To Balance of Interest		33	3	10			
30		To Balance		.....	....	....	1,488	3	10
				33	4	8	1,533	3	10

Dr.   WILLIAM TRUEMAN,

1817.			4 per Cent. Interest.					
			£.	s.	d.	£.	s.	d.
June 28	2	To Cash	0	0	2	50	0	0
30		To Balance of Interest	14	19	10			
30		To Balance	.....	....	....	714	19	10
			15	0	0	764	19	10

Dr.   MARY BRANDON,

1817.		4 per Cent. Interest.					
		£.	s.	d.	£.	s.	d.
June 30	To Balance of Interest	10	0	0			
30	To Balance	.....	....	....	510	0	0
		10	0	0	510	0	0

Dr.   ELLEN WILTON,

1817.		4 per Cent. Interest.					
		£.	s.	d.	£.	s.	d.
June 30	To Balance of Interest..................	4	1	1			
30	To Balance	.....	....	....	229	1	1
		4	1	1	229	1	1

(18)   **LEEDS.**   *Cr.*

1817.			4 per Cent. Interest.					
			£.	s.	d.	£.	s.	d.
May 31		By Balance	33	4	8	1,500	0	0
June 30	2	By Interest				33	3	10
			33	4	8	1,533	3	10
June 30		By Balance				1,488	3	10

LEEDS.   *Cr.*

1817.			4 per Cent. Interest.					
May 31		By Balance	15	0	0	750	0	0
June 30	2	By Interest				14	19	10
			15	0	0	764	19	10
June 30		By Balance				714	19	10

LEEDS.   *Cr.*

1817.			4 per Cent. Interest.					
May 31		By Balance	10	0	0	500	0	0
June 30	2	By Interest				10	0	0
			10	0	0	510	0	0
June 30		By Balance				510	0	0

LEEDS.   *Cr.*

1817.			4 per Cent. Interest.					
May 31		By Balance	4	0	0	200	0	0
June 11	1	By Cash	0	1	1	25	0	0
30	2	By Interest				4	1	1
			4	1	1	229	1	1
June 30		By Balance				229	1	1

Dr.   SIR HENRY WATSON,   (19)

1817.			5 per Cent. Interest.					
			£.	s.	d.	£.	s.	d.
May 31		To Balance	187	10	0	7,500	0	0
June 30	2	To Interest				187	10	0
			187	10	0	7,687	10	0
June 30		To Balance				7,687	10	0

Dr.   JOHN DAVISON,

1817.			5 per Cent. Interest.					
May 31		To Balance	85	0	0	3,400	0	0
June 30	2	To Interest				85	0	0
			85	0	0	3,485	0	0
June 30		To Balance				3,485	0	0

Dr.   SAMUEL BARNARD,

1817.			5 per Cent. Interest.					
May 31		To Balance	125	0	0	5,000	0	0
June 30	2	To Interest				125	0	0
			125	0	0	5,125	0	0
June 30		To Balance				5,125	0	0

(19)	LEEDS.							Cr.
		5 per Cent. Interest.						
1817.		£.	s.	d.	£.	s.	d.	
June 30	By Balance of Interest	187	10	0				
30	By Balance	......	....	....	7,687	10	0	
		187	10	0	7,687	10	0	

	LEEDS.							Cr.
		5 per Cent. Interest.						
1817.								
June 30	By Balance of Interest	85	0	0				
30	By Balance	......	....	....	3,485	0	0	
		85	0	0	3,485	0	0	

	LEEDS.							Cr.
		5 per Cent. Interest.						
1817.								
June 30	By Balance of Interest	125	0	0				
30	By Balance	......	....	....	5,125	0	0	
		125	0	0	5,125	0	0	

Dr.   PETER SMITH,   (20)

1817.				4 per Cent. Interest.					
				£.	s.	d.	£.	s.	d.
June 7	1	To Cash		0	5	1	100	0	0
30		To Balance of Interest		14	12	1			
30		To Balance		......	....	....	1,892	12	8
				14	17	2	1,992	12	8

Dr.   JOHN BROWN,

1817.				4 per Cent. Interest.					
				£.	s.	d.	£.	s.	d.
May 31		To Balance		2	13	2	287	16	6
June 11	1	To Cash............................		0	2	1	50	0	0
30	2	To Interest		....	....	....	2	15	3
30		To Balance		......	....	....	485	7	5
				2	15	3	825	19	2

| (20) | | | PRIVATE ACCOUNT. | | | | | | | **Cr.** | | |

				4 per Cent. Interest.					
				£.	s.	d.	£.	s.	d.
1817.									
May 31		By Balance		14	17	2	876	15	0
June 30	2	By Interest		......	....	....	14	12	1
30	1	By Profit this Half Year, ⅓d		......	....	....	1,101	5	7
				14	17	2	1,992	12	8
June 30		By Balance		......	....	....	1,892	12	8

| | | | PRIVATE ACCOUNT. | | | | | | | **Cr.** | | |

				4 per Cent. Interest.					
1817.									
June 30		By Balance of Interest		2	15	3			
30	1	By Profit this Half Year, ¼th		......	....	....	825	19	2
				2	15	3	825	19	2
June 30		By Balance		......	....	....	485	7	5

Dr.   CHARLES LANGDON,   (21)

1817.			4 per Cent. Interest.					
			£.	s.	d.	£.	s.	d.
May 31		To Balance	3	1	9	321	11	0
June 2	1	To Cash	0	3	1	50	0	0
20	2	To Ditto	0	0	8	30	0	0
30	2	To Interest	....	....	....	3	5	6
30		To Balance	....	....	....	421	2	8
			3	5	6	825	19	2

Dr.   GEORGE WILLIAMS,

1817.			4 per Cent. Interest.					
May 31		To Balance	1	19	6	195	8	4
June 5	1	To Cash	0	2	2	40	0	0
16	1	To Ditto	0	0	7	20	0	0
30	2	To Interest	....	....	....	2	2	3
30		To Balance	....	....	....	293	2	2
			2	2	3	550	12	9

(21)		PRIVATE ACCOUNT.						_Cr._

1817.			4 per Cent. Interest.					
			£.	s.	d.	£.	s.	d.
June 30		By Balance of Interest	3	5	6			
30	1	By Profit this Half Year, ¼th	.....	....	....	825	19	2
			3	5	6	825	19	2
June 30		By Balance	.....	....	....	421	2	8

		PRIVATE ACCOUNT.						_Cr._

1817.			4 per Cent. Interest.					
June 30		By Balance of Interest	2	2	3			
30	1	By Profit this Half Year, ⅙th	.....	....	....	550	12	9
			2	2	3	550	12	9
June 30		By Balance	.....	....	....	293	2	2

3 B

Dr.   CHARLES WILFRED,   (22)

1817.				£.	s.	d.
May 31		To Balance...		130	0	0
June 30	2	To Cash		20	0	0
				150	0	0

Dr.   JOHN SIMPSON,

1817.						
May 31		To Balance.........		60	0	0
June 30	2	To Cash		15	0	0
				75	0	0

Dr.   GEORGE RILEY,

1817.						
May 31		To Balance...		40	0	0
June 30	2	To Cash		10	0	0
				50	0	0

Dr.   JOHN WILKES,

1817.						
May 31		To Balance...		20	0	0
June 30	2	To Cash		5	0	0
				25	0	0

Dr.   JAMES THOMPSON,

1817.						
May 31		To Balance...		20	0	0
June 30	2	To Cash		5	0	0
				25	0	0

(22)			CASHIER.	*Cr.*		
				£.	s.	d.
1817.						
June 30	3		By Bank Expenses, ½ Year's Salary	150	0	0

			ACCOUNTANT.	*Cr.*		
1817.						
June 30	3		By Bank Expenses, ½ Year's Salary	75	0	0

			SUB-ACCOUNTANT.	*Cr.*		
1817.						
June 30	3		By Bank Expenses, ½ Year's Salary	50	0	0

			OUT-DOOR CLERK.	*Cr.*		
1817.						
June 30	3		By Bank Expenses, ½ Year's Salary	25	0	0

			OUT-DOOR CLERK.	*Cr.*		
1817.						
June 30	3		By Bank Expenses, ½ Year's Salary	25	0	0

Dr.　　　　(1)　　　　THE JOINT ESTATE OF PETER SMITH, JOHN BROWN,

		May 31st, 1817.	£.	s.	d.
L	4	To Promiscuous Discounts, Balance of Profit....................	589	14	8
L	6	To Notes on Demand, Amount in Circulation	96,500	0	0
* *	....	To Grandison Neville & Co. London, Balance due to them...........	1,760	8	6
L	12	To Johnson & Sons .... Leeds... Ditto .. ditto.................	132	7	2
L	14	To John Evergreen........ Ditto ... Ditto .. to him..............	267	12	0
L	16	To Samuel Winsford & Co.. Ditto ... Ditto .. to them..............	81	3	9
L	17	To Sir Charles Slade.... .. Ditto ... Ditto .. to him..............	3,000	0	0
L	17	To Henry Bath.......... Ditto ... Ditto .. ditto..............	1,000	0	0
L	18	To Mrs. Risingham .... Ditto ... Ditto .. to her..............	1,500	0	0
L	18	To William Trueman...... Ditto ... Ditto .. to him	750	0	0
L	18	To Mary Brandon......... Ditto ... Ditto .. to her..............	500	0	0
L	18	To Ellen Wilton.......... Ditto ... Ditto .. to ditto..............	200	0	0
L	20	To Peter Smith........ .... Ditto ... Ditto .. to him	876	15	0
			107,158	1	5
L	1	To Joint Stock, our Net and Permanent Capital....................	30,000	0	0
			137,158	1	5

* *　　　　　Grandison, Neville and Co. per Our Account.

L	8	Crs. By Balance of Acceptances outstanding £46,278 14 1
L	9	Drs. To Balance of Bills in hand..... £38,596 18 10
L	10	Drs. To Balance of Cash........... 5,921 6 9
		———— 44,518 5 7
		Crs. By General Balance ...... £ 1,760 8 6

....　....Con-

CHARLES LANGDON, AND GEORGE WILLIAMS, LEEDS. *Cr.* (1)

		May 31st. 1817.	£.	s.	d.
C	1	By Cash .... Balance in hand.......	12,050	7	11
B R	1	By Bills Receivable...................... Ditto .... ditto........	6,758	15	0
L	3	By Stamps .... Ditto .... disbursed....	217	13	6
L	3	By Bank Expenses........................ Ditto .... ditto	59	11	2
L	7	By Three Per Cent. Funds .... Cost of £80,000	44,000	0	0
L	7	By Five per Cent. Funds .... Ditto 40,000	36,000	0	0
L	7	By India Stock .... Ditto 10,000	15,000	0	0
L	11	By Simpson & White .... Leeds, ... Balance due from them	4,173	15	8
L	13	By Billington & Co. .... Ditto .... Ditto...... ditto......	1,285	4	10
L	15	By Hunt & Milner................ Ditto .... Ditto...... ditto......	216	12	6
L	17	By James Arnold's Assignees........ Ditto .... Ditto...... ditto......	421	5	0
L	19	By Sir Henry Watson.............. Ditto .... Ditto...... ditto him..	7,500	0	0
L	19	By John Davison .... Ditto .... Ditto...... ditto......	3,400	0	0
L	19	By Samuel Barnard .... Ditto .... Ditto...... ditto......	5,000	0	0
L	20	By John Brown .... Ditto .... Ditto...... ditto......	287	16	6
L	21	By Charles Langdon............... Ditto .... Ditto..... ditto......	321	11	0
L	21	By George Williams............... Ditto .... Ditto..... ditto......	195	8	4
L	22	By Charles Wilfred............... Ditto .... Ditto...... ditto.....	130	0	0
L	22	By John Simpson .... Ditto .... Ditto...... ditto......	60	0	0
L	22	By George Riley.................. Ditto .... Ditto..... ditto......	40	0	0
L	22	By John Wilkes .... Ditto .... Ditto...... ditto.....	20	0	0
L	22	By James Thompson .... Ditto .... Ditto..... ditto......	20	0	0
			137,158	1	5

		Grandison, Neville & Co. per their Account.			
* *					
L	8	Crs. By Balance of Acceptances outstanding.........£46,916 6 7			
L	9	Drs. To Balance of Bills in hand £38,796 18 10			
L	10	Drs. To Balance of Cash 6,358 19 3			
		45,155 18 1			
formity..		.... Crs. By General Balance........£ 1,760 8 6			

(2)   *Dr.*   THE JOINT ESTATE OF PETER SMITH, JOHN BROWN,

		June 30th, 1817.	£.	s.	d.
L	6	To Notes on Demand, Amount in Circulation.	100,000	0	0
L	17	To Sir Charles Slade. . . . . Leeds . . . . Balance due to him.	2,806	19	10
L	17	To Henry Bath. . . . . , . Ditto . . . . Ditto. . . . . . ditto.	1,460	15	8
L	18	To Mrs. Risingham . . , . , . Ditto . . . . Ditto. . . . . to her.	1,488	3	10
L	18	To William Trueman . . . . Ditto . . . . Ditto. . . . . to him	714	19	10
L	18	To Mary Brandon . . . . Ditto . . . . Ditto. . . . . to her.	510	0	0
L	18	To Ellen Wilton. . . . . Ditto . . . . Ditto. . . . . to her.	229	1	1
L	20	To Peter Smith . . . . Private Account . . . . . Ditto. . . . . to him	1,892	12	8
L	20	To John Brown . . . . . Ditto . . . . Ditto. . . . . to him	485	7	5
L	21	To Charles Langdon . . Ditto . . . . Ditto. . . . . to him	421	2	8
L	21	To George Williams . . Ditto . . . . Ditto. . . . . to him	293	2	2
			110,302	5	2
L	1	To Joint Stock, our Net and Permanent Capital . . , ... ,	30,000	0	0
			140,302	5	2

		Grandison, Neville, & Co. per our Account,			
L	9	Drs. To Balance of Bills in hand £40,501 8 5			
L	10	Drs. To Balance of Cash 7,162 16 5			
		47,664 4 10			
L	8	Crs. By Balance of Acceptances outstanding 42,857 8 0			
		Drs. To General Balance £4,806 16 10	. . . .	. . . .	Con-

CHARLES LANGDON, AND GEORGE WILLIAMS, LEEDS.   *Cr.*   (2)

June 30th, 1817.

			£.	s.	d.
C	2	By Cash...................... Balance in hand..........	11,070	16	2
B R	4	By Bills Receivable .... Ditto.... Ditto............	3,990	12	7
L	7	By Three per Cent. Funds.......... Cost of £80,000...........	44,000	0	0
L	7	By Five per Cent. Funds........... Ditto.... 40,000...........	36,000	0	0
L	7	By India Stock.................. Ditto.... 10,000...........	15,000	0	0
L	6	By Stock Dividends	2,600	0	0
*		By Grandison, Neville, & Co. London, Balance due from them	4,806	16	10
L	11	By Simpson & White .... Leeds ....,Ditto .... ditto.........	4,379	13	5
L	12	By Johnson & Sons .... Ditto...... Ditto .... ditto.........	104	11	3
L	13	By Billington & Co. .... Ditto....... Ditto .... ditto.........	1,461	18	9
L	14	By John Evergreen .... Ditto..... Ditto ...... him.........	154	7	1
L	15	By Hunt & Milner .... Ditto..... Ditto .... them	395	0	9
L	16	By Samuel Winsford & Co. .. Ditto..... Ditto .... ditto.........	40	18	4
L	19	By Sir Henry Watson ...... Ditto..... Ditto ...... him.........	7,687	10	0
L	19	By John Davison .... Ditto..... Ditto ...... ditto.........	3,485	0	0
L	19	By Samuel Barnard .... Ditto..... Ditto .... ditto.........	5,125	0	0
			140,302	5	2

* *   Grandison, Neville, & Co. per their Account.

L	9	Drs. To Balance of Bills in hand £40,801	8	5	
L	10	Drs. To Balance of Cash 7,230	6	5	
			48,031	14	10
L	8	Crs. By Balance of Acceptances outstanding 43,224	18	0	
formity..		.... Drs. To General Balance.......... £4,806	16	10	

Dr.   JOINT CAPITAL.   (1)

1800.			£.	s.	d.
January 1	To Sundry Co-Partners, Permanent Amount		30,000	0	0

Dr.   PETER SMITH.

Dr.   JOHN BROWN.

Dr.   CHARLES LANGDON.

Dr.   GEORGE WILLIAMS.

(1)	PER CONTRA.				Cr.

PER CONTRA.				Cr.

1800.		£.	s.	d.
January 1	By Joint Capital, $\frac{1}{3}$d Share Permanent	10,000	0	0

PER CONTRA.				Cr.

1800.				
January 1	By Joint Capital, $\frac{1}{4}$th Share Permanent	7,500	0	0

PER CONTRA.				Cr.

1800.				
January 1	By Joint Capital, $\frac{1}{4}$th Share Permanent	7,500	0	0

PER CONTRA.				Cr.

1800.				
January 1	By Joint Capital, $\frac{1}{6}$th Share Permanent	5,000	0	0

THE END.

Bensley & Sons, Printers,
Bolt Court, Fleet Street, London.

THE DEVELOPMENT OF
CONTEMPORARY ACCOUNTING THOUGHT

An Arno Press Collection

Baldwin, H[arry] G[len]. **Accounting for Value As Well as Original Cost** *and* Castenholz, William B. **A Solution to the Appreciation Problem.** 2 Vols. in 1. 1927/1931

Baxter, William. **Collected Papers on Accounting.** 1978

Brief, Richard P., Ed. **Selections from Encyclopaedia of Accounting, 1903.** 1978

Broaker, Frank and Richard M. Chapman. **The American Accountants' Manual.** 1897

Canning, John B. **The Economics of Accountancy.** 1929

Chatfield, Michael, Ed. **The English View of Accountant's Duties and Responsibilities.** 1978

Cole, William Morse. **The Fundamentals of Accounting.** 1921

Congress of Accountants. **Official Record of the Proceedings of the Congress of Accountants.** 1904

Cronhelm, F[rederick] W[illiam]. **Double Entry by Single.** 1818

Davidson, Sidney. **The Plant Accounting Regulations of the Federal Power Commission.** 1952

De Paula, F[rederic] R[udolf] M[ackley]. **Developments in Accounting.** 1948

Epstein, Marc Jay. **The Effect of Scientific Management on the Development of the Standard Cost System** (Doctoral Dissertation, University of Oregon, 1973). 1978

Esquerré, Paul-Joseph. **The Applied Theory of Accounts.** 1914

Fitzgerald, A[dolf] A[lexander]. **Current Accounting Trends.** 1952

Garner, S. Paul and Marilynn Hughes, Eds. **Readings on Accounting Development.** 1978

Haskins, Charles Waldo. **Business Education and Accountancy.** 1904

Hein, Leonard William. **The British Companies Acts and the Practice of Accountancy 1844-1962** (Doctoral Dissertation, University of California, Los Angeles, 1962). 1978

Hendriksen, Eldon S. **Capital Expenditures in the Steel Industry, 1900 to 1953** (Doctoral Dissertation, University of California, Berkeley, 1956). 1978

Holmes, William, Linda H. Kistler and Louis S. Corsini. **Three Centuries of Accounting in Massachusetts.** 1978

Horngren, Charles T. **Implications for Accountants of the Uses of Financial Statements by Security Analysts** (Doctoral Dissertation, University of Chicago, 1955). 1978

Horrigan, James O., Ed. **Financial Ratio Analysis—An Historical Perspective.** 1978

Jones, [Edward Thomas]. **Jones's English System of Book-keeping.** 1796

Lamden, Charles William. **The Securities and Exchange Commission** (Doctoral Dissertation, University of California, Berkeley, 1949). 1978

Langer, Russell Davis. **Accounting As A Variable in Mergers** (Doctoral Dissertation, University of California, Berkeley, 1976). 1978

Lewis, J. Slater. **The Commercial Organisation of Factories.** 1896

Littleton, A[nanias] C[harles] and B[asil] S. Yamey, Eds. **Studies in the History of Accounting.** 1956

Mair, John. **Book-keeping Moderniz'd.** 1793

Mann, Helen Scott. **Charles Ezra Sprague.** 1931

Marsh, C[hristopher] C[olumbus]. **The Theory and Practice of Bank Book-keeping.** 1856

Mitchell, William. **A New and Complete System of Book-keeping by an Improved Method of Double Entry.** 1796

Montgomery, Robert H. **Fifty Years of Accountancy.** 1939

Moonitz, Maurice. **The Entity Theory of Consolidated Statements.** 1951

Moonitz, Maurice, Ed. **Three Contributions to the Development of Accounting Thought.** 1978

Murray, David. **Chapters in the History of Bookkeeping, Accountancy & Commercial Arithmetic.** 1930

Nicholson, J[erome] Lee. **Cost Accounting.** 1913

Paton, William Andrew and Russell Alger Stevenson. **Principles of Accounting.** 1918

Pixley, Francis W[illiam]. **The Profession of a Chartered Accountant and Other Lectures.** 1897

Preinreich, Gabriel A. D. **The Nature of Dividends.** 1935

Previts, Gary John, Ed. **Early 20th Century Developments in American Accounting Thought.** 1978

Ronen, Joshua and George H. Sorter. **Relevant Financial Statements.** 1978

Shenkir, William G., Ed. **Carman G. Blough: His Professional Career and Accounting Thought.** 1978

Simpson, Kemper. **Economics for the Accountant.** 1921

Sneed, Florence R. **Parallelism in Two Disciplines.** (M.A. Thesis, University of Texas, Arlington, 1974). 1978

Sorter, George H. **The Boundaries of the Accounting Universe** (Doctoral Dissertation, University of Chicago, 1963). 1978

Storey, Reed K[arl]. **Matching Revenues with Costs** (Doctoral Dissertation, University of California, Berkeley, 1958). 1978

Sweeney, Henry W[hitcomb]. **Stabilized Accounting.** 1936

Van de Linde, Gérard. **Reminiscences.** 1917

Vatter, William J[oseph]. **The Fund Theory of Accounting and Its Implications for Financial Reports.** 1947

Walker, R. G. **Consolidated Statements.** 1978

Webster, Norman E., Comp. **The American Association of Public Accountants.** 1954

Wells, M. C., Ed. **American Engineers' Contributions to Cost Accounting.** 1978

Worthington, Beresford. **Professional Accountants.** 1895

Yamey, Basil S. **Essays on the History of Accounting.** 1978

Yamey, Basil S., Ed. **The Historical Development of Accounting.** 1978

Yang, J[u] M[ei]. **Goodwill and Other Intangibles.** 1927

Zeff, Stephen Addam. **A Critical Examination of the Orientation Postulate in Accounting, with Particular Attention to its Historical Development** (Doctoral Dissertation, University of Michigan, 1961). 1978

Zeff, Stephen A., Ed. **Selected Dickinson Lectures in Accounting.** 1978